Java for the COBOL Programmer

Advances in Object Technology Series
Dr. Richard S. Wiener, Series Editor
and Editor-in-Chief of
Journal of Object-Oriented Programming
SIGS Publications, Inc.
New York, New York

and

Department of Computer Science
University of Colorado
Colorado Springs, Colorado

1. Object Lessons: Lessons Learned in Object-Oriented Development Projects • Tom Love

2. Objectifying Real-Time Systems • John R. Ellis

3. Object Development Methods • edited by Andy Carmichael

4. Inside the Object Model: The Sensible Use of C++ • David M. Papurt

5. Using Motif with C++ • Daniel J. Bernstein

6. Using CRC Cards: An Informal Approach to Object-Oriented Development • Nancy M. Wilkinson

7. Rapid Software Development with Smalltalk • Mark Lorenz

8. Applying OMT: A Practical Step-By Step Guide to Using the Object Modeling Technique • Kurt W. Derr

9. The Smalltalk Developer's Guide to VisualWorks • Tim Howard

10. Objectifying Motif • Charles F. Bowman

11. Reliable Object-Oriented Software: Applying Analysis & Design • Ed Seidewitz & Mike Stark

12. Developing Visual Programming Applications Using Smalltalk • Michael Linderman

13. Object-Oriented COBOL • Edmund C. Arranga & Frank P. Coyle

14. Visual Object-Oriented Programming Using Delphi • Richard Wiener & Claude Wiatrowski

15. Object Modeling and Design Strategies: Tips and Techniques • Sanjiv Gossain

16. The VisualAge for Smalltalk Primer • Liwu Li

17. Java Programming by Example • Rajiv Sharma & Vivek Sharma

18. Rethinking Smart Objects: Building Artificial Intelligence with Objects • Daniel W. Rasmus

19. The Distributed Smalltalk Survival Guide • Terry Montlick

20. Java for the COBOL Programmer • E. Reed Doke, Ph.D. and Bill C. Hardgrave, Ph.D.

Additional Volumes in Preparation

Java for the COBOL Programmer

E. Reed Doke, Ph.D.
Bill C. Hardgrave, Ph.D.

PUBLISHED BY THE PRESS SYNDICATE OF THE UNIVERSITY OF CAMBRIDGE
The Pitt Building, Trumpington Street, Cambridge, United Kingdom

CAMBRIDGE UNIVERSITY PRESS
The Edinburgh Building, Cambridge CB2 2RU, UK
40 West 20th Street, New York, NY 10011-4211, USA
10 Stamford Road, Oakleigh, Melbourne 3166, Australia
Ruiz de Alarcón 13, 28014 Madrid, Spain
Dock House, The Waterfront, Cape Town 8001, South Africa

http://www.cambridge.org

Published in association with SIGS Books

First published 1999
Reprinted 2000

Design and composition by Andrea Cammarata
Cover design by Tom Jezek

Printed in the United States of America

A catalog record for this book is available from the British Library

Library of Congress Cataloging in Publication data is available

ISBN 0 521 465892 6 paperback

To the millions of
COBOL programmers in the world.

Contents

Foreword

COBOL programmers are, above all else, practical. They have seen languages come and go, each providing 15 megabytes of fame before vanishing in the night with little fanfare and less regret. COBOL programmers, meanwhile, quietly go about the business of developing and delivering the systems essential to business. Why then, given the hype and history of broken language promises, should COBOL programmers care about a language that more has been written about, than in?

Surprisingly, in many respects Java is much like COBOL. Each was defined with a very specific role to play, each eschews complexity for the sake of productivity, each strives for openness, and each is being defined by ISO to protect and promote corporate as well as personal investments in the language. Yet it takes more for a language to grow and prosper—it takes the right problem, or stated in slightly different terms—the right *opportunity*. The Internet is the opportunity for Java to prove its mettle.

Learning Java means many things. It does not mean abandoning COBOL, which will continue to thrive in the next century. The size of the information technology pie is exploding (and by pie we mean the business tasks, both existing and new, that require automation). We have only scratched the digital surface in terms of providing the systems that the company of tomorrow will demand. Our obsession with focusing inward will dramatically change to an outwardly directed view of the world. This fundamental shift will take us from systems integration to business integration. Building the infrastructure, constructing the numerous connections, and doing it right will require many sharp tools. COBOL and Java will serve complementary roles. COBOL excels in some areas, Java in others. The business/software engineers of today and tomorrow will exploit the best of both to make the age of information a reality.

First, learning Java means you will be exposed to a greater range of programming styles and new and exciting patterns of thought. A larger vocabulary of programming ideas will always stand you in good stead. Second, in that circular reinforcing way that knowledge works, knowing

Java will make you a better COBOL programmer, and knowing COBOL will make you a better Java programmer. Third, learning Java will enhance your ability to pick the right tool for the right job. Fourth, you will be in a position to increase the value of legacy systems and you will increase your own value to a company. And fifth, Java is fun.

I have the pleasure of knowing both Reed Doke and Bill Hardgrave. They come from the world of COBOL. They both teach COBOL and have written an excellent book called *An Introduction to Object COBOL* (John Wiley & Sons, 1998). In a nutshell, they know their COBOL. From this position they are able to build a bridge between the two languages. *Java for the COBOL Programmer* is clear, crisp, and concise. Brimming with insight and presented in an easy-to-follow, straightforward manner any COBOL programmer will appreciate, Doke and Hardgrave make learning Java easy and fun. Do yourself a favor and get a copy of this book, and then sit down and enjoy a good read. You will learn a lot. I know I did.

Edmund C. Arranga
Editor-in-Chief, *The COBOL Report*

Preface

If you are like most of us, you have probably been thinking about updating your technical skills. You have been hearing a lot about Java, object-oriented (OO) development, and Internet applications. These topics have been getting a tremendous amount of press lately. In the fanfare, you may have heard someone suggest that COBOL programmers will be obsolete and can't possibly make the switch to OO programming. Can this possibly be true?

We wrote this book because we believe it is important that you learn Java and OO development. Although, we don't claim learning a new programming language is a trivial task, the fact that you already know COBOL gives you a head start on learning Java. Don't let what others say frighten you.

We work with COBOL as consultants for industry, in our classrooms, and as authors. However, we also work with Java and OO development. From our perspective, we believe COBOL and Java are highly complementary development tools in the evolving computing environment. COBOL does a super job of processing and maintaining a firm's data. Java plays an equally important role by capturing and reporting data by connecting clients to the server across a variety of networked computers, with little concern about the specific hardware and operating systems involved.

Today's business environment is diverse. A single platform and/or single language cannot meet the needs of most organizations. The business environment is becoming one of interconnectivity, requiring many different organizations with many different computing environments to communicate. Perhaps your organization is moving in this direction. Has your manager inquired about your interests in client-server computing or Java? The fact that you are reading this suggests you have been thinking about your future. We urge you to learn Java...not as a replacement for COBOL, but to make yourself even more valuable and make an even greater contribution to your firm's computing projects. Plus, we find writing Java fun and we think you will too!

Many COBOL programmers are asking questions such as: What is Java? How does it differ from COBOL? How is it similar? What is the impact of Java on COBOL? What is object technology? We wrote this book to answer these questions for you.

Can you learn Java? Of course you can. Java has only 48 reserved words. At last count, COBOL had over 600! These numbers suggest the Java language set is much easier to learn and remember than many others, including COBOL, and our experience with Java corroborates this. Although it is not immediately obvious, there are many similarities between COBOL and Java. In fact, some of the statements are almost identical. We include a lot of Java code in the book and for most of it we have the corresponding COBOL code. Finally, you already know programming constructs – you need learn only the new syntax. But, you must also learn OO concepts and about half a dozen OO terms. Although not particularly difficult to learn, without these concepts, you will find it nearly impossible to learn Java. Therefore, before we get into programming statements, Chapter 2 explains OO for you in simple straightforward terms.

Good luck, have fun,
and let us hear from you.

Reed   (ReedDoke@mail.smsu.edu)
Bill   (whardgra@comp.uark.edu)

Acknowledgments

We want to thank all of the people who assisted us in making this book a reality:

- Lothlórien Homet, the managing editor at SIGS Books, who kept all of us (mostly) on schedule.

- Edmund C. Arranga, President of Object-Z and editor of the *COBOL Report* for writing a very nice foreword and for his constructive comments about the approach and tone of the first few chapters.

- Dr. Neil Marple, technical area manager at SIAC in McLean, Virginia, for all of his encouragement and constructive suggestions, in addition to contributing a very sharp pencil to the technical editing process.

- Lisa McCumber, process specialist at Southwestern Bell in St. Louis for her astute and speedy technical review.

- Mike Hellebush, technical architect at Edward Jones in St. Louis, for providing a lot of real-world experience and insight, in addition to some technical editing chores.

- Dr. Lou Glorfeld at the University of Arkansas for some timely technical assistance with the database programs.

Introduction

We organized the chapters in this book to be read in sequence. However, each chapter begins with a clear statement of what we assume you know before reading the chapter, so you can jump around a little bit, depending on your background and experience. You can use the book as a reference and jump in anywhere once you have the fundamentals.

Chapter 1 presents reasons why you should learn Java and describes the many similarities between COBOL and Java.

Chapter 2 explains what OO is, and what it is not. OO terms and concepts are described using several everyday examples.

Chapter 3 describes the overall structure and format of a Java program. Several small programs are developed to show you how to create object instances and call methods.

Chapter 4 shows you how to define Java data items and use them in a program. Java data definition is somewhat different than COBOL and these differences are clearly explained and demonstrated in the program examples.

Chapter 5 introduces Java computation and again, several small programs are written to illustrate the idea and concepts presented. You will see that some Java computation is nearly identical to COBOL.

Chapter 6 illustrates how to use the Java decision-making statements. We develop programs using the Java IF (sound familiar?) and the Java counterpart to the COBOL EVALUATE verb.

Chapter 7 describes how to write Java loops. As you will see, Java looping is different from COBOL.

Chapter 8 shows you how to define and work with Java arrays which are really the old COBOL tables with a more technical-sounding name. There are a lot of parallels between Java arrays and COBOL tables.

Chapter 9 explains how to access data in sequential files, relational databases and on networks. You will appreciate Java's approach to accessing relational databases using standard SQL statements.

Chapter 10 illustrates how to develop Graphical User Interfaces for user input and output. This is an interesting and important chapter, even though there are few COBOL similarities.

Chapter 11 discusses OO development in a broader context. Both software and hardware issues are explored. Three-tier software design is illustrated using a GUI front end and a relational database back end.

The Accompanying CD-ROM

The accompanying CD-ROM contains the Java programs we developed in the book. These programs are named the same as in the book, and are placed in separate folders for each chapter.

The CD also includes a TrialWare copy of Symantec's Visual Café Database Edition version 3.0 for Windows. Documentation for using Café is included on the CD.

If you wish to run the programs on a platform other than Windows, visit the Sun Java web site (http://www.java.sun.com/) to download the Java Development Kit (JDK) for your system.

Chapter 1

Why You Should Learn Java

Objectives

In this chapter you will study:
- An overview and history of Java
- Some unique characteristics of Java
- Reasons for learning Java
- An overview of the book

So you want to learn Java? Why? You probably want to learn because:

- as a COBOL programmer, you feel a need to update your skills

- Java is hot and so are the jobs for Java programmers

- object technology is hot and Java fits perfectly with the object development your boss is requiring you to learn

- you are a naturally curious person and you want to see what this Java stuff is all about

Whatever your reasons, we're glad you're here!

1

In this book, the emphasis is on learning Java from a COBOL perspective. There are several million COBOL programmers worldwide and a significant number of you are, or soon will be, learning Java. We have designed this book to help you with that task. We will take what you know about COBOL and apply as much of it as possible to learning Java. But first, let's learn a little bit about Java in general, nontechnical terms, and about object-oriented development. Chapters 1 and 2, respectively, have been set aside for these purposes.

This chapter presents a general description of Java and an overview of the book. Our purpose is to present a brief history of Java, give you an overview of Java, describe why Java is becoming so popular, and discuss Java's impact on the future of COBOL.

Java is a very young language (circa 1995) and its explosive popularity indicates it is rapidly becoming the language of choice for many firms. Three main forces are supporting Java's popularity in information systems:

- the need to increase developer productivity,

- the adoption of the client-server model, and

- the growing number of Internet applications.

Java has received a lot of notice because it can be imbedded in Web pages to do input/output and animation. Java, however, is much more. Java is a complete, industrial-strength, full-featured application development language. It is also object-oriented, which facilitates implementation of the client-server model and Internet applications, plus it can significantly improve your productivity in developing all applications.

On the surface, Java appears to be a totally different language than COBOL. This appearance is because Java is object-oriented and uses a more concise (some say cryptic) syntax than COBOL. Java has numerous similarities with COBOL, however, that can be used to enhance your learning process and ease the transition from COBOL to Java. Learning a new subject (Java) is much easier when you can base it on something you already know (COBOL). That is precisely the basis for this book. We describe Java features and syntax in light of similar features and syntax that exist in COBOL.

History and Overview of Java

According to Sun Microsystems, the creator of Java, Java is:

> *"a simple, object-oriented, network-savvy, interpreted, robust, secure, architecture neutral, portable, high-performance, multithreaded, dynamic language."*

Enough said? This statement certainly touts many of the benefits of Java, but it doesn't say much about what Java really is. Perhaps we should start with a brief history of Java.

Java began in the early 1990s as a project at Sun Microsystems. The idea was to create a language to support the development of systems embedded in consumer electronic devices. The project, headed by James Gosling, produced a language originally called Oak (named for the tree outside Gosling's window). Unknown at the time, another language had already taken the Oak name. The name was later changed from Oak to Java (the idea for the new name was generated during a visit to a local coffee shop).

C and C++ were available at the time and widely used. However, Sun was concerned about many of the limitations of the popular C++ language. Java is similar to C++, but avoids many of its problems.

After a few years and many changes, the Java language was redirected to the Internet. Fueled by the rapid growth of the Internet and Web applications, Sun officially introduced Java in May 1995. Although Java initially gained recognition and acceptance because of its use on Web pages, it has grown to a full-blown development language capable of producing mission-critical systems on a wide range of hardware and operating systems.

NOTE

1. You may visit Sun Microsystems at *http://java.sun.com/*

2. A glossary of Java and related terms is available at *http://java.sun.com/docs/glossary.print.html*

3. The complete Java Language Specification is available at *http://java.sun.com/docs/books/jls/html/index.html*

4. The Java Language Environment: A White Paper is available at *http://java.sun.com/docs/white/langenv/*

Table 1-1. *Some common Java terms and their meanings*

Applet	A program written in Java that can be embedded inside Web pages and executed in Java-compatible browsers
Bean (i.e., JavaBean)	An independent, reusable software component. Beans can be combined to create an application.
Bytecode	Code generated by a Java compiler. Bytecode is platform independent and must be interpreted by a Java interpreter.
Java Archive files (JAR files)	A Java file format used for compressing many files into one to improve transmission speed across network connections.
Java Development Kit (JDK)	Sun's software development environment for writing Applets and applications in Java.
Java Integrated Development Environment (IDE)	A complete Java development environment including text editors, compilers, debuggers, interpreters, and so forth.
JavaScript	A Web scripting language developed by Netscape; has similar constructs to Java, but is a separate language. Typically used for user interface features within HTML documents, but can also be used on the server side.
Java Virtual Machine (JVM)	A Java interpreter; responsible for interpreting bytecodes.
Servlet	Similar to an Applet, but is located on the server; provides added functionality to Java-enabled servers

The Java name is trademarked by Sun Microsystems, making it a commercial proprietary product. Java is in the pubic domain, however, and a Java compiler can be obtained from Sun free of charge. Sun has been restrictive in its official licensing of the Java name to assure developers that anything bearing the Java seal meets the language standards and will run reliably in their environment.

During its brief history, Java has created a large following of software developers and a corresponding vocabulary. Many of the commonly used Java terms are listed in Table 1-1.

The Popularity of Java

The popularity of Java is evident. Look at the number of Java books available (including this one!). You cannot pick up an industry newspaper or magazine (such as ComputerWorld or InfoWorld) without seeing numerous Java-related items. Java seems to be everywhere—or, at least, everyone is talking about it. In March 1998, the month following the release of version 1.1 of Sun's Java Development Kit, more than 220,000 copies were downloaded from Sun's Web site. The next month, more than 8,000 developers attended the Java One Conference.

But, is Java actually being used? The answer is an emphatic YES! According to Signhal and Nguyen (1998): "Java is being used on a wider range of applications than any other language, including C and C++." In higher education, Java has also gained rapid growth. Java's use in university curricula jumped from 0 percent in 1995 to 42.5 percent in February 1998—not bad for a language officially less than three years old.

Will Java's meteoric growth continue? Only time will tell. Initially, the growth of Java mirrored the growth of the Web, as Java was primarily used as a tool for building Applets. Java's recent growth, however, is in the area of business applications. The popularity of JDK may be a sign of continued growth for Java in business applications.

In its short life, Java has grown faster and gained a wider acceptance than any other language before. Why? What propelled Java, a spin-off of C++, to such success? Certainly, the growth of the Web and Java Applets fueled its growth. However, Java offers many advantages not available in other languages. As an outgrowth of C++, Java specifically avoided some of the problems with C++. Let's take a closer look at how Java differs from other languages.

What Makes Java Different?

Java is just another programming language—right? Yes, it is another programming language, but it is also much more. Some would say the language is simple. For example, Java has only 48 reserved words. At last count, COBOL had over 600! These numbers suggest the language set is much easier to learn and remember than many others, including COBOL—our experience with Java makes us believe this is true.

Java is unarguably object-oriented, which puts it in select company (along with other pure object-oriented languages such as Smalltalk and Eiffel). Java is also portable, enabling it to run on many different platforms. Combined, these factors, and more, create an environment of improved development productivity and programming excellence. Let's explore the issues of simplicity, object-orientation, and portability further.

Java Is Simple

Java really is simple, especially if you know C++ because it closely resembles the language. Is it simpler than COBOL? Is it more difficult than Smalltalk? The answers to these questions vary by the individual. It is probably safe to say, however, that Java is easier to learn than C++, but more difficult than BASIC. How's that for a wide range? Our goal in this book is to make Java simple for you, the COBOL programmer. We think you will quickly conclude Java is certainly no more difficult than COBOL to use, and you will come to appreciate and even to prefer its syntax.

Remember the history of Java: Gosling's group at Sun took C++ as the foundation and eliminated many of the negatives. The Eiffel, Smalltalk, and Objective-C languages, among others, also influenced Java. From C++, the troublesome features such as operator overloading, multiple inheritance, and pointers were removed. Features lacking from C++, such as automatic garbage collection and memory management, were added. Overall, Java represents some of the best features and avoids some of the negatives, of several popular languages.

Java Is Object-Oriented

Java is a *pure* object-oriented language. *Pure* means everything is represented as an object and all the major characteristics of object-orientation, such as inheritance, classes, and polymorphism are supported (the next chapter explores the characteristics of object-orientation). Smalltalk and Eiffel are examples of other pure OO languages.

In Java, everything is an object except primitive data types (we discuss these in Chapter 4). Single inheritance and polymorphism are supported. A *hybrid* language, on the other hand, uses an existing language as its base and adds object-oriented features and syntax. For example,

C++ (derived from C), Object COBOL (derived from COBOL), and Object Pascal (derived from Pascal), are all hybrid languages. In many cases, hybrid languages do not fully support all OO characteristics.

The motivation for hybrid languages is a shorter learning curve. Developers can use their familiar language as the base and simply learn the OO extensions. The danger, of course, is developers do not truly learn OO development. Rather, they learn how to write procedural programs in an OO context. Java forces compliance to object-oriented development. With Java, it is difficult to revert back to procedural programming. However, the use of Java does not ensure a successful development project. Good analysis and design remain essential prerequisites to writing the program code.

In the true spirit of OO, Java applications can be built by assembling JavaBeans in a Java Integrated Development Environment (IDE). In other words, JavaBeans (independent software components or objects) can be combined to form an application. For example, a customer object and bank account object can be combined to form a banking application. Reusable independent software components are the foundation of object-oriented development. Soon, you will write these components using Java and then assemble them into functioning software.

Java Is Portable

Portability is the capability to run an application on different platforms (hardware and software configurations) without making changes to the code. Many of us have experienced the problems associated with moving an application from one platform to another. Typically, it required us to identify code that needed changing and then recompiling and testing every program in the application. Our task would have been trivial if our application had been portable.

With the multitude of platforms available, such as Windows, Windows NT, UNIX, MVS, and OS/2, portability is a most useful feature. Portability is, perhaps, Java's most appealing feature. In fact, "write once, run anywhere" is a common Java slogan.

What gives Java the portability so many other languages lack? Bytecode and Java Virtual Machines (JVM) are key to Java's portability. In most cases, when a program is compiled, machine code is created. For example, a COBOL program is compiled into machine code that can be executed directly by a computer. Machine code is not portable across various platforms, however, and must be created specifically for the platform to be used. A COBOL program that runs on UNIX probably will not run on MVS and most certainly will not execute on a Windows NT system. In the traditional compiled environment, multiple platforms means multiple compilers, as illustrated in Figure 1-1. If I want my COBOL program to run on UNIX and MVS and Windows NT, I need a compiler for UNIX and MVS and Windows NT. Unfortunately, even with multiple compilers, no assurance exists that the source code will compile and run correctly across all the platforms.

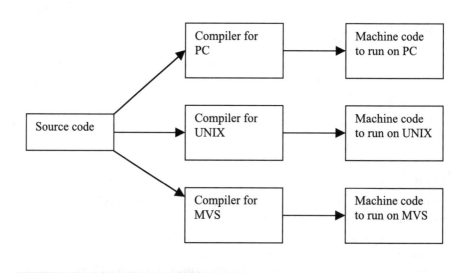

Figure 1-1. *Multiple compilers for multiple platforms*

When Java source code is compiled, it can be compiled into bytecode. Bytecode is not machine code and, therefore, is not directly executable. Instead, bytecode is an intermediate format—somewhere between source code and machine code. For bytecode to be executed on a computer, another tool, called a virtual machine is needed to interpret the bytecodes. A Java Virtual Machine (JVM) is a program that interfaces with the local operating system and hardware. The JVM interprets the bytecode at runtime so the Java program can run on the local platform, as illustrated in Figure 1-2.

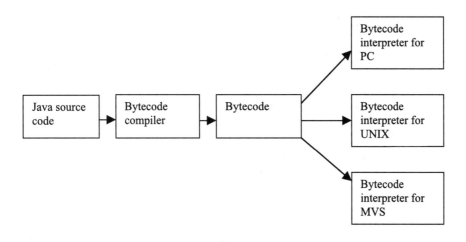

Figure 1-2. *Java running on multiple platforms*

Many different JVMs exist to accommodate the many different platforms. Therefore, only one version of the bytecode file is needed to run on many platforms. Bytecodes are platform independent and portable as long as a JVM is available for the platform for which you want to run the bytecodes. The combination of bytecodes and JVM guarantees portability—no need to re-compile the program for each platform and no need to have multiple compilers for multiple platforms.

Many operating systems fortunately are providing JVMs for their environment. Currently, Windows, Windows NT, Windows CE, Solaris, HP-UX, IRIX, AIW, and MacOS, among others, support Java. And Internet Web browsers such as Netscape and Internet Explorer contain bytecode interpreters, so when a Java Applet is recognized, it is interpreted and executed.

As you probably have begun to suspect, however, interpreting a bytecode program is slower than executing native code for a particular platform. In situations where execution speed is an issue, Java can be compiled into native code (just like COBOL) and then it will run as fast as any other application language.

Will Java Replace COBOL?

COBOL's demise has been predicted since its introduction, yet it continues to thrive. Two obvious reasons exist for COBOL's strength. First, it does an incredibly good job of processing and maintaining large quantities of data—the backbone of modern businesses. Second, the language continues to evolve and improve. Each new ANSI standard provides additional features and boosts programmer productivity. The forthcoming COBOL-XX standard provides additional improvements including OO extensions. No, COBOL is not dying. In our view, it isn't even sick!

More than 3 million COBOL programmers are in the world. More than 80 percent of all code, representing as much as 200 billion lines of code, is written in COBOL. Will Java replace COBOL anytime soon? We doubt it. The year 2000 (Y2K) problem has certainly rekindled the demand and interest in COBOL programming, but will this interest continue after January 1, 2000? You may have asked yourself this question. To set the record straight, an increasing demand has occurred for COBOL programmers for many years. Y2K projects may have caused a blip in the demand curve, but the shortage of COBOL people did not begin with Y2K cleanup efforts and will certainly not end with the arrival of the new millennium. Will Java replace COBOL as the primary development language in the long run? Several unanswered questions impact the long run use of COBOL:

- Will OO development continue to be adopted by organizations? The increase, or decrease, in use of OO development in organizations will affect the use of object-oriented languages overall.

- Will Object COBOL be widely accepted? If Object COBOL is widely accepted as the next generation of COBOL, then a smooth migration path is provided to OO development. As such, companies may stick with COBOL (albeit Object COBOL) rather than switching to Java.

- What will happen to all those new COBOL programmers hired to deal with Y2K? Will these programmers continue to use COBOL after January 1, 2000, or will they move into a new area of programming, such as Java?

- Will Microsoft continue to pursue its own Java strategy? A major threat to the future of Java is the separation of Java into two camps: Microsoft in one and the consortium led by Sun Microsystems in the other. The incompatibilities between the two groups could hinder Java's portability and ultimate acceptance.

One indication of Java's encroachment into COBOL's camp is the use of the two languages in higher education information systems curricula. During the period June 1995 (remember, Java was officially introduced in May 1995) to February 1998, the teaching of Java increased from 0 percent to 42.5 percent in information systems programs of study. On the other hand, COBOL declined from 89.7 percent to 52.8 percent during the same time period (see Table 1-2).

Table 1-2: *Primary languages in undergraduate IS programs*

Language	Taught (June 95)	Taught (Feb. 98)
COBOL	89.7%	52.8%
C	54.9%	26.4%
C++	59.7%	52.8%
Object COBOL	---	6.6%
Java	---	42.5%
Smalltalk	12.7%	4.7%
Visual Basic	59.1%	69.8%
(Source: Douglas and Hardgrave, 1998)		

Let's say that again:

- Java increased from 0 to 42.5 percent

- COBOL decreased from 89.7 percent to 52.8 percent

Because adding a course to a curriculum without removing a course is difficult, one would expect that Java replaced COBOL in many college curricula.

Alchemy Computing, Ltd. suggests COBOL programmers make good client-server developers. Some of their reasons are directly applicable to Java. Why should COBOL programmers be retrained in Java? Why should YOU learn Java?

- COBOL programmers typically have a high-quality, zero-defect attitude. This type of attitude is needed to develop reusable objects that must be of high quality.

- COBOL programmers have a strong development process discipline. This discipline is needed in a Java OO development environment. Adherence to a methodical analysis and design is crucial to the successful development of an OO system.

- COBOL programmers already know the business. COBOL programmers are familiar with important business issues and processes. This knowledge gives you an edge when developing Java applications.

- COBOL programmers already know programming. You already know the logic of the various programming structures: sequence, selection, and iteration. You need learn only the new syntax.

Knowing two languages gives you a sharper perspective when designing systems. You can see solutions that are not necessarily tied to a single language.

From our perspective, we don't see Java as COBOL's replacement. Instead, we believe COBOL and Java are complementary development tools in the evolving client-server environment. COBOL's job is to process and maintain the firm's data. Java plays a complementary role by capturing and reporting data by connecting the client to the server across a variety of networked computers, with little concern about the specific hardware and operating systems involved. Today's business environment is diverse. A single platform and/or single language cannot meet the needs of most organizations. The business environment is becoming one of interconnectivity, requiring many different organizations with many different computing environments to communicate.

The Goal of This Book

After reading this book, you will be the world's best object-oriented software developer!

We wish such a claim were true. Realistically, you will learn *some* Java, but you will want to learn more. Learning about object-oriented development is equally as important as learning Java. Object-oriented development represents a new paradigm in software development and, as such, can be as challenging as learning a new programming language. In fact, one of the primary obstacles to adopting object-oriented development is many people view OO as a new programming paradigm. OO is, in fact, a new software development approach encompassing analysis, design, and programming. The next chapter gives you a good understanding of OO.

Our main goal throughout this book is to show you how to make the transition from COBOL to Java by using your existing COBOL knowledge. As you will see as you progress through the various chapters—although not everything in Java can be compared to COBOL—a significant part can be compared. Table 1-3 lists several examples.

Table 1-3: *A comparison of COBOL and Java.*

COBOL	Java
Arithmetic Operators	Arithmetic Operators
Boolean Operators	Boolean Operators
Calling Subprograms	Invoking Methods
Compute	Assignment
Conditions	Boolean expression
Evaluate Verb	Switch Statement
If-Then-Else	If-Then-Else
Intrinsic Functions	Class Library
Literals	Literals
Move	Assignment
Passing Arguments	Passing Arguments
Perform-Until	While
Perform-Until-Test After	Do – While
Perform-Varying	For Loop
Tables	Arrays

Several approaches exist to using the material in this book. One method is to read the book from the beginning to the end. This will give you an excellent overall understanding of Java and the similarities and differences between COBOL and Java.

This book can also be used as a reference by looking up only those things you need when you need them. If you are interested in defining variables, for example, read Chapter 3. If you only want to know how to change variable data types, see the section entitled "Changing Variable Types" in Chapter 4.

Each chapter provides the necessary translation of COBOL to Java for the major programming components, such as data definition, decision making, arithmetic operations, looping, tables and arrays, and input and output. Samples of COBOL code and corresponding Java code are provided to illustrate the similarities and differences between the two languages. All our program code is also packaged with the Java Café software on the accompanying CD-ROM.

Overall, you will learn the basics of Java in this book. You will not learn all the details of the Java language. For example, we deliberately avoid building Web-based Java Applets for two reasons: First, COBOL has no counterpart, and, perhaps more important, numerous excellent books dealing with this topic already exist. See the bibliography at the end of this chapter for more information.

Neither will you learn everything about developing OO software, especially OO analysis and design. Again, the focus here is moving from COBOL to Java and other books are available. We encourage you to continue learning about OO development and the Java language before building critical applications.

We think you will find Java is an easy language to learn despite what you might have heard. Your COBOL knowledge base and your programming experience will prove useful in the transition.

Remember: understanding both COBOL and Java makes you a more valuable programming professional.

Summary of Key Points

1. Java is a new language, originally created in the early 1990s and released in May 1995 by Sun Microsystems.

2. Java can do a lot more than make cute Web page animations. It is a full-featured industrial strength application development language.

3. Java is based on the C++ language, thus making it easy for C++ programmers to learn Java. Java removed the trouble-prone features of C++ and added some helpful tools.

4. Java is a pure object-oriented language, which means everything, except primitive data types, is represented as an object. This means you need to know a little about OO before you can learn Java. Chapter 2 introduces you to OO. You will be surprised how simple it really is!

5. Java is portable. It can run on many different platforms without making changes to the code. A program called the Java compiler produces a bytecode file (an intermediate compiled code) and the Java Virtual Machine interprets the bytecode. Where execution speed is an issue, native Java code can be produced to bypass the interpretation process.

6. Many issues face Java in the near future. However, Java appears to be poised as one of the most popular programming languages.

7. Many similarities exist between COBOL and Java, which will enhance and simplify your learning Java.

Glossary

Applet A program written in Java that can be embedded inside Web pages and executed in Java-compatible browsers.

Bean (aka JavaBean) An independent, reusable software component. Beans can be combined to create an application.

bytecode The code generated by a Java compiler. Bytecode is platform independent and must be interpreted by a Java interpreter.

compiled code Machine-readable code, converted from computer language syntax via a compiler.

hybrid object-oriented language A language that uses an existing language as its base and adds object-oriented features and syntax.

Java archive files (JAR files) A Java file format used for compressing many files into one to improve transmission speed across network connections.

Java Development Kit (JDK) Sun's software development environment for writing Applets and applications in Java.

Java integrated development environment (IDE) A complete Java development environment including text editors, compilers, debuggers, interpreters, and so forth.

Java virtual machine (JVM) A Java interpreter; responsible for interpreting bytecode.

JavaScript A Web scripting language developed by Netscape; has similar constructs to Java, but is a separate language. Typically used for user interface features within HTML documents, but can also be used on the server side.

portability The capability to run an application on different platforms without making changes to the code.

pure object-oriented language A language in which everything is represented as an object and all major characteristics of object-orientation such as inheritance, classes, and polymorphism are supported.

Servlet Similar to an Applet, but is located on the server; provides added functionality to Java-enabled servers.

Bibliography

Dietel, H. M., and Dietel, P. J., *Java: How to Program*, Upper Saddle River, NJ: Prentice Hall, 1997.

Douglas, D. E., and Hardgrave, B. C., "The Changing Language Mix in Information Systems Curricula," *1998 Proceedings of the National Decision Sciences Institute*, November 1998.

Garside, R., and Mariani, J., *Java: First Contact*, Cambridge, MA: Course Technology, 1998.

"Glossary of Java and Related Terms," available at *http://www.java.sun.com/docs/glossary.print.html*

Gosling, J., Joy, B., and Steele, G., *The Java Language Specification*, available at *http://java.sun.com/docs/books/jls/html/index.html*

Gosling, J., and McGilton, H., "The Java Language Environment: A White Paper," available at *http://java.sun.com/docs/white/langenv/*

Harrington, J. L., *Java Programming: An IS Perspective*, New York, NY: John Wiley & Sons, Inc., 1998.

Nilsen, K., "Adding Real-Time Capabilities to Java," *Communications of the ACM*, 41 (6), June 1998, 49-56.

Radding, A., "Tool Immaturity Tempers Java Buzz," *Software Magazine*, 17 (8), July 1997, 51-54.

"Retraining COBOL Programmers for Client-Server," available at *http://www.alchemy-computing.co.uk/coboltrn.htm*

Singhal, S., and Nguyen, B., "The Java Factor," *Communications of the ACM*, 41 (6), June 1998, 34-37.

"The Java Language: An Overview," available at *http://java.sun.com/docs/overviews/java/java-overview-1.html*

Tyma, P., "Why Are We Using Java Again?" *Communications of the ACM*, 41 (6), June 1998, 38-42.

Chapter 2

An Introduction to Object-Oriented Programming

Objectives
In this chapter you will study:
- The history of OO
- What it means to be OO
- Key OO concepts

This chapter is devoted to the introduction of the key concepts essential to your understanding of the OO paradigm, in general, and writing OO code, in particular. This chapter describes the primary OO concepts: objects, classes, inheritance, encapsulation, polymorphism, and dynamic binding. A basic understanding of these ideas will enable you to begin writing Java programs and developing OO systems.

Several examples are used throughout the chapter to illustrate the concepts. In most cases, the examples are based on everyday things with which you are already familiar. A case study (The Community National Bank Case) is introduced at the beginning of the chapter and is used to illustrate OO concepts. This case study continues to be used throughout the remainder of the book.

21

1. OO development is a **new way of thinking** about the development of systems—it is not simply a programming technique.

2. Although programming languages were the first to use the ideas of OO, the concepts of OO are prevalent throughout the entire development of a system.

3. It is important for you to understand the basics of OO before you attempt to write a Java program.

This chapter assumes a basic understanding of computing and programming; it does not, however, assume a prior knowledge of OO concepts.

The Community National Bank

The Community National Bank (CNB) is a small, privately owned bank located in a medium-sized city in the Midwestern United States. The bank was established during the early 1900s and is owned and managed by the descendants of the founder. CNB offers the typical small bank services such as checking and savings accounts, certificates of deposit, safe deposit box rental, and loans.

Defying a nationwide trend, CNB remains independent and privately owned. The bank has nearly $200 million in deposits and 60 employees.

CNB takes advantage of its relatively small size by providing personalized attentive service to its customers, especially its small business accounts.

As you learn about OO and Java, we will develop software to provide processing for CNB and its customers.

History of OO

With the recent growth in interest in OO development, you may think OO represents a new set of ideas and concepts. On the contrary, OO is not new. In fact, the beginning of OO can be traced to the mid-1960s!

Many credit the beginning of OO to the introduction of Simula, a **simu**lation **la**nguage, developed by Dahl and Nygaard in 1966. The language was officially known at that time as Simula-67. Many of the core elements of today's OO languages were contained in this early language. Also during this period of time, a professor at the University of Utah, Alan Kay, was working on the FLEX system. His goal was to develop a computer that could be used by nonexperts. Simula was a guiding force for his work. A few years later, Kay headed the Dynabook project at the Xerox Palo Alto Research Center (PARC). The outcome of the project was some new hardware, plus a new programming language named **Smalltalk**, the first OO programming language (OOPL). In fact, Kay is credited with coining the terms "object-oriented" and "object-oriented programming." Smalltalk was officially released in 1972, and remains in use today.

After Smalltalk's introduction, several years passed before OO programming received widespread attention. During the mid-1980s, new OO languages such as Objective-C, Eiffel, Flavors, and C++ were introduced. Some of the languages, such as Eiffel, were *pure* OO languages; others, such as C++, were *hybrids*. Pure OO languages view everything as an object and encompass the OO concepts discussed later in the chapter. Hybrid languages are a modification of an existing language with OO capabilities. One advantage of the hybrid languages is a short learning curve. For example, C++ quickly found a large following due in large part to the popularity of its immediate predecessor, the C language. In 1996, early versions of Object COBOL, another hybrid language, were released.

In May 1995, Sun Microsystems introduced Java, another *pure* OOPL. Perhaps no other programming language in history has witnessed the tremendous amount of attention and subsequent use as Java. Fueled by its Web applications and client-server architecture, Java has exploded onto the programming scene. Many believe Java will be the next COBOL of programming languages. As you soon see, Java is a very powerful language.

In addition to the proliferation of OOPL introductions in the mid-1980s, OO analysis and design methods began to appear. Led by the design method developed by Grady Booch, largely from his work with the Ada programming language, a plethora of methods appeared such as Objectory, OMT, Shlaer/Mellor, and Coad/Yourdon, among others. This was both good news and bad news for the software development industry. It was good because OO was beginning to receive increased attention by researchers, academicians, and industry leaders and several methods were emerging to assist in the development of OO systems. It was bad because the methods were very different, employing different approaches and notation. This divergence of methods and notation sets undoubtedly slowed the adoption of OO. Recently (circa November 1997), however, the Unified Modeling Language (UML) was adopted by the Object Management Group (OMG) as a standard notation set and metamodel for OO modeling. UML represents the efforts of many different individuals and organizations, but is primarily based on the prior work of Grady Booch, Jim Rumbaugh, and Ivar Jacobson. The adoption of a standard should help ease the burden of adopting organizations. This book uses UML notation.

With a standard notation set, the future will focus on the establishment of a standard development methodology that will use UML, a set of standards for OO databases, and OO CASE tools to support software development. Programming languages will always be an issue, but it appears that a few languages, particularly Java will be dominant.

Objects

Look around you—you probably see familiar items such as chairs, tables, books, and pencils. Could you describe these items to a person so he or she would understand what you are describing? If you close your eyes and someone hands you a pencil, could you determine the item without looking? The answer to both is (hopefully) yes. Let's think about how you would describe, for example, a pencil. One might say the item is about six inches long, wooden, round, sharp on one end, dull on one end, can write, and can erase. By describing the item (in this case, a pencil), data about the item (length, material, and so forth), and descriptions of what the item can do (write and erase) are used. In OO terminology, you have described an object. An *object* contains both data (what it knows about itself) and behavior (what it can do). In this case, the pencil knows its length, material, shape, and ends; and, it can write and erase. In OO parlance, the things an object knows about itself are called *attributes*; the things it can do are called *methods*. Thus, an object can be defined as data (attributes) and a set of behaviors (methods).

In OO programming, we write software that models real-world objects. Real-world objects can be tangible things such as a car, an airplane, a computer, and a person, or less tangible things such as a transaction. The Community National Bank system will have numerous objects such as customer, employee, and account. Can you think of some attributes and methods for each of these objects?

Attributes for an <u>Account</u> object would certainly include *accountNumber* and *balance*. Methods may include **computeServiceCharge** and **recordACheck**.

NOTE

We use the following notation:

1. **Class names:** underlined, mixed case with the first letter of each word capitalized, no spaces or hyphens.
   Example: <u>CheckingAccount</u>.

2. **Attribute names:** italicized, mixed case with the first letter lowercase, first letter of remaining words capitalized, no spaces or hyphens.
   Example: *accountNumber*.

3. **Method Names:** boldface, mixed case the first letter lowercase, first letter of remaining words capitalized, no spaces or hyphens, begins with a verb.
   Example: **recordACheck**.

Classes

A *class* is a group of objects that share common attributes and common methods. Using our earlier pencil example, we could have a drawer full of pencils of various colors, shapes, and sizes. Although different, each would be considered a pencil. They would all have a length, a shape, and could write and erase. The values of those attributes, however, would vary depending on the pencil. For example, one pencil could be six inches long, plastic, square, use #2 lead, and have a big eraser, while another pencil might be eight inches long, wooden, round, use #3 lead, and have a small eraser. Both of these are still considered pencils because they belong to the class of pencils—they share common attributes and methods. The value of the attributes and the way in which the methods (behaviors) are conducted differentiate members of the class and allow us to identify particular pencil objects. Think of a class as the epitome of all objects in the class; it describes a collection of objects, or an object type, but not any one particular object (that is, it lacks sufficient detail, such as values of attributes and details of the behaviors).

In the next chapter, we write a Java program to describe the attributes and methods of a class. This program is called a ***class program***. For the Community National Bank system, we write class programs to represent Account, Customer, and others.

Java refers to specific objects as ***instances***. In developing the CNB system, we write a class program to define and describe Account. Specific accounts are called *instances* of Account. We actually have one instance for each account at CNB. If the bank has 5,000 accounts, then there will be 5,000 instances of the account class, but we have only one account class. Remember, the actual data (account number and balance) reside in the instance, but the description of the data is defined in the class program.

You should also be aware that the definitions of class, object, and instances are not universal and, unfortunately, vary by the OO method or the OO language used. For example, some use the terms instance and object interchangeably. Here we follow the definitions that correspond to the way in which they are used by the Java language.

Diagramming Classes and Instances

Throughout this book, the Unified Modeling Language notation is used where appropriate. Figure 2-1 illustrates the UML notation for a class. Note that it has three sections: the name of the class, its attributes, and its methods. Here we italicize attribute names and bold method names.

We also use UML to diagram an instance as shown in Figure 2-2. The name aPencil is called the instance name or instance pointer. We develop this idea in much more detail in the next chapter.

The pencil (instance), is six inches long, is made of wood, is round, has an eraser on one end and lead on the other end, can write, and can erase. This particular pencil (instance) belongs to the class of all pencils.

My dog Fido (instance), weighs 20 pounds, is 15 inches tall, can bark, and can bite. Fido belongs to the class Dog.

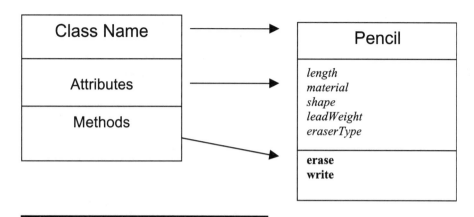

Figure 2-1. *A class symbol using UML notation*

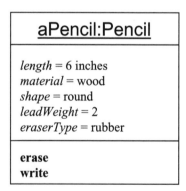

Figure 2-2. *An instance of the Pencil class*

An employee Joe (instance), has a SSN of 123-45-6789, a salary of $35,000, and can increase his salary (by earning a raise).

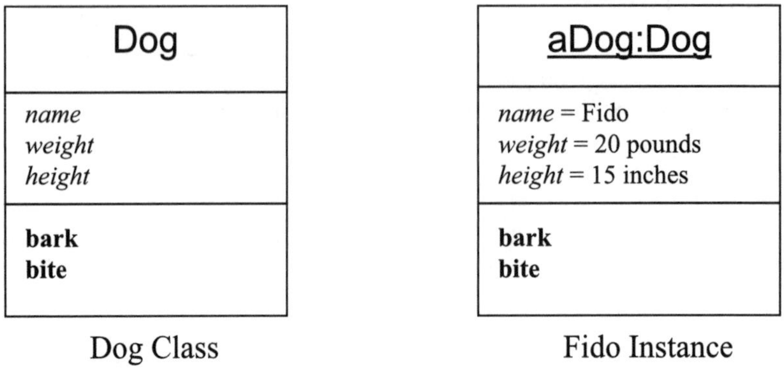

Dog
name *weight* *height*
bark **bite**

Dog Class

aDog:Dog
name = Fido *weight* = 20 pounds *height* = 15 inches
bark **bite**

Fido Instance

Figure 2-3. *A Dog class and instance*

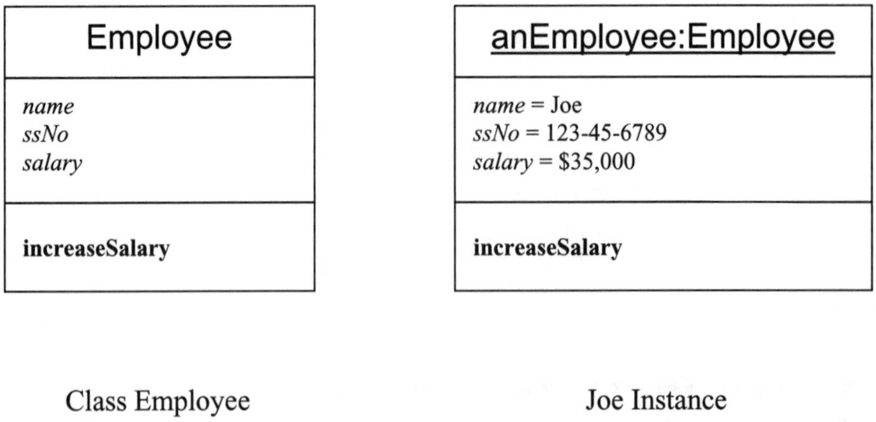

Employee
name *ssNo* *salary*
increaseSalary

Class Employee

anEmployee:Employee
name = Joe *ssNo* = 123-45-6789 *salary* = $35,000
increaseSalary

Joe Instance

Figure 2-4. *An Employee class and instance*

The Community National Bank system has several classes, shown in Figure 2-5.

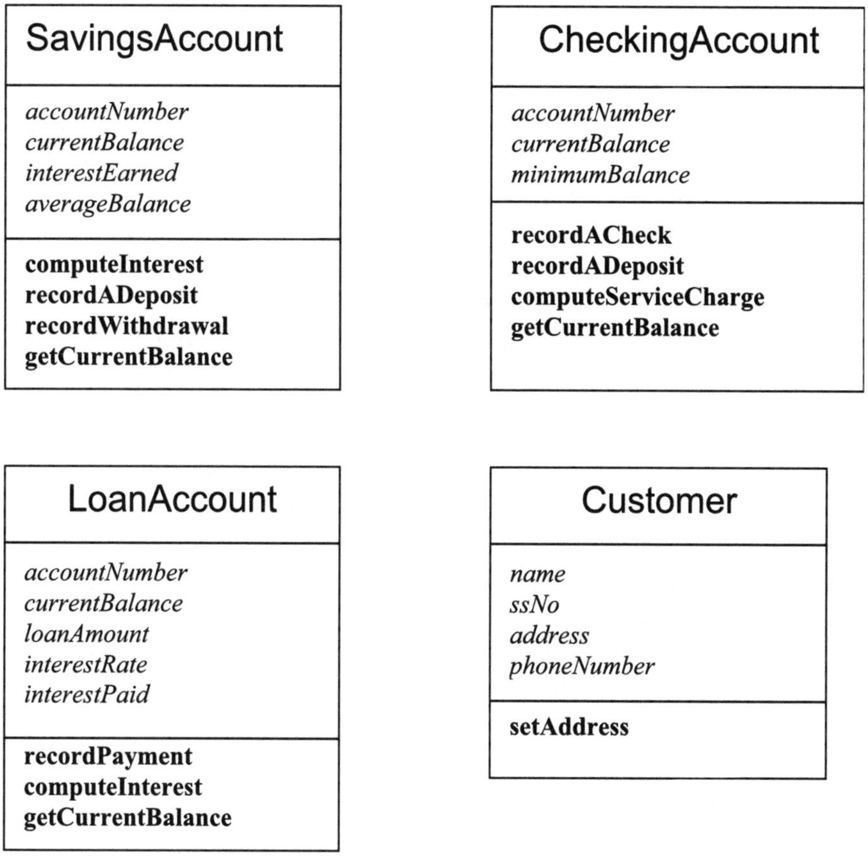

SavingsAccount
accountNumber *currentBalance* *interestEarned* *averageBalance*
computeInterest **recordADeposit** **recordWithdrawal** **getCurrentBalance**

CheckingAccount
accountNumber *currentBalance* *minimumBalance*
recordACheck **recordADeposit** **computeServiceCharge** **getCurrentBalance**

LoanAccount
accountNumber *currentBalance* *loanAmount* *interestRate* *interestPaid*
recordPayment **computeInterest** **getCurrentBalance**

Customer
name *ssNo* *address* *phoneNumber*
setAddress

Figure 2-5. *Community National Bank classes*

Understanding OO analysis and design enhances your OO programming. Unlike structured development where design is separate from programming, OO programming, OO analysis, and OO design are well integrated. This book focuses on OO programming, and enables you to begin writing OO programs using Java, but to understand OO completely, you should investigate OO analysis and design. Many excellent books exist on the subject and several are listed at the end of this chapter.

Inheritance

Inheritance is a relationship among classes wherein one class shares the attributes and/or methods defined in other classes. Inheritance permits the sharing of attributes and methods among similar classes and provides a means of locating a common set of information and behavior in one area. Inheritance is a very important concept of OO technology and is used to distinguish between *OO* languages, those that support inheritance, and *object-based* languages, those that do not support inheritance.

We saw earlier that there are many different pencil objects (wooden, plastic, long, short, and so forth) that belong to the class of Pencil. However, pencil is not the only thing in our desk drawer that we can use to write—pens and markers are also included. When we look at the various writing instruments—pencils, pens, markers—we see a common set of attributes and behaviors. In this case, all writing instruments have some type of writing tip (felt, lead, ball, and so forth), a shape (round, square, and so forth), a length, a weight, and they all can write.

We create a new class called WritingInstrument that has attributes and methods common to all types of writing instruments (in this case, pencils, pens, and markers). Specifically, all writing instruments have some type of writing tip, are composed of material, have a shape, a length, a weight, and can write.

In Figure 2-6, we take the Pencil class from Figure 2-1, but we remove the attributes *(length, material,* and *shape)* and method (**write**) that are inherited from WritingInstrument.

The arrow running from Pencil to WritingInstrument is UML notation for the inheritance relationship.

In this diagram, Pencil is called a *subclass* or *child* and WritingInstrument is the *superclass* or *parent.* Subclasses (children) inherit from their superclasses (parents). In the UML notation, the arrow points from the subclass to the superclass.

Now, let's add classes to illustrate the importance of inheritance.

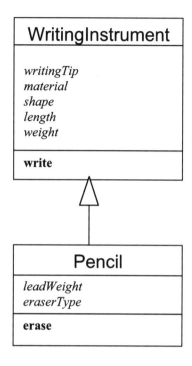

Figure 2-6. *Subclasses and superclasses*

From the earlier discussion, pens and markers can be added as subclasses of writing instruments, as Figure 2-7 illustrates.

To describe a pen, we would know its ink color, ink type, writing tip, material, shape, length, and weight, and we would know it can write. A marker has a tip size, ink color, writing tip, material, shape,

> **NOTE**
>
> 1. Java permits children to have only **one** parent. This means a subclass can have only one superclass.
>
> 2. A child with one parent is called *single inheritance*. If a child has more than one parent, it is called *multiple inheritance*. Java does **NOT** support multiple inheritance.
>
> 3. A child can also have children. If a subclass has subclasses, then it is **both** a superclass and a subclass. Its subclasses can inherit attributes and methods from its superclass.

length, and weight, and it can write. Notice all three subclasses inherit writing tip, material, shape, length, and weight attributes and the write method from their superclass.

Inheritance is often depicted as a hierarchical structure (as previously shown) and is referred to as an **IS-A** relationship. The IS-A name is derived from the way in which the diagram is translated in prose: a pencil *IS-A* writing instrument, a pen *IS-A* writing instrument, a marker *IS-A* writing instrument.

In the Community National Bank system, we noted earlier that we have three types of accounts: checking, savings, and loan. In addition, these accounts share common attributes and methods. Specifically, referring to Figure 2-5, we see all three have *accountNumber* and *currentBalance* attributes and the method **getCurrentBalance**. We can then create a superclass named <u>Account</u> and place these shared attributes and method

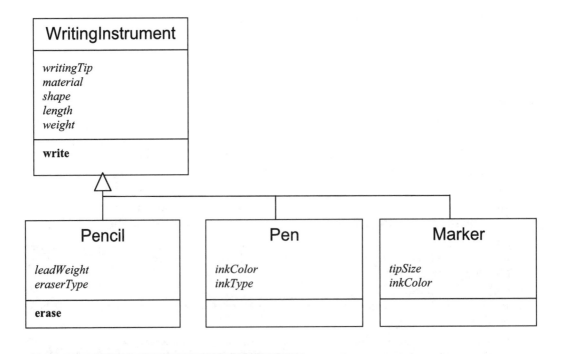

Figure 2-7. *Subclasses of WritingInstruments*

there. The new diagram is shown in Figure 2-8.

The interpretation of the diagram would be: a savings account is an account; a checking account is an account; and a loan account is an account. All accounts have an account number and a current balance and can tell you their current balance. These attributes and method are *inherited* by the three subclasses of Account.

Inheritance is extremely important in OO development for two reasons. First, the maintenance task is greatly simplified. By abstracting common attributes and behaviors, changes are localized. Using the previous CNB example, suppose we want to track the date the account was opened. We need only add this attribute to Account and it will be inherited by all subclasses. What if the bank decided to offer two types of loan

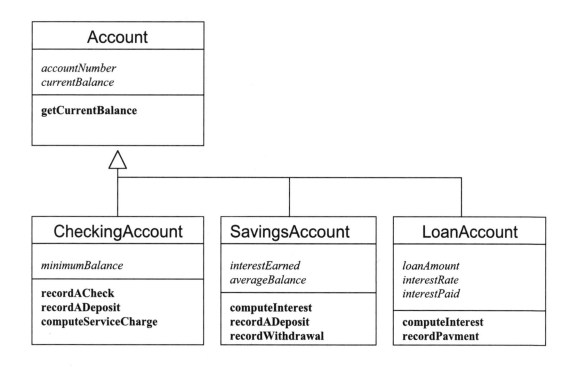

Figure 2-8. *Subclasses at CNB*

accounts, say home loans and automobile loans? We simply create these two subclasses under the existing <u>LoanAccount</u> and include only those attributes and methods unique to the new classes.

Second, inheritance gives us an excellent tool for code reuse. We have the attributes and methods written only once. We then reuse them taking advantage of inheritance.

Class Relationships

In the previous section, one type of relationship among classes was presented: the inheritance or IS-A relationship. There are, in fact, three distinguishable types of relationships:

1. Inheritance

2. Aggregation

3. Association

The inheritance relationship, also known as the IS-A or generalization/specialization relationship (*gen-spec* for short), is appropriate for those situations where one class needs to share attributes or behavior with other classes. *Aggregation*, also referred to as HAS-A, CONSISTS-OF, and PART-WHOLE, is used to illustrate a relationship among classes wherein one class is a component or part of another class. An *association* is a relationship between classes that is not an inheritance or aggregation, but rather a general linkage between classes.

Aggregation

Suppose we had a situation where it was necessary to show a PC (class) consisting of a keyboard, a monitor, and one or more secondary storage devices. One way would be to create a PC class with each of these items as attributes (as well as the typical attributes of manufacturer, date purchased, and so forth), as shown in Figure 2-9.

If we need more information beyond a simple fact about, for example, keyboards such as Yes/No or keyboard model, then the previous class structure will not work. The keyboard attribute, as part of PC, only allows for a single value. If more information is needed about the key-

PC

---

manufacturer
datePurchased
purchasePrice
keyboard
monitor
storageDevice
....

Figure 2-9. *The PC class containing all attributes*

board, such as number of keys and manufacturer, then a new class for keyboards should be created.

For discussion purposes, let's assume we need to know various pieces of information about keyboards, monitors, and storage devices. Each of those classes could be constructed as seen in Figure 2-10. (For simplicity, no methods are shown).

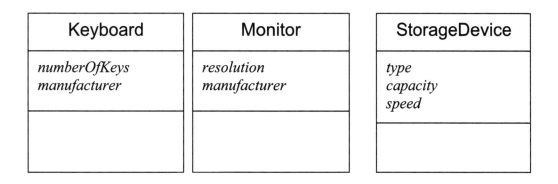

Figure 2-10. *Classes for PC components*

Now, we want to show these classes as components of the PC class. Using the UML notation, aggregation is shown in Figure 2-11.

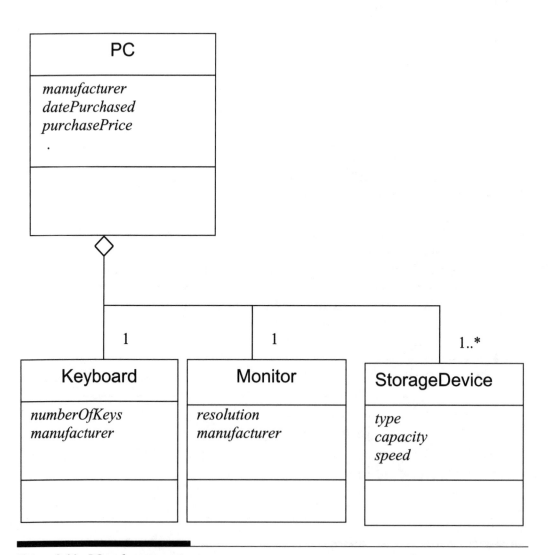

Figure 2-11. *PC and components*

In this case, the diagram is interpreted as: a PC consists of a keyboard, a monitor, and one or more storage devices. Conversely, one can say a keyboard is part of a PC, a monitor is part of a PC, and a storage device is part of a PC. The diamond symbol indicates aggregation and is connected to the class that contains the parts (often called the *WHOLE*, in the *PART-WHOLE* relationship). The PC is the WHOLE; keyboard, monitor, and storage device are the PARTS. The numbers/characters on the lines connecting the parts indicate the number of parts involved in the relationship. An indication of the number of instances of a class involved in a relationship is called **multiplicity**. Multiplicity can be stated as

1 == only 1

n == only *n* number can be involved (*n* can be stated as any number)

* == zero or more

1..* == 1 or more

n..* == *n* or more, where *n* is specified

n..*m* == *n* to *m*, where both *n* and *m* are specified

In the previous example, a PC has one (and only 1) keyboard, one (and only 1) monitor, and one or more storage devices.

> **NOTE**
> 1. An aggregation relationship does not involve inheritance.
> 2. In the previous example, a keyboard does not inherit attributes or behavior from PC. It is a part of the PC, but it does not share the PC's structure and behavior.

Association

In many cases, classes are related without sharing attributes or behavior (that is, inheritance), or without being a part of, or containing, other classes (that is, aggregation). In these cases, the relationship is simply an **association**. An association indicates a connection (not considered inheritance or aggregation) between two or more classes. For example, an employee uses a PC (Figure 2-12).

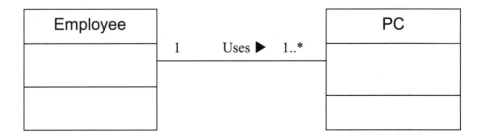

Figure 2-12. *An association relationship*

Multiplicity is interpreted as illustrated with aggregation. The previous diagram is interpreted as: an employee uses one or more PCs; a PC is used by only one employee. The previous relationship involves two classes and is thus termed a binary association. Note, a class can have an association with itself (that is, a unary association), two (binary association) classes, three (ternary association) classes, or more (n-ary association) than three classes. Introducing and explaining the various types and details of associations is beyond the scope of this book. We encourage you to seek additional sources illustrating UML notation (for example, see the Fowler & Scott book in the Bibliography at the end of this chapter).

Returning to the CNB example, we need to complete the class diagram by adding the customer class to the inheritance hierarchy. In this example, the customer owns one or more accounts; an account can only be owned by one customer (we realize that, in reality, most accounts can have more than one owner; for simplicity, we are limiting each account to one owner). The complete (at this point) class diagram from the CNB example is shown in Figure 2-13.

Object Communication

Objects communicate by sending messages that invoke methods. In fact, OO systems operate by object communication—without object communication, the system does not function. Thus, knowing what objects are

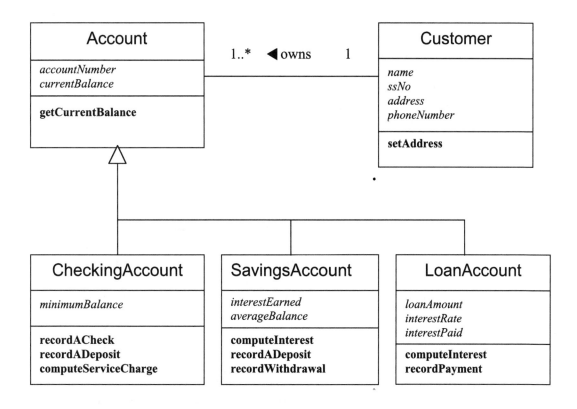

Figure 2-13. *A more complete CNB class diagram*

capable of doing (their methods) and how to communicate (send messages) with that object is important. In general, a ***message*** consists of the class or instance name, a method name, and required arguments. For example, to change the customer's address in our CNB example, the following message (in Java syntax) would be used:

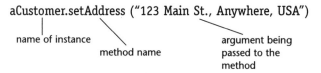

aCustomer.setAddress ("123 Main St., Anywhere, USA")

   name of instance　　　method name　　　argument being
                            passed to the
                            method

If the class does not contain the method **setAddress**, then the communication fails, unless it inherits the method. In this case, <u>Customer</u> does not inherit any attributes or methods. Notice we direct the message to an instance rather than the class. This is done because the method **setAddress**, applies to a specific customer, not the general group of customers the class represents.

Suppose we wish to know the current balance in our checking account, then the message to be used would be:

aCheckingAccount.getCurrentBalance()

The message is sent to the checking account, but looking at Figure 2-13, we see that <u>CheckingAccount</u> does not have the specified method **getCurrentBalance** and is unable to satisfy the request. In this case, <u>CheckingAccount</u> will look to its superclass, <u>Account</u>, for help. <u>CheckingAccount</u> inherits the method **getCurrentBalance** from its superclass, <u>Account</u>.

Notice the sender of the message, the client, does not know (or care) how the message request is satisfied. For example, when the message is sent to <u>CheckingAccount</u>, the sender is unaware that <u>Account</u> actually satisfies the request. Additionally, the sender does not know how the request is satisfied. In fact, the sender should not care who satisfies the request or how the request is satisfied, only that it is accomplished. The sender need know only the name of the object, the method name, and required arguments.

The goal is to protect the data in an object from everything outside the object—only the object's methods are allowed to access the object's data. The hiding of information from everything outside the object, and providing access only via methods, is called *encapsulation* (sometimes referred to as information hiding). Nothing outside the object should be aware of the object's internal structure or how its methods are implemented. Outside the object, others only need to know the object's name, the method name, and the required parameters. In fact, one can think of this as the object's interface to the outside world.

Consider the impact on maintenance that encapsulation provides. If everything is hidden within an object, then the only place a change needs be made is inside the object—nothing outside the object is affected unless the object interface changes (it never should!). For example, using our CNB example, we could add the attribute *dateOpened* to Account without affecting anything outside of the account class. We could also change the manner in which the current balance is stored, but nothing outside the account class would be affected.

Polymorphism

Polymorphism means the same message can elicit a different response, depending on the receiver of the message. Using the CNB example, both SavingsAccount and LoanAccount have methods called **computeInterest**. Thus, we could send the following messages:

> aSavingsAccount.computeInterest()
> aLoanAccount.computeInterest()

The message is the same (**computeInterest**), but the receiver of the message is different. Will both messages be handled the same way? One would hope not! The savings account's interest is based on an average monthly balance and varies by current interest rates. A loan's interest is based on a fixed interest rate (CNB does not have variable rate loans). The procedure for calculating interest for a savings account is different from calculating interest for a loan. Thus, the receiver of the message—SavingsAccount or LoanAccount—determines how the message is satisfied. Remember, because of encapsulation, those outside the object do not know how the message is satisfied (the methods could be exactly the same—we would not know!). Polymorphism provides a consistent and natural way to use messages without worrying about how or who satisfies the message. A message is sent to an object and the object handles it. It is confusing to use specific messages such as **computeSavingsInterest** and **computeLoanInterest**, when, in reality, they are both simply **computeInterest**.

Dynamic Binding

What happens when you compile a COBOL program that has the following statement, but in the data division, only *X* was defined?

```
MOVE X TO Y
```

Of course, you get an error and you can't continue until you define *Y*. Now, in the context of OO, assume an object *X* sends the following message to object *Y*:

Y.doSomething ('data')

If, at compile time, the compiler (1) finds *Y*, (2) determines that **doSomething** is a valid method (either in *Y* or in its inheritance hierarchy), and (3) links the message to the appropriate memory location (the method), then we have achieved ***static binding***. Static binding means all classes and methods are validated at compile time. Now, consider a different scenario. *Y* sends the same message, but the compiler does not check the validity. Instead, the message is only validated at runtime. In this case, ***dynamic binding*** is used. Dynamic binding means the messages are not validated until runtime.

What is the importance of static and dynamic binding? Static binding increases reliability (no runtime crashes due to undeliverable messages) and improved performance (doesn't have to look up the methods), but reduces flexibility (if a class is added or a new message is sent, the program may need to be recompiled). In contrast, dynamic binding provides increased flexibility, but less reliability and perhaps lower performance. Not all languages support both types of binding. Thus, we must be aware of the language features while developing a system. Java supports both static and dynamic binding. COBOL does support static binding, but has no provision for dynamic association.

Summary of Key Points

1. OO is not new but began in the mid-1960s.

2. OOPLs are classified as *pure* or *hybrid.* Pure OOPLs, such as Java and Smalltalk, view everything as an object; hybrids, such as C++ and Object COBOL, are extensions of non-OO languages.

3. In OO development, everything is represented as an *object.* An object contains data (attributes) and a set of operations (methods). An *instance* is a specific object (e.g., Fido is an instance of the object DOG). A *class* is a set of objects that share a common structure and a common behavior (for example, a DOG object, Fido, belongs to the class of all DOGS). Classes represent an abstraction; it is the essence of the object.

4. *Inheritance* is a relationship among classes wherein one class shares the attributes and/or methods defined in one (single inheritance) or more (multiple inheritance) other classes. Classes are represented via a hierarchy that shows the inheritance from one class to another. An inheritance relationship is also referred to as an *IS-A*, or generalization/specialization relationship.

5. There are three primary forms of relationships among classes: (1) inheritance; (2) aggregation; and (3) association. *Aggregation*, also referred to as HAS-A, CONSISTS-OF, and PART-WHOLE, is used to illustrate a relationship among classes wherein one class is a component of another class. An *association* is a relationship between classes that is not an inheritance or aggregation, but rather a general linkage between classes.

6. Objects communicate by sending *messages* that invoke methods. When we send a message, we don't know how or where it will be satisfied.

7. Information hiding is called *encapsulation.* Encapsulation means an object's data is hidden within, and protected by, a shell of procedures.

8. *Polymorphism* means the same message can elicit different responses depending on the object receiving the message. This allows com-

mon names to be used for methods (such as start, stop, run, and so forth).

9. *Dynamic binding* means the messages are not validated until runtime. This allows greater flexibility in adding objects and messages to the system, but can reduce reliability and performance. *Static binding* means messages are resolved at compile time.

Glossary

aggregation A relationship among classes wherein one class is a component or part of another class.

association A connection (not considered inheritance or aggregation) between two or more classes.

attributes The things an object knows about itself; an object's data.

binary association An association involving two classes.

class A group of objects that share common attributes and common methods.

class program Java program to describe the attributes and methods of a class.

dynamic binding Classes and methods are not validated until runtime.

encapsulation (aka information hiding) The hiding of an object's internals from everything outside the object.

inheritance A relationship among classes wherein one class shares the attributes and/or methods defined in other classes.

instance name (aka instance pointer) A unique identifier for a specific object.

instance A specific object.

message An operation that one object performs upon another; usually consists of the class or instance name, a method name, and required arguments.

methods The things an object can do; its behavior.

multiple inheritance A subclass (child) with more than one superclass (parent).

multiplicity An indication of the number of instances of a class involved in a relationship.

n-ary association An association involving n classes (usually more than three).

object An entity containing both data (what it knows about itself) and behavior (what it can do).

object interface What others outside the object see of the object; usually the object name, method name, and required parameters

object-based language A programming language that supports some OO concepts, but does not support inheritance.

object-oriented language A programming language that supports all OO concepts, including inheritance.

polymorphism The same message can elicit a different response, depending on the receiver of the message.

single inheritance A subclass (child) with only one superclass (parent).

static binding All classes and methods are validated at compile time.

subclass (aka child) Inherits attributes and/or methods from another class.

superclass (aka parent) Is inherited from by other classes.

ternary association An association involving three classes.

unary association An association involving only one class.

Bibliography

Booch, G., *Object-Oriented Analysis and Design with Applications*, The Benjamin/Cummings Publishing Company, Inc., Redwood City, CA, 1994.

Booch, G., "Object Oriented Development," *IEEE Transactions on Software Engineering*, SE-12 (2), February 1986, 211-221.

Brown, D., *Object-Oriented Analysis: Objects in Plain English*, John Wiley & Sons, New York, NY, 1997.

Deitel, H. M., and Deitel, P. J., *Java: How to Program*, Prentice-Hall, Englewood Cliffs, NJ, 1997.

Doke, E. R., and Hardgrave, B. C., *An Introduction to Object COBOL*, John Wiley & Sons, New York, NY, 1998.

Fowler, M. and Scott, K., *UML Distilled, Applying the Standard Object Modeling Language*, Addison Wesley Longman, Inc., New York, NY, 1997.

Henderson-Sellers, B., and Edwards, J., *Book Two of Object-Oriented Knowledge: The Working Object*, Prentice-Hall, Englewood Cliffs, NJ, 1994.

Kay, A. C., "The Early History of Smalltalk," *SIGPLAN Notices*, 28 (3), March 1993, 69-95.

Chapter 3

Java Structure

Objectives

In this chapter you will study:
- Java Program Structure
- Writing Class Programs
- Writing Java Comments
- Naming Rules & Conventions
- Calling Methods
- Creating Object Instances
- Working With Subclasses

The purpose of this chapter is to introduce you to the structure of Java programs. You see how to write and execute simple Java programs. By working with real functioning programs, instead of just code segments, you quickly learn the major structural differences between COBOL and Java.

This chapter begins with a program that models the customer class from the Community National Bank system introduced in Chapter 2. This program is used to illustrate Java program structure.

We show you how to write Java comments and review the simple rules for naming variables, methods, classes, and programs. We also explain the Java coding conventions and style guidelines that can greatly improve the readability of your programs.

We then execute methods in the customer class program to show how object instances are created and to demonstrate calling methods. We conclude the chapter by developing programs for the account and checking account classes to illustrate working with subclasses.

49

This chapter assumes you understand the following:

COBOL:

- COBOL program structure
- column restrictions—area A and B
- continuation column 7
- comments and remarks
- uses of periods, commas, parentheses, spaces
- scope terminators
- rules for programmer-supplied names

Java:

- OO Concepts (Chapter 2)

A Class Program

Chapter 2 introduced OO concepts and described classes and object instances. You also read about the Community National Bank's classes. The class diagram for CNB is presented again in Figure 3-1.

Programs that model classes are called *class programs* and are written to define the attributes and methods for the class they represent. For Figure 3–1, for example, we would write five class programs, one for each of the classes shown. A class program consists of Java code that defines attributes followed by method code.

A class program begins with a *class header* followed by the body of the class program enclosed in braces ({ }). The body of the class program is made up of variable (attribute) definitions followed by one or methods. Each method, in turn, consists of its own *method header* followed

---

| **NOTE** | 1. In COBOL, we use the term *data item* or *field* for attribute. |
| | 2. Java, and many other languages, use the term ***variable***. We use the term *variable* here. |

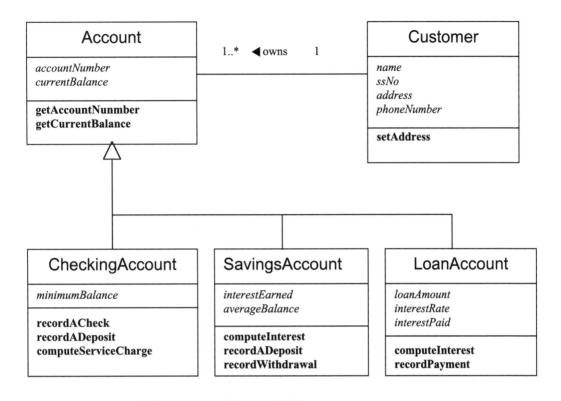

Figure 3-1. *Community National Bank classes*

by variable definitions and Java procedural statements. This structure is shown in Figure 3-2.

Let's begin our exploration of Java program structure by looking at a small class program named Customer.java, written to model the customer class for Community National Bank. From Figure 3–1, we see <u>Customer</u> has four attributes *name, ssNo, address,* and *phoneNumber*, plus the method **setAddress()**. Customer.java (see Listing 3-1) defines these four variables and the code for **setAddress()**.

Class header

{   beginning of the class program

        variable definitions for this class

We can have
several methods
for each class

Method header

{   beginning of method

    variable definitions
    java procedural statements

}   end of method

}   end of the class program

Figure 3-2. *Java class program structure*

Listing 3-1: *Customer.java*

public class Customer ——————— The class header marks the beginning
                                  of the class and names the class
    {
            // customer attribute definitions
            private String name; ——————— Java statements end with ;
            private String ssNo;
            private String address;
braces enclose private String phoneNumber;
the class and
method definitions   The method header marks the
                                          beginning of the method and
                                          names the method
            // setAddress method
              public void setAddress (String newAdr)
              {
                  address = newAdr; ——————— Java statements end with ;
              } // end of setAddress method

    } // end of Customer Class

As a programmer, you probably want to understand every line of code in this program and you soon will, but for now, be patient and let's focus on the overall structure. This simple program has the class header and then all the class code enclosed in braces. Java makes extensive use of braces to indicate the beginning and end of blocks of code. Within the class definition code, we have the attribute definitions and the method code. Notice braces also surround the method definition code.

As you may suspect, the lines with the double slash (//) are comments. We include them in the program to help you see the various components. In the next section, we describe writing comments in more detail.

Notice the Java statements terminate with a semicolon (;). At first, this may seem a bother, like the notorious period (.) we use in terminating COBOL statements. However, the Java semicolon has an important purpose—it tells the compiler this is the end of the statement. This means, like COBOL, we can write multiline Java statements and simply terminate the statement with the semicolon. This gives us flexibility in including indentation and white space in our programs to improve readability.

> **NOTE**
>
> Java does not provide us with scope terminating statements, such as END-IF, END-COMPUTE, and so forth. We must rely on semicolons and braces to indicate end of statements and blocks of code. Although this may seem at first to be cryptic, you will soon come to appreciate the brevity of this approach.

Let's look at the details of Customer.java beginning with the class header:

This is a *public* class   Its name is Customer

```
public class Customer
```

The class header serves to indicate the start of the class, to name the class, and to define *accessibility* to the class. This header specifies **public** accessibility, which means any program may access the class.

The four attributes of Customer are defined as:

```
private String name;
private String ssNo;              Don't forget the semicolons!
private String address;
private String phoneNumber;       String is the type of data. It is
                                  similar to COBOL's PIC X
```

As you probably have guessed, the word *private* in each line indicates no other program may access these attributes—their accessibility is private. String simply means the contents will be alphanumeric (similar to PIC X in COBOL). Following String is the name of the attribute, which you will notice matches the attribute names in our class diagram (Figure 3–1). Java calls these statements "variable definition statements."

NOTE

1. Like COBOL, each Java variable definition must include a datatype.

2. Chapter 4 describes Java data definition and data types.

The **setAddress()** method consists of a method header followed by a single statement sandwiched between two braces. The method header appears as:

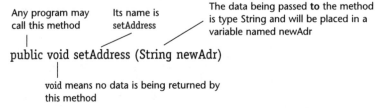

In general, a method header follows the format

access   return_data_type   method_name (parameter_list)

- *access* is either *public* (the method may be called by anyone), *private* (may be called only from within this class), or *restricted* (may be called from within this class or its subclasses).

- *return_data_type* indicates the type of data (String, integer, and so forth) that will be returned to the method. Only one "piece" of data can be returned, although the data can be a variable or an object instance. A data type of *void* is also legitimate and indicates that no data is returned.

- *method_name* specifies the name of the method.

- *parameter_list* contains the data types and variable names of the values being passed to the method. The method name combined with the parameter list is called the **method signature**.

The single statement in **setAddress()** is called an *assignment* statement because it *assigns* or stores a value into a variable. Here, this statement stores the value passed (the new customer address) into the attribute named address.

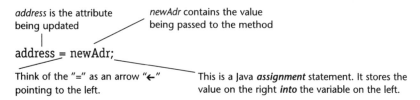

address is the attribute being updated

newAdr contains the value being passed to the method

address = newAdr;

Think of the "=" as an arrow "←" pointing to the left.

This is a Java *assignment* statement. It stores the value on the right *into* the variable on the left.

We demonstrate the execution of this program later in the chapter, but first we want to describe Java structure in a little more detail.

Java Column Restrictions

In general, the column restrictions and margin rules of COBOL are much more strict than Java. For example, COBOL has reserved the first six columns for sequence numbers (page and line numbers carried over from the days of coding forms and punched cards), and the seventh column for comments and continuation characters. COBOL has a part of the coding line named Area A and another named Area B. Certain COBOL code must begin in one area or the other.

Fortunately, Java has no such column restrictions. To be fair, however, the next COBOL release (COBOL-XX) promises to remove some column restrictions (in addition to giving us OO language extensions).

Like COBOL, good Java programming style suggests we adopt the practice of using indentation and white space to improve program readability.

Writing Comments in Java

Because Java programs are less self-documenting than COBOL programs, we make more use of comments in our Java programs. The Java language provides three types of comments:

1. Single Line

2. Multiple Line

3. Documentation

A *single line comment* begins with two forward slashes (//). Some examples are:

```
// This is a comment line
if (minimumBalance < 500)  // The service charge is $5.00
    serviceCharge = 5.00F;  // if minimum balance is below
                            // $500.00
```

The second example here combines an instruction and a comment. (The new COBOL-XX standard will also give us this capability.) The Java compiler simply ignores everything on a line following double slashes (//).

A multiple line comment begins with a forward slash followed by an asterisk (/*) and terminates with an asterisk followed by a forward slash (*/). The multiple line comment is a handy tool whenever you want to write several lines of comments in a program. This is a little dangerous, however, because when the compiler encounters the slash-asterisk (/*), it assumes everything following is a comment until it detects the terminating asterisk-slash (*/). If you forget to write the (*/), the compiler will ignore the remainder of your program statements!

```
/****************************************
*     You can write very long           *
*     comments using the multiple        *
*     line comment                       *
****************************************/
/*
    You don't need all of the
    asterisks in the previous
    example unless you like
    their appearance
*/
```

```
/*    Don't forget to terminate
      multiple line comments or
      the compiler will ignore
      the remainder of your program!
      Oops! The following 'if' is ignored!
      if (minimumBalance < 500)
          serviceCharge = 5.00F;
```

Documentation comments are also multiline, but begin with a slash followed by two asterisks (/**) and terminate with asterisk-slash (*/). These comments are called documentation comments because they can be used to produce program documentation. A supplied program named javadoc reads your source program and generates a report containing the documentation comments. This report contains hyperlinks and can be read with a Web browser.

Naming Rules and Conventions

Java names for classes, methods, and variables are officially called *identifiers*. Java's rules for naming identifiers are quite simple. An identifier name has only two requirements. It may

1. be as long as you wish, but must start with a letter of the alphabet (A–Z, a–z), $, or underscore

2. include any character except space (we generally avoid using the Java operators +, -, *, /).

For example, the following are *not* valid Java identifier names:

- 4Score (does not begin with a letter, $ or _. Note: fourScore is OK.)

- Student Name (contains a space. studentName is OK)

NOTE

1. COBOL programmers are accustomed to using the hyphen (-). Java programmers **do not** use the hyphen as part of an identifier because the compiler will interpret it as the **subtract** operator!

2. Be careful—Java is case-sensitive. Java makes a distinction between CustomerName and customerName.

Java programmers, like COBOL programmers, have adopted a convention or style for writing code. Specific naming conventions have evolved and we suggest you use them in your code. In addition to the obvious rule that all identifiers should be meaningful and descriptive we suggest:

- Class Names begin with the first word and successive words capitalized
  Account, SavingsAccount, Customer

- Constant names are all uppercase with an underscore separating each word
  PRIME_INTEREST_RATE, PERCENT_CASH_DISCOUNT

- Method names begin with lowercase but have the remaining words capitalized
  getCurrentBalance, computeInterest

- Program names are the class name followed by ".java"
  Account.java, Customer.java

- Variable names begin with lowercase but have the remaining words capitalized
  customerName, currentBalance, accountNumber

> **NOTE**
>
> 1. Although Java enables us to have more than one class within a program, there can be only one **public** class. The program name is the same as the public class name. In the examples in this book, we use only one class per program.
>
> 2. Because both method names and variable names begin with a lowercase letter, we generally include a verb in the method name to indicate its primary task—for example, **recordACheck()** and **computeServiceCharge()**. Note the methods also have parentheses following the name.

Creating Instances

Chapter 2 made an important distinction between a *class* and an *object instance*. Recall that a class serves to define the attributes and methods for the class. For example, <u>Customer</u> represents *all* the customers of Community National Bank. An instance of <u>Customer</u>, however, represents a **single specific customer**. The class program Customer.java describes the four attributes every customer will have. Each instance, however, will have its own values for *name, ssNo, address*, and *phoneNumber*.

To do any processing for a specific customer, say Jed Muzzy, we must first create an *instance* for Jed. This instance will contain values for Jed's *name, ssNo, address*, and *phoneNumber*. Figure 3-3 illustrates both the customer class and an instance of the class for customer Jed Muzzy.

Customer
name *ssNo* *address* *phoneNumber*
setAddress

The Customer Class

aCustomer:Customer
name = Jed Muzzy *ssNo* = 499444471 *address* = P.O. Box 1881,   Great Falls, MT 59601 *phoneNumber* = None
setAddress

An Instance of Customer

Figure 3-3. *Customer class & instance*

We create an object instance by executing a special method in the class program called a ***constructor.*** A constructor method is similar to other methods in that it has a method header and statements sandwiched between braces. The constructor method, however, always has the same name as the class. The constructor method for <u>Customer</u> is:

The constructor method name is the same as the class name

The parameters contain the attribute values for the new instance

```
public Customer (String newName, String newSSNo, String newAdr, String
    newPhone)
{
  name = newName;
  ssNo = newSSNo;
  address = newAdr;
  phoneNumber = newPhone;
} // end constructor
```

These assignment statements populate the attributes for this particular customer instance

Notice the constructor method has a slightly different format from other methods. As specified earlier, a method follows the form:

access   return_data_type   method_name   (parameter_list)

What is missing from the constructor method? The return_data_type is not specified. Constructor methods never return data. Thus, for constructor headers, a return_data_type is not included.

Most Java classes also include methods to report the values of the attributes. Our program, for example, should have methods to tell us the *name, ssNo, address,* and *phoneNumber* of a customer. Methods that report attribute values are called ***accessor*** methods. Let's add the accessor methods to Customer.java.

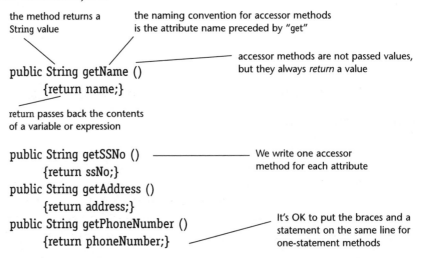

the method returns a
String value

the naming convention for accessor methods
is the attribute name preceded by "get"

accessor methods are not passed values,
but they always *return* a value

```
public String getName ()
     {return name;}
```

return passes back the contents
of a variable or expression

```
public String getSSNo ()
     {return ssNo;}
public String getAddress ()
     {return address;}
public String getPhoneNumber ()
     {return phoneNumber;}
```

We write one accessor
method for each attribute

It's OK to put the braces and a
statement on the same line for
one-statement methods

Java classes also generally include methods to change attribute values. These are called ***mutator methods***. Their names traditionally begin with "set", followed by the variable name. For example, the mutator for *address* is **setAddress()**. Technically, we should also have mutator methods for the other attributes, but we have omitted them here for brevity. Feel free to add them yourself.

We now have a complete working class program that models Customer (see Listing 3-2). It has the four attributes, a constructor method to create instances, the mutator method **setAddress()** to change the customer's address, and the four accessor methods to report the attribute values.

Listing 3-2: *Customer.java*

```
public class Customer
{ // customer attribute definitions
    private String name; // private scope limits access to this class
    private String ssNo;
    private String address;
    private String phoneNumber;
    // constructor method to create an instance
    public Customer (String newName, String newSSNo, String newAdr,
String newPhone)
    {
        name = newName;
        ssNo = newSSNo;
        address = newAdr;
        phoneNumber = newPhone;
    } // end constructor
    // setAddress mutator method
    public void setAddress (String newAdr)
    { address = newAdr;
    } // end setAddress

    // accessor methods
    public String getName ()
        {return name;}
    public String getSSNo ()
        {return ssNo;}
    public String getAddress ()
        {return address;}
    public String getPhoneNumber ()
        {return phoneNumber;}
} // end Customer.java
```

Invoking Methods

As you can see, we write methods to do things—whatever processing is required. A Java method, although different, can be compared to a

COBOL subprogram. We execute subprograms in COBOL using the CALL statement and we can pass values to and from a subprogram. Figure 3-4 illustrates the use of a COBOL subprogram to compute an employee's pay.

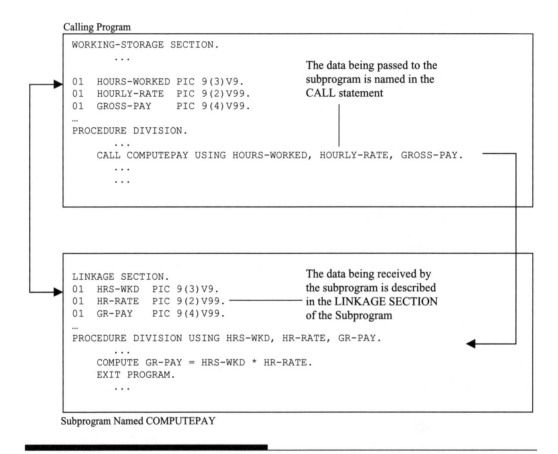

Calling Program

```
WORKING-STORAGE SECTION.
    ...
                                      The data being passed to the
01  HOURS-WORKED PIC 9(3)V9.         subprogram is named in the
01  HOURLY-RATE  PIC 9(2)V99.        CALL statement
01  GROSS-PAY    PIC 9(4)V99.
...
PROCEDURE DIVISION.
    ...
      CALL COMPUTEPAY USING HOURS-WORKED, HOURLY-RATE, GROSS-PAY.
      ...
      ...
```

```
LINKAGE SECTION.                     The data being received by
01  HRS-WKD  PIC 9(3)V9.             the subprogram is described
01  HR-RATE  PIC 9(2)V99.            in the LINKAGE SECTION
01  GR-PAY   PIC 9(4)V99.            of the Subprogram
...
PROCEDURE DIVISION USING HRS-WKD, HR-RATE, GR-PAY.
    ...
      COMPUTE GR-PAY = HRS-WKD * HR-RATE.
      EXIT PROGRAM.
      ...
```

Subprogram Named COMPUTEPAY

Figure 3-4. *Execution of a COBOL subprogram*

Similarly, we execute Java methods by calling them and we can pass and receive values. Figure 3-5 shows the execution of a Java method similar to the previous COBOL example.

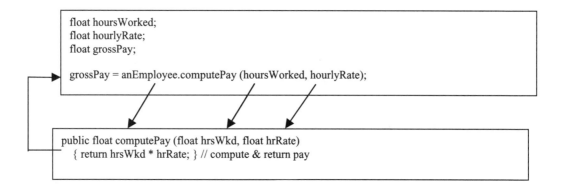

Figure 3-5. *Execution of a Java method*

In general, we call a method by specifying the name of the instance, the method name, and the argument we wish to pass to the method. For example, to change the customer's address in our CNB example, we simply execute the following statement:

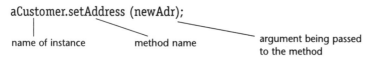

aCustomer.setAddress (newAdr);

name of instance   method name   argument being passed to the method

To obtain a customer's address, we would write:

customerAddress = aCustomer.getAddress ();

This statement calls the method **getAddress()**, and stores the value returned by the method in the variable customerAddress. Of course, the variable customerAddress would have to be previously defined.

NOTE

1. An *argument* is the data passed **to** a method.

2. A *parameter* is the data received **by** the method.

3. We pass an *argument* into a *parameter*.

4. The parameter list in the method header creates local variables to contain the argument values being passed to the method. Changing the contents of these variables **does not change** the original argument values.

To illustrate how all this actually works, let's write a real functioning program to call the various methods in Customer.java. We will name this new program CustomerProcessor.java. This program does not model a class and it has only one method named **main()**. This is a special Java method that is automatically executed when the program is loaded—we don't call it.

Listing 3-3: *CustomerProcessor.java*

```
1. public class CustomerProcessor
2. {
3.   public static void main (String args[]) // main is first method
                                             // executed
4.   { // customer attribute definitions
5.     String name = "Jed Muzzy";
6.     String ssNo = "499444471";
7.     String address = "P.O. Box 1881, Great Falls, MT 59601";
8.     String phoneNumber = "None";
9.     // create an account instance
10.    Customer aCustomer = new Customer(name, ssNo, address,
          phoneNumber);
11.    // retrieve and display customer information
12.    System.out.println ("Name: " + aCustomer.getName());
13.    System.out.println ("SS No: " + aCustomer.getSSNo());
14.    System.out.println ("Address: " + aCustomer.getAddress());
15.    System.out.println ("Phone: " + aCustomer.getPhoneNumber());
16.    // change address then redisplay
17.    aCustomer.setAddress ("P.O. Box 1998, St. Louis, MO 63105");
18.    System.out.println ("Address: " + aCustomer.getAddress());
19. } // end main
20. } // end CustomerProcessor.java
```

This parameter doesn't do anything, but it is required for the main method

NOTE Although the method header for main() (line 3) appears a little strange, it is required as is by the Java compiler. For now, don't worry about the header.

CustomerProcessor.java does five things:

1. Establishes values for the attributes (lines 5–8)
   These four statements declare the four variables and assign their values

2. Creates an instance of customer (line 10)
   Line 10 calls the constructor method in Customer.java and passes it the values for the four attributes. The instance reference is then stored in the variable aCustomer.

   aCustomer is a reference variable of   Customer() is the constructor
   type Customer   method in Customer.java

   Customer aCustomer = new Customer(name, ssNo, address, phoneNumber);

   An *instance reference variable*, aCustomer in this example, is simply a variable that contains the memory address of the instance. In other words, it is a *pointer* to the memory location of the instance. When Java creates an instance, memory space is allocated to contain the attribute values for the instance.

3. Retrieves and displays attribute values (lines 12–15)
   println() is a system method used to display output. Notice we pass the argument ("Name: " + aCustomer.getName()). Java, working from the inside parentheses out, first executes **getName()** for the instance specified by aCustomer. Then the literal "Name: " is concatenated with the value returned by **getName()**, and this concatenated value is the argument passed to the method println().

4. Changes the address value (line 17)
   Here we simply pass the new address, a literal value this time, instead of a variable, to **setAddress()**. The method stores the new address in the attribute *address* for this instance.

5. Once more, retrieve and display the address (line 18)

The output from the program is:

```
Name: Jed Muzzy
SS No: 499444471
Address: P.O. Box 1881, Great Falls, MT 59601
Phone: None
Address: P.O. Box 1998, St. Louis, MO 63105
```

NOTE   The CD-ROM included with this book contains a Java compiler, plus all of the program examples in the book.

As with all of the programs in the book, we encourage you not only to execute them, but experiment with them by making changes and examining the output. For example, an excellent exercise here is to modify CustomerProcessor.java to create two instances of the customer class and then execute various methods for each instance. Note you needn't make any changes to Customer.java, only to CustomerProcessor.java. You will, however, need to have two instance reference variables. You could use aCustomer and aSecondCustomer, for example.

Working With Subclasses

Recall from Figure 3–1 that the Account class has three subclasses: CheckingAccount, SavingsAccount, and LoanAccount. We show Account and CheckingAcccount in Figure 3-6.

This class diagram tells us several important things. First, Account is a superclass of CheckingAccount and CheckingAccount is a subclass of Account. Also, recall from Chapter 2 that the diagram indicates we have an Inheritance or IS-A relationship. A CheckingAccount IS-A Account. The subclass CheckingAccount inherits methods and relationships from its superclass, Account.

Let's first write a class program for Account. This program will be named Account.java and will have two attributes, *accountNumber* and *currentBalance* plus two accessor methods **getAccountNumber()** and **getCurrentBalance()**. In addition, we will add the constructor method named **Account()** and the mutator method **setCurrentBalance()**. We will not include a mutator for *accountNumber*.

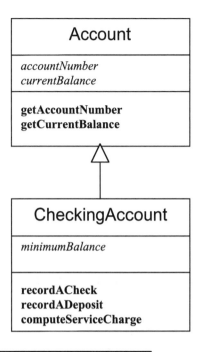

Figure 3-6. *Account and subclass CheckingAccount*

Listing 3-4: *Account.java*

abstract means this class will not have an instance.
Instead, we create instances of the subclass

1. public abstract class Account // abstract classes do not have instances
2. {   // account attribute definitions
3.   private int accountNumber; // private scope limits access to this class
4.   private float currentBalance;

private means only this program has access

5. // constructor method for abstract class only populates attributes
6. public Account (int newAccountNumber, float newCurrentBalance)

int means datatype integer.   float means datatype floating point.
Chapter 4 discusses data types.   Chapter 4 discusses datatypes.

```
7. {
8.    accountNumber  = newAccountNumber; // populate the attributes
9.    currentBalance = newCurrentBalance;
10.   } // end constructor
11.   // accessor methods
```

```
          getAccountNumber()           getAccountNumber()
          returns an integer value     receives no values
                         \                          \
12. public int getAccountNumber ()
13.    { return accountNumber; }
14.    public float getCurrentBalance ()
15.    { return currentBalance; }
16.    // mutator method
```

```
           protected limits access to this and subclasses
           |
17.   protected void setCurrentBalance (float newCurrentBalance)
18. {   currentBalance = newCurrentBalance;
19.   } // end setCurrentBalance
20. }  // end of Account.java
```

Notice the header for Account.java contains the word ***abstract***. This means we will not create an instance of <u>Account</u>. Instead, we create instances of the subclass <u>CheckingAccount</u> that inherits <u>Account</u> methods. Here the superclass exists only so its subclasses <u>CheckingAccount</u>, <u>SavingsAccount</u>, and <u>LoanAccount</u> can inherit from it.

The accessibility for the attributes is private in this program. Private accessibility means only this program may access the attribute. Other programs must use the accessor methods to obtain attribute values such as the balance and account number. This example illustrates data encapsulation.

Next, let's write the class program for <u>CheckingAccount</u>. This program has only one attribute, *minimumBalance*, and five methods. It has a constructor method, an accessor method, **getMinimumBalance()**, plus two ***custom methods*** recordACheck() and recordADeposit(). A custom method is one we write to do some processing, such as record a check or deposit. To keep this example simple and the program a little smaller, we have omitted the custom method **computeServiceCharge()**. We develop this method later in Chapter 6.

Listing 3-5: *CheckingAccount.java*

extends Account means <u>CheckingAcccount</u>
is a subclass of <u>Account</u>

```
1. public class CheckingAccount extends Account  // superclass is account
2. {  // class variable
3.    private float minimumBalance;// private limits access to this class
4. // constructor method
5. public CheckingAccount (int newAccountNumber,float newCurrentBalance)
6. {  // invoke account constructor to populate account attributes
7.    super (newAccountNumber, newCurrentBalance); // super is the superclass
8.    minimumBalance = newCurrentBalance;   // populate checkingAccount
                                            // attribute
9. } // end constructor
10. // accessor method
11. public float getMinimumBalance ()
12.   { return minimumBalance; }
13. // post a check to this account
14. public void recordACheck (float checkAmount)
15.   { float balance = getCurrentBalance(); // retrieve balance
16.   balance = balance - checkAmount;       // subtract check
17.   setCurrentBalance(balance);            // store new balance
18. } // end recordACheck
19. // post a deposit to this account
20. public void recordADeposit (float depositAmount)
21. { float balance = getCurrentBalance();   // retrieve balance
22.    balance = balance + depositAmount;    // add deposit
23.    setCurrentBalance(balance);           // store new balance
24. } // end recordADeposit
25. }  // end of checking account class
```

Let's look a little closer at one of the custom methods, **recordACheck()**.

```
// post a check to this account
 public void recordACheck (float checkAmount)
    { float balance = getCurrentBalance(); // retrieve balance
```

```
        balance = balance - checkAmount;    // subtract check
        setCurrentBalance(balance);         // store new balance
    } // end recordACheck
```

recordACheck() does three things:

1. retrieves the balance from the account instance

2. subtracts the check from the balance

3. stores the new balance in the instance

Notice the method calls **getCurrentBalance()** to retrieve the account balance and store it in the variable balance. **getCurrentBalance()** is inherited from Account.java. The method resides in Account.java, not in CheckingAccount.java. Similarly, **recordACheck()** calls the inherited method **setCurrentBalance()** to store the new balance.

Finally we write a little program named AccountProcessor.java to create a checking account instance and then we execute methods in CheckingAccount.java.

Listing 3-6: *AccountProcessor.java*

```
1. public class AccountProcessor
2. {
3.   public static void main (String args[])    // main is the first method
                                                 // executed
4.   {
5.   // attribute values
6.   int accountNumber = 12345;
7.   float currentBalance = 50.00F;          "F" means the value is
                                             floating point

     anAccount is a variable containing the
     memory address of the instance
                                             pass the account number and balance
                                             to the constructor method
8. // create a checking account instance
9. CheckingAccount anAccount = new CheckingAccount(accountNumber,
       currentBalance);
10. // retrieve and display current balance
11. System.out.println ("Beginning Balance: " +
```

anAccount.getCurrentBalance());

12. // post a $20 check then again retrieve and display current balance

13. anAccount.recordACheck (20.00F); ——— notice we pass a literal, but we could pass a variable

14. System.out.println ("Balance After $20 check:"+
    anAccount.getCurrentBalance());

15. // post a $15 deposit then again retrieve and display current balance

16. anAccount.recordADeposit (15.00F);

17. System.out.println ("Balance After $15
    deposit:"+anAccount.getCurrentBalance());

18. } // end main

19. } // end accountProcessor.java

As you can see, this program does several things:

1. Creates a checking account instance with account number 12345 and a current balance of $50.00 (line 9)

2. Retrieves and displays the current balance (line 11)

3. Records a $20 check (line 13)

4. Retrieves and displays the current balance (line 14)

5. Records a $15.00 deposit to the account (line 16)

6. Again retrieves and displays the current balance (line 17)

The output from AccountProcessor.java is

```
Beginning Balance: 50.0
Balance After $20 check: 30.0
Balance After $15 deposit: 45.0
```

Summary of Key Points

1. Java programs that model classes are called *class programs.* Class programs must have the same name as the class they represent, with the ".java" extension. For example, the class program for Account is Account.java.

2. Class programs consist of a class header followed by the class attribute (variable) definitions and one or more methods. Methods consist of variable definitions and Java procedural code. Java uses braces ({}) to enclose class and method definitions.

3. Java lacks the column restrictions of COBOL. Statements may begin and end in any column. Java statements terminate with a semicolon (;).

4. Java has three different types of comments:
   - Single Line—begins with double slash
     // this is a comment

   - Multiple Line—begins with slash-asterisk and ends with asterisk-slash
     /* this is a multiline comment */

   - Documentation—begins with a slash-double asterisk and ends with asterisk-slash.
     /** this is an example of a documentation comment */

5. The names of Java classes, methods, and variables are called *identifiers.* An identifier may be any length, but it must begin with a letter or & or underscore and may include any character but space.

6. Access to Java classes, methods, and variables is either *public* (all programs have access), *private* (only this class has access), or *protected* (this class and its subclasses have access).

7. An important distinction exists between a *class* and an *object instance.* A class, such as Account, represents the attribute definitions and method code for all accounts. An *instance* of Account, on the other hand, represents a **specific** customer's account and contains the **values** for the account number and current balance of the account.

8. We write a special method called a ***constructor*** to create instances of a class. A constructor has the same name as the class.

9. We write ***accessor*** methods to report attribute values for specific instances, ***mutator*** methods to change attribute values, and ***custom*** methods to do processing.

10. Java methods are executed by calling them, similar to calling COBOL subprograms. The Java call statement has the following format:

    instance_name.method_name (argument_list)

11. ***Arguments*** are passed to methods and ***parameters*** are received by methods.

12. Subclasses ***inherit*** from their superclass. We define superclasses as ***abstract*** to indicate instances of the superclass will not exist.

13. A method name combined with the parameter list is called the ***method signature***.

14. The Java ***assignment*** statement *assigns* or stores a value into a variable.

Glossary

abstract Java keyword used in class header to indicate the class will not have instances. Instead, we create instances of its subclass.

accessor method a method that returns an attribute value. Named with a prefix "get" plus the variable name.

argument the variable or variables passed to a method.

assignment statement Java uses the assignment to store a value into a variable. The expression on the right side of the equal sign is evaluated and the result is placed in the variable on the left of the equal sign.

class header the first line in a class definition containing accessibility, class name, and other keywords.

class program a Java program written to model a class. The program contains the attribute definitions and method code for the class.

constructor method a method to create object instances. It has the same name as the class.

custom method a method designed and written to do some custom processing.

data type the type of data—String, integer, floating point, and so forth.

identifier a term used for the name associated with Java programs, classes, methods, and variables.

method header the first line of a method definition indicating accessibility, return data type, method name, and parameter list.

method signature the method name and its parameter list.

mutator method a method that changes the contents of an attribute. Named with a prefix "set" plus the variable name.

object instance an area of memory containing values for a specific member of a class.

parameter the variables received by a method.

private access only this program has access to this method or variable.

protected access only this program and its subclasses have access to this method or variable.

public access any program has access to this method or variable.

reference variable a variable that *points to* an object instance.

return a Java statement that *returns* a specified variable to the calling program.

variable a variable is a place in memory used to store data. The data can be either a value or a *pointer* to an object instance.

Chapter 4

Defining Data

Objectives

In this chapter you will study:
- Defining Java Data
- Java Data Types
- Variable Scope
- Using Literals
- Defining Constants
- Changing Data Types
- Using Java's String Class

In this chapter, you learn how to define data using Java. We write data definition statements for alphanumeric, numeric, and Boolean data (arrays are described and illustrated in Chapter 8). You see how to use a supplied Java class program named String to simplify the definition and manipulation of alphanumeric data. You also learn about the *scope* of variables. Scope determines which parts of your program can access a variable or method.

At the end of this chapter, we develop the complete data definition statements for the attributes of the Community National Bank classes developed in the previous chapter.

COBOL uses the term *Data Item* or *Field*.   **NOTE**

Java uses the term *Variable*.

In keeping with the spirit of Java, here we use *Variable*.

This chapter assumes you know about:

COBOL

- Data Division code
- Picture clauses
- Usage clause
- bits and bytes

Java

- OO concepts (Chapter 2)
- Java Program Structure (Chapter 3)

COBOL Picture Clause

Those of us writing COBOL programs are accustomed to using the PICTURE clause to describe data items. The PICTURE clause, always contained in the Data Division of a COBOL program, establishes the *data type* of data (numeric or alphanumeric), the size of the data item, the number of decimal positions for numeric values, and indicates if the item is signed. To illustrate:

```
                                        1 Byte Alphanumeric

05  ACCOUNT-TYPE          PIC X(1).
                                        7 Bytes, Numeric, Signed, 2 Decimals

05  MINIMUM-BALANCE       PIC S9(5)V99.
```

COBOL also uses the terms *group item* and *elementary item*. In the following example, ACCOUNT-INFORMATION is a group item, while ACCOUNT-TYPE and MINIMUM-BALANCE are elementary items. A group item is simply a concatenation of elementary items.

```
01  ACCOUNT-INFORMATION.
    05  ACCOUNT-TYPE       PIC X(1).
    05  MINIMUM-BALANCE    PIC S9(5)V99.
```

In addition, COBOL has a USAGE clause to specify how data is stored, such as USAGE DISPLAY and USAGE COMP-3.

Defining Java Variables

Java's data definition is somewhat different from COBOL. Like COBOL, all variables must be defined as a specific data type. However, variables are declared in a different way.

Unlike COBOL, Java has no Data Division, which means we can define our variables anywhere in the program. Good programming style, however, recommends we write data definition code at the beginning of our program.

In Chapter 3, you saw the rules for writing Java variable names are quite similar to COBOL: No imbedded spaces, limited use of special characters, first character must be alphabetic. One of the most important things to remember when specifying variable names is to use descriptive names. A variable name of *X* does not say much about the purpose of a variable; customerName is a much better variable name. Chapter 3 discusses naming rules and conventions for Java identifiers in detail.

Java has eight basic (Java uses the term primitive) data types grouped into four general categories: Two are numeric, one is alphanumeric, and one is Boolean. Table 4-1 lists the details.

Table 4-1. *Java Data Types*

Category	Type	Range of Values*	Size
1. Integer	int	± 2.1 trillion	4 bytes
	short	± 32 thousand	2 bytes
	long	± 9 E18	8 bytes
	byte	± 127	1 byte
2. Floating Point	float	± 3.4 E+38	4 bytes, 7 decimal positions
	double	± 1.79 E+308	8 bytes, 15 decimal positions
3. Character	char	any Unicode**	2 bytes
4. Boolean	boolean	true/false	

* Actually, to be precise, the most negative value is 1 more than the value shown here. For example, byte has a range from -128 to +127.
** see following Unicode Note

> **NOTE** *Unicode* is a standard character set used by Java and created to accommodate all the characters in international languages (English, Spanish, Chinese, Russian, and so forth). Each Unicode character requires 2 bytes which provides 65,535 unique characters. The first 255 characters correspond to the familiar ASCII character set.

We define a Java variable by simply specifying its data type and name using the following format:

datatype variablename;

To define our account number, for example, we write:

int   accountNumber;

variable data type   variable name is
is integer   accountNumber

COBOL Equivalent:
    05 ACCOUNT-NUMBER   PIC 9(5).

Similar to COBOL, we can also assign a value to a variable when we write its definition.

int   accountNumber = 12345;

type is floating point

COBOL Equivalent:
    05 ACCOUNT-NUMBER   PIC 9(5)
        VALUE 12345.

float   minimumBalance = 50.00F;

we use *F* to indicate a
floating point value

COBOL Equivalent:
05 MINIMUM-BALANCE PIC S9(5)V99
   VALUE 50.00.

Some other examples of Java data definition are

boolean businessAccount = true;
char billingCycle = 'M';

> **NOTE**
>
> **1.** Single character data values are enclosed in single quotes:
> char billingCycle = 'M';
>
> **2.** The data type char is used only for **single** characters. Use the String class for multiple characters.
>
> **3.** Character strings, discussed a little later in this chapter, are enclosed in double quotes:
> String customerName = "Jed Muzzy";

Writing Java Literals

Writing literals in Java is similar to COBOL. For example, when we wanted to store a value of 12345 in the accountNumber variable, we simply wrote the value 12345 and assigned it to the variable:

```
int     accountNumber = 12345;
```

As we said in Chapter 3, we call this an assignment statement because it assigns a value to the variable. We use the VALUE clause or a MOVE statement to assign values to variables in COBOL.

When we write a literal value, Java makes some assumptions about the data type of the value we are writing. We can override this assumption by explicitly writing the data type. For example, when we previously wrote:

```
float   minimumBalance = 50.00F;
```

We included the *F* after the value to specify a data type of float. This is because Java assumes literal values with decimals, such as 50.00, are type double. Because we wanted to use type float, we wrote the *F* after the value to tell Java it was a floating point value.

We did not have to indicate the value was integer in the statement.

```
int     accountNumber = 12345;
```

Java assumes numbers without decimals are data type int (integer).

The Scope of Variables

The scope of a variable determines its accessibility by other parts of your program.

Java scope is more of an issue than in COBOL because we make much greater use of scope with Java. For example, Java variables can have *class scope*, *instance scope*, *method scope*, or even *instruction scope*! Where and how we define a variable determines its scope. As we define variables in program examples, we emphasize their scope for you.

If we declare a variable within a Java statement, its scope is limited to that statement. Instruction scope is discussed more thoroughly in subsequent chapters.

Variables declared within a method have method scope. They are accessible only to the method where they are declared. This is in sharp contrast to COBOL, where a data item declared in the data division can be accessed by the entire program. Incidentally, variables declared within a method are erased when the method terminates. In other words, method scope variables exist only while the method is executing.

Class scope exists for variables declared within a class program, but outside all methods. All methods within the class have access to variables with class scope. These variables generally represent *attributes* and each time we create an object instance, we get another set of variables. In other words, we have a set of variables with their individual values for each object instance. Each instance of <u>Customer</u>, for example, will have its own values for *name*, *ssNo*, *address* and *phoneNumber*.

If, however, we want to have only one copy of a variable for a class, regardless of the number of instances, we specify the variable as *static*. Static variables are also called *class variables* because only one copy of the variable exists for the entire class. To illustrate, assume we have a class variable for the prime interest rate for loan accounts. (We will apply the same prime rate to all accounts.) We declare the variable as:

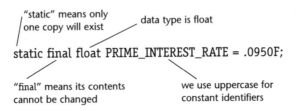

"static" means only one copy will exist

data type is float

static final float PRIME_INTEREST_RATE = .0950F;

"final" means its contents cannot be changed

we use uppercase for constant identifiers

When we use the keyword static in defining a variable, or constant, it means the variable applies to the class as a whole and is not associated with an individual instance. Only one copy of the variable exists—individual instances will not have separate copies.

Defining Java Constants

Just like COBOL, Java enables us to define variables with constant data. Once we define a constant, however, Java does not permit us to change its value.

The general format for defining a Java constant is

final datatype CONSTANT_NAME = value;

> The keyword final means the variable value **cannot** be changed—this is the final value. The Java compiler will not allow statements that attempt to change it.

For example, when we write:

final char BILLING_CYCLE = 'M';

We define a character variable named BILLING_CYCLE, initialize it to a value of M, and then do not allow its value to be changed. Here we follow the Java style of capitalizing constant names and we separate the words within the name with the underscore character.

String Variables

We previously described the eight primitive Java data types and said a character string of data (an alphanumeric value such as a person's name) uses the String class provided by Java. This class gives us several nice tools, as we learn shortly. Incidentally, data objects like String are called *complex* data types in Java.

When we define and initialize a character string, it actually looks like a primitive data type. We cannot do much with the string value unless we use the methods in the string class, however. For example, we cannot compare the contents of two string instances without using the **equals**() method, in String.

The format to define a character string is similar to the other data definition statements:

String variablename;

\
    Note the class name String is
    capitalized – it is case-sensitive

For example:

String customerName = "Jed Muzzy";

    The value is enclosed in ⟋
    double quotes

> **COBOL Equivalent:**
> 05 CUSTOMER-NAME PIC X(9)
>   VALUE 'Jed Muzzy'.

NOTE

1. The statement
   String customerName = "Jed Muzzy";
   creates an object **instance** of the String class named customerName.

2. This instance contains the value (attribute value) "Jed Muzzy."

3. Like all instances, we cannot directly access its attributes—we must use **methods** defined by the class.

The String class provides us with numerous methods to access, compare, and manipulate string values. To list just a few (assume s1 and s2 are two String instance reference variables):

1. s1.charAt(n)—returns the character in the string at position n in s1 (relative to zero)

2. s1.equals(s2)—compares values character by character in s1 and s2 and returns either true or false

3. s1.equalsIgnoreCase(s2)—same as **equals()** method, except case is ignored

4. s1.length()—returns the number of characters in s1

5. s1.substring(n1,n2)—returns a string of characters in s1 beginning at position n1 and ending at n2 (relative to zero)

Let's look at a small Java program that illustrates the creation and manipulation of a couple of string objects. The program named StringDemo.java is shown in Listing 4-1. This program has a single method named **main()** whose purpose is to demonstrate the creation of two string objects and then to illustrate the execution of three <u>String</u> instance methods: **length()**, **charAt()** and **substring()**.

Listing 4-1: *StringDemo.java*

```
1. public class StringDemo ——————— the class header names the class
2. {
3. public static void main (String args[]) ——————— main() is the first method
4. {                                                executed when the program
5.     String s1 = "COBOL Programmers";            begins
6.     String s2 = "can learn Java";
7.     System.out.println ("The length of s1 is " + s1.length());
8.     System.out.println ("The 7th character of s1 is " + s1.charAt(6));
                                   println() is a method of the
                                   System.out class that displays
                                   output on the screen
9.     System.out.println (s2.substring (10,13) + " is FUN!");
10. } // end of main method
11. } // end of StringDemo.java
```

Let's briefly look at the program before we run it. The program has only one method named **main()**. The main method is where execution begins when the program is loaded.

Lines 5 and 6 create two string object instances named s1 (17 characters) and s2 (14 characters).

s1	COBOL Programmers

s2	can learn Java

Line 7 does three things. First, it invokes the method **length()** for the instance s1 and then concatenates the value returned with the literal "The length of s1 is ", and then invokes the method **println()**. <u>System.out</u> is a special Java class that gives us tools for outputting data.

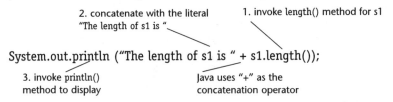

2. concatenate with the literal   1. invoke length() method for s1
"The length of s1 is "

System.out.println ("The length of s1 is " + s1.length());

3. invoke println()   Java uses "+" as the
method to display   concatenation operator

Similarly, line 8 invokes the **charAt()** method and line 9 invokes **subString()**. The output from StringDemo.java is

```
The length of s1 is 17
The 7th character of s1 is P
Java is FUN!
```

NOTE

1. **The length of a string object is the number of characters, not the number of bytes.** Because Java uses *Unicode*, there are two bytes per character.

2. Remember: the first character is located at position 0 (that is, everything is relative to 0). Thus, the seventh character of s1 is *P*, but it is referenced as position number 6.

Similar to <u>String</u>, Java also has a class named <u>StringBuffer</u> that behaves a little more like a COBOL alphanumeric field. You can create a string buffer object with a given size and then store data in it, up to the size of the buffer.

Changing Variable Types

Java gives us the ability to change the data type of a variable. This capability is called *type casting* or simply *casting*. Let's illustrate casting with an example.

First, let's look quickly at using the Java assignment statement to do computation. The COBOL statement:

```
COMPUTE ANSWER = 1.5 + INTEGER1 / INTEGER2
```

looks almost the same when written in Java:

```
answer = 1.5 + integer1 / integer2;
```

The same rules of operator precedence apply (division before addition) and the result of the computation is placed in the variable answer.

So, we have a variable named answer defined as:

```
double answer;
```

Let's also have two integer variables named integer1 and integer2 defined and initialized as follows:

```
int integer1 = 3;
```

```
int integer1 = 2;
```

When we execute the following computation statement, what do you think answer will contain?

```
answer = 1.5 + integer1 / integer2;
System.out.println ("The answer is " + answer);
```

```
OUTPUT:     The answer is 2.5
```

Wait a minute! When we divide 3 by 2, we get 1.5. Then, when we add 1.5 we get 3—right? Why, then, did we get 2.5 instead of 3? The variables integer1 and integer2 are integer values and the result of the division is 1, not 1.5. Just like COBOL, the decimal is truncated unless we specify decimal positions.

We can correct this error by casting the integer division to type double, which tracks up to 15 decimal positions. Now answer contains 3.

the literal 1.5 is assumed
to be type double

converts the result of the
division to type double

answer = 1.5 + (double) integer1 / integer2;

OUTPUT: The answer is 3.0

The program CastDemo.java executes this example and is shown in Listing 4-2.

Listing 4-2: *CastDemo.java*

```
public class CastDemo
{
    public static void main (String args [])
    {
    double answer;
    int integer1 = 3;
    int integer2 = 2;
    answer = 1.5 + integer1 / integer2;
    System.out.println ("The first answer is " + answer);

    answer = 1.5 + (double) integer1 / integer2;
    System.out.println ("The second answer is " + answer);
    } // end of main method
} // end of CastDemo.java
```

Program Output:

```
The answer is 2.5
The second answer is 3.0
```

In COBOL, if we move a PIC 9(3)V99 field to a PIC 9(1) field, we risk losing data because of truncation. The Java compiler helps us avoid truncation errors when we mix data types in an assignment statement.

The compiler usually enables us to assign a type with a smaller potential range of values to a type with a larger range of values, but produces an error when we attempt to assign a larger type to a smaller type. To illustrate, two of the four integer data types are byte with a range of -128 to + 127 and short with a range of -32,768 to +32,767. We can assign byte values to short values. For example, given the following variable definitions and value assignments:

```
byte aByteVariable; ——————— Range: -128 to +127
short aShortVariable; ———————Range: -32,768 to +32767
aByteVariable = 112;
aShortVariable = 12623;
```

We can execute the statement:

```
aShortVariable = aByteVariable; —— Value = 112
```

After executing the previous statement, *aShortVariable* is assigned the value of 112.

The following statement, however, produces a compiler error because we are at risk of truncation (assuming originally assigned values):

```
aByteVariable = aShortVariable;
```

Valid range = -128 to +127   Value = 12623

aByteVariable cannot hold a value greater than 127, thus the statement will fail to compile. To rectify the previous situation, we can override the truncation and explicitly cast the statement:

```
(short) aByteVariable = aShortVariable;
```

aByteVariable has now been recast as a short type, thus avoiding a truncation problem and a compiler error.

Variables for Community National Bank

In Chapter 2, we developed the following class diagram for CNB showing the classes Customer, Account, CheckingAccount, SavingsAccount, and LoanAccount, as illustrated in Figure 4–1.

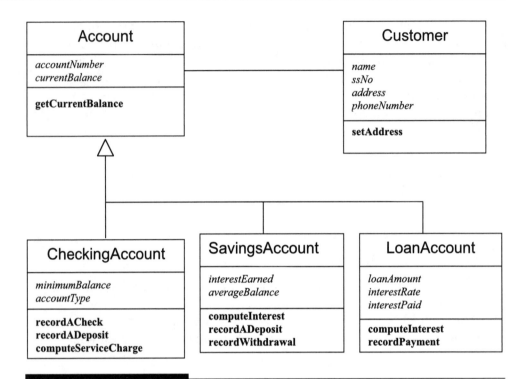

Figure 4-1. *CNB class diagram*

The data declarations for each of these classes are as follows:

<u>Account</u>
int accountNumber;
float currentBalance;

<u>Customer</u>
String name;
String ssNo;
String address;
String phoneNumber;

<u>CheckingAccount</u>
float minimumBalance;
int accountType;

<u>SavingsAccount</u>
float interestEarned;
float averageBalance;

<u>LoanAccount</u>
float loanAmount;
float interestRate;
float interestPaid;

Summary of Key Points

1. Java has eight *primitive* data types grouped into four general categories.

Category	Type	Range of Values	Size
1. Integer	int	± 2.1 trillion	4 bytes
	short	± 32 thousand	2 bytes
	long	± 9 E18	8 bytes
	byte	± 127	1 byte
2. Floating Point	float	± 3.4 E±38	4 bytes, 7 decimal positions
	double	± 1.79 E±308	8 bytes, 15 decimal positions
3. Character	char	any Unicode	2 bytes
4. Boolean	boolean	true/false	

2. We define a Java variable by specifying its data type and name:
    datatype variablename;
   and can assign a value as part of the definition:
    datatype variablename = initialvalue;

3. The *scope* of a variable determines its accessibility by various parts of a program. Java variables may have **class scope, instance scope, method scope**, and even **instruction scope**. A variable's scope is determined by where it is defined.

4. Use the keyword **static** to declare a class variable. Only one copy of the variable will exist and all methods in the class have access. If you want to have a copy of a variable for each object instance, omit static.
    static datatype variablename = value;

5. Use the keyword final to define constant data:
    final datatype CONSTANT_NAME = value;

6. Character string data is stored in an instance of the <u>String</u> class that provides methods to access the data:
    String variablename = "string value";

7. The Java compiler will not enable us to use an assignment statement in which truncation may occur without explicitly *casting* the value that may be truncated.

Glossary

casting the process to change the data type of a variable in an assignment statement to override a potential truncation error.

class scope applies to variables in a class that are accessible by all methods within the class.

complex data type an object instance; not one of the eight Java primitive data types (see primitive data type).

constant a variable defined using the keyword final; its value cannot be changed.

data type the type of data that must be explicitly stated when declaring a variable. Java has eight primitive types.

final a keyword used to define constants.

instruction scope a variable declared within a statement has instruction scope.

method scope a variable declared within a method has method scope; it is accessible only within the method.

primitive data type one of the eight basic types of data in Java (int, short, long, byte, float, double, char, Boolean).

scope the accessibility of a variable. Java variables have either class, instance, method, or instruction scope.

static a keyword meaning only one copy is to exist; sometimes called *class variables*.

String A supplied Java class whose instances contain character string data; these instances are *complex* data type.

Unicode A standard character set used by Java; each Unicode character requires 2 bytes.

Chapter 5

Computation

Objectives

In this chapter you will study:

- Exceptions
- Data Types
- Type Casting
- Wrapper Classes
- Arithmetic Operators
- The Math Class
- The NumberFormat Class

The purpose of this chapter is to introduce you to Java computation. The basic arithmetic operators—add, subtract, multiply, and divide (+, -, *, /)—are the same as those we use in COBOL's COMPUTE statement. However, Java operations such as exponentiation (raising a value to a power) and rounding, are accomplished using methods in the Math class. Java also has operators that enable us to write computation shortcuts, if we wish.

Also, you may recall from Chapter 4, Java is particular about data types. This sensitivity is raised to a higher level when we do computation, as discussed more thoroughly in this chapter.

This chapter begins with a discussion of Java Exceptions. An exception is Java's way of informing us of some condition that occurs while our program is running. While doing computation, for example, this could be an error, such as dividing by zero. Exceptions are not limited to arithmetic, however. You will see how exceptions are used to signal us about any condition, ranging from computation errors to hardware problems. In this chapter, we illustrate the use of custom exceptions using the familiar <u>CheckingAccount</u> class developed in Chapter 3.

We review Java's primitive data types. Then we describe and illustrate **wrapper** classes for the primitive data types. Methods in these classes for converting data from numeric to String and back are explored and demonstrated. Next, we present and discuss the language's arithmetic operators. Changing data types (casting) is also reviewed and illustrated.

The Math class is introduced and some of its methods are demonstrated. And, although it's not directly related to computation, we demonstrate how to format numerical data using the <u>NumberFormat</u> class. This class has some useful methods to format data with commas and dollar signs. We write a small program to illustrate the use of these methods.

This chapter assumes you understand the following:

COBOL:

- COMPUTE verb

- SIZE ERROR clause

- COBOL Edit Characters

- Arithmetic Operators

Java:

- OO Concepts (Chapter 2)

- Java Program Structure (Chapter 3)

- Defining Data (Chapter 4)

Exceptions

Java uses **exceptions** as a tool to help us deal with errors and conditions that occur while our program is running. Exceptions can be genuine errors, such as divide by zero or file not found, or simply situations we need to do something about, such as end of file or nonnumeric data entered by a user.

Like nearly everything else in Java, an exception is an instance (of the Exception class or one of its subclasses) created while our program is running. The steps for dealing with exceptions are

1. Our program executes code that can cause an exception.

2. Java detects the condition, creates an exception instance describing the condition, and sends the exception instance to our program.

3. Our program recognizes the exception and takes appropriate action. Note, if an exception is produced and sent to our program, but we fail to recognize it, Java terminates our program.

An exception is an instance of a class derived from the Exception class. Part of the class hierarchy is shown in Table 5–1. The classes in **boldface** are demonstrated in this chapter (unless otherwise noted).

Table 5-1. *Partial Exception Class Hierarchy*

```
Exception
        IOException (described and illustrated in Chapter 9)
                EOFException
                FileNotFoundException
        RuntimeException
                ArithmeticException (illustrated below)
                NumberFormatException (illustrated below)
```

The process of creating an exception instance and sending it to our program is called ***throwing an exception***. Our program then ***catches the exception*** when it receives the exception instance and takes appropriate action.

In keeping with this terminology, Java uses a structure called ***try-catch*** whenever we execute code that has the potential for creating an exception. Incidentally, when we call any method that can throw an exception, we must use the try-catch structure, otherwise the Java compiler generates an error message and will not compile our program. In other words, we must learn to recognize when a method may throw us an exception. The Java API documentation specifies which methods can throw exceptions.

The try-catch structure is shown in Listing 5-1.

Listing 5-1: *try-catch structure*

```
try
{
  // code that can cause an exception
  // execution transfers to the appropriate catch block when
  // the exception is thrown
}
catch (exception_class reference_variable_name)
{
  // this code is executed only if the specified exception
  // is thrown
}
finally  // the finally block is optional
{
  // this code is executed whether or not an exception is thrown
}
```

The code in a catch block will be executed only if the specific exception identified in the catch parameter is thrown. For example, if we write a catch block for ArithmeticException, it will catch only an ArithmeticException. It will ignore for example, a NumberFormatException. However, if we catch a superclass of ArithmeticException, say Exception, then it will be caught if an ArithmeticException occurs. Notice we can have multiple catch blocks—one for each different type of exception we wish to catch. Also, note that whenever a statement in the try block triggers an exception, any remaining statements in the try block are not executed and execution goes to the appropriate catch block. In other words, the execution of the try block stops as soon as an exception is thrown.

The following program, named ArithmeticExceptionDemo.java, is a simple example of exception handling for a divide by zero error. The program attempts to divide by zero. Because we are using the try-catch structure, however, Java detects the error and transfers control to the catch block. The specific exception being caught is ArithmeticException (refer to Table 5–1). When the error occurs, the catch block is executed and the output is displayed, as shown in the following. The error description contained in the exception instance is "/ by zero."

Listing 5-2: *ArithmeticExceptionDemo.java*

```
public class ArithmeticExceptionDemo
{
    public static void main(String args[])
    {
      int a = 5;
      int b = 0;
      int c = 0;

      try                    a divide by zero triggers the
      {                      creation of an exception
        c = a / b;
        System.out.println ("Successful divide by zero");
      } // end try
                                          the ArithmeticException
                                          is caught
      catch (ArithmeticException anException)
      {
        System.out.println ("Caught  ArithmeticException" + anException);
      } // end catch
    } // end main               anException Contains
} // end ArithmeticExceptionDemo.java     "/ by zero"
```

The output is

Caught ArithmeticException java.lang.ArithmeticException: / by zero

If we were to remove the try-catch and rerun the program, Java terminates our program with the message:

java.lang.ArithmeticException: / by zero

The difference is, if we use try-catch to intercept the exception, we can deal with the condition without allowing Java to terminate our program.

Similarly, COBOL uses the ON SIZE ERROR clause to trap computational errors. Rewriting the previous Java code segment in COBOL we have

```
01  A PIC 9(2) VALUE 5.
01  B PIC 9(2) VALUE 0.
01  C PIC 9(2) VALUE 0.
COMPUTE C = A / B
   ON SIZE ERROR
      DISPLAY "CANNOT DIVIDE BY ZERO"
   NOT ON SIZE ERROR
      DISPLAY "SUCCESSFUL DIVIDE BY ZERO"
END-COMPUTE
```

The output is

```
CANNOT DIVIDE BY ZERO
```

Custom Exception Classes

Times occur when we may wish to use an exception that is not part of the Java Exception class hierarchy to deal with some condition we encounter. This is a simple matter for us to define a new exception class and to use it in a program.

Recall that the CheckingAccount class for Community National Bank has an instance method named **recordACheck()** shown again in the following:

```
// post a check to this account
public void recordACheck (float checkAmount)
{  float balance = getCurrentBalance();  // retrieve balance
   balance = balance - checkAmount;    // subtract check
   setCurrentBalance(balance);         // store new balance
} // end recordACheck
```

The logic in this method records a check without considering if the account has a sufficient balance to pay the check. To call this method, we write

```
   the CheckingAccount instance        amount to be posted
         |                               /
anAccount.recordACheck(checkAmount);
```

Let's assume we wish to have **recordACheck()** throw an exception to notify the calling program that the account does not have sufficient funds to pay the check.

We have **recordACheck()** create and throw a *custom* exception. The steps are

1. Write a class program for the new custom exception by extending the Exception class. This is a short program because the only method it needs is a constructor.

NSFException is a subclass of Exception

```
public class NSFException extends Exception // not sufficient funds
{
  public NSFException (String errorMessage)  // constructor
      {super(errorMessage);}            // call superclass constructor
  } // end NSFException
```

2. Add "throws NSFException" to the **recordACheck()** method header. This forces any call to this method to use try-catch.

```
public void recordACheck (float checkAmount) throws NSFException
```

3. When insufficient funds are detected, create and throw the exception:

```
if (balance >= checkAmount) // see if sufficient balance
{   // if yes, record the check
  balance = balance - checkAmount;
  setCurrentBalance(balance);    // store new balance
{
else
{ // not sufficient funds – create & throw NSFException
  NSFException e = new NSFException("Not Sufficient Funds");
  throw e;
} end if
```

throw sends the exception instance to the calling program

this message is stored in the exception instance

4. Then, when we call **recordACheck()** we must use the try-catch structure to detect the insufficient funds exception if it is thrown:

```
try
{
    anAccount.recordACheck(checkAmount); // post the check
}
catch (NSFException e)  // catch insufficient funds exception
{
    // do whatever needed for insufficient funds
} // end try-catch
```

CheckingAccount.java with the custom exception NSFException added is shown in Listing 5–3. Notice we have changed only the **recordACheck()** method. No other changes are necessary.

Listing 5-3: *CheckingAccount.java with NSFException*

```
public class CheckingAccount extends Account  // superclass is account
{ // attribute definition
    private float minimumBalance; // private scope limited to this class
    // constructor method
public CheckingAccount (int newAccountNumber,float newCurrentBalance)
{ // invoke account constructor to populate account attributes
    super (newAccountNumber, newCurrentBalance);
    minimumBalance = newCurrentBalance; // populate attribute
} // end constructor

// accessor method
public float getMinimumBalance ()
    { return minimumBalance; }

// instance method to post a check to this account
public void recordACheck (float checkAmount) throws NSFException
{ float balance = getCurrentBalance();
    if (balance >= checkAmount)  // see if sufficient funds
        {
        balance = currentBalance - checkAmount;
        setCurrentBalance(balance);    // store new balance
        }
```

```
    else
      {// if not, throw an exception
      NSFException e = new NSFException("Not Sufficient Funds");
      throw e;
    } // end if
} // end instance method recordACheck

// post a deposit to this account
public void recordADeposit (float depositAmount)
{
    float balance = getCurrentBalance();    // retrieve balance
    balance = balance + depositAmount;      // add deposit
    setCurrentBalance(balance);             // store new balance
    } // end recordADeposit
} // end of checking account class
```

We then modify AccountProcessor.java from Chapter 3 to exercise the revised **recordACheck()** method. Here we use the try-catch structure to call **recordACheck()**. As you can see, we create a checking account instance with an initial balance of $50. Next, we post a $20 check and a $15 deposit, leaving a balance of $45. Then we attempt to post a $100 check but, because the balance is less than the amount of the check, **recordACheck()** throws the NSFException and the catch block displays the message "Not sufficient Funds."

Listing 5-4: *AccountProcessor.java with try-catch*

```
    public class AccountProcessor
    {
        public static void main (String args[])  // main is executed first
        {
        // attribute values
        int accountNumber = 12345;
        float currentBalance = 50.00F;

        // create a checking account instance
        CheckingAccount anAccount = new CheckingAccount(accountNumber,
```

```
    currentBalance);
// retrieve and display current balance
System.out.println ("Beginning Balance: " +
    anAccount.getCurrentBalance());

try
{// post a $20 check then again retrieve and display current balance
    anAccount.recordACheck (20.00F);
    System.out.println ("Balance After $20 check: " +
        anAccount.getCurrentBalance());
//   post a $15 deposit then again retrieve and display balance
    anAccount.recordADeposit (15.00F);
    System.out.println ("Balance After $15 deposit: " +
        anAccount.getCurrentBalance());
//   now try posting a $100 check
    anAccount.recordACheck (100.00F);
    System.out.println ("Balance After $100 check: " +
        anAccount.getCurrentBalance());
} // end try block

catch (NSFException e)
{
    System.out.println ("Caught NSFException" + e);
} // end catch

} // end main}
}// end of accountProcessor.java
```

The output from AccountProcessor.java is shown in the following:

```
Beginning Balance: 50.0
Balance After $20 check: 30.0
Balance After $15 deposit: 45.0
Caught NSFExceptionNSFException: Not Sufficient Funds
```

A Review of Primitive Data Types

Chapter 4 described how to define Java data. You may recall Java has eight primitive data types. Six of these types are numeric, one is alphanumeric, and one is Boolean. In this chapter, we focus on the six numeric types. Four of these contain whole numbers (int, short, long, byte) and two allow decimal positions (float and double). Table 5-2 lists the detailed characteristics of these numeric data types.

Table 5-2: *Java Numeric Data Types*

Type	Range of Values*	Size
int	± 2.1 trillion	4 bytes
short	± 32 thousand	2 bytes
long	± 9 E18	8 bytes
byte	± 127	1 byte
float	± 3.4 E+38	4 bytes, 7 decimal positions
double	± 1.79 E+308	8 bytes, 15 decimal positions

* Actually, to be precise, the most negative value is 1 more than the value shown here. For example, byte has a range from –128 to +127.

Also, recall from Chapter 4 that Java is particular about converting one data type to another because it does not want to truncate numerical data without our specific approval and knowledge. The Java compiler helps us avoid truncation errors when we mix data types. In general, the compiler permits us to assign a type with a smaller potential range of values to a type with a larger range of values, but generates an error when we attempt to assign a larger type to a smaller type. We use type casting to convert numeric data from one type to another whenever truncation could occur.

Table 5-3 lists the data types in ascending range of value order. Conversions can be made without explicit casts when going from a lower type to a higher type, but not the reverse. Explicit casts are required when converting from a larger range of values to a smaller. Also, when an arithmetic expression contains mixed data types, Java converts the result to the type with the largest range of values. For example, if we use int and float in an expression, the result must be float.

Table 5-3: *Data Type Value Ranges*

Type	Range
byte	± 127
short	± 32 thousand
int	± 2.1 trillion
long	± 9 E18
float	± 3.4 E+38
double	± 1.79 E+308

We can explicitly cast one data type to another. For example if we have a data type double we want to convert to float, we could write

aFloatValue = (float) aDoubleValue;

Cast to float

The contents of aFloatValue is now type float.

Wrapper Classes

The java.lang class library contains classes for each of the primitive data types. All of these, except <u>Integer</u>, are named the same as their corresponding primitive (int is *Integer*), where the first letter of the name is capitalized. For example, type double has the class <u>Double</u>, float has <u>Float</u>, and so forth. Be careful however, because the only difference between the primitive float and the class <u>Float</u>, is the uppercase *F*!

These classes are often called **wrapper** classes because they *wrap* an object instance around the data: the data is encapsulated. The instance contains a value of the type indicated. For example, an instance of the <u>Integer</u> class contains an *int* value.

The code to create an instance of one of these classes looks like that for any other object instance creation. To create instances of <u>Double</u>, <u>Float</u>, <u>Integer</u>, and <u>Long</u> we write

```
Double aDouble = new Double(123.456);
Float aFloat = new Float(123.456F); // we specify "F" for float
```

```
Integer anInteger = new Integer (123);
Long aLong = new Long(123456);
```

Note, these variables (aDouble, aFloat, anInteger, and aLong) are now *instance reference variables*. They contain references to instances instead of data values. This means we cannot treat them as data items in computation statements. For example, we cannot write a statement like this:

```
i = anInteger + 1;
```

This is because anInteger does not contain the integer value 123. Instead, it contains a reference to an instance of the Integer class that contains the integer value 123. If we wish to add 1 to the value contained in the anInteger instance and store it in an integer variable *i*, we must use a method to obtain the value stored in the instance:

```
i = anInteger.intValue() + 1;
```

anInteger **refers** to or points to the instance that contains the integer value 123.

intValue() returns the integer value (123) contained in the instance. Note that it is an *instance* method.

These classes also provide some useful methods to convert numeric data to <u>String</u>. (Remember, a String variable is also a reference variable pointing to an instance of the <u>String</u> class.) For example, to convert the integer value in anInteger to <u>String</u>, we use the Integer class method **toString()**:

```
String aStringFromInteger;  // declare a String reference variable
aStringFromInteger = new String(Integer.toString(anInteger.intValue()));
```

we now have a new String instance named aStringFromInteger that contains 123

toString() is an Integer **class** method that converts an integer to a String

intValue() is an **instance** method that returns the value in anInteger

We can then convert the string value back to an integer value using the Integer class method **valueOf()**. The following code converts the contents of **aStringFromInteger** back to int and puts it into a new Integer instance named anIntegerFromString:

```
Integer anIntegerFromString = Integer.valueOf(aStringFromInteger);
```

the Integer instance now contains 123

valueOf() converts String to integer

Many of these methods throw an exception if the argument passed is inappropriate. For example, if we try to convert a nonnumeric value with the **valueOf()** method, it will throw a <u>NumberFormatException</u>. In fact, this is a useful technique for detecting nonnumeric data. Try to convert it to Integer using the **valueOf()** method. If it is not numeric, you will catch <u>NumberFormatException</u>. An example of this code is

```
try
{Integer anIntegerFromString=Integer.valueOf(aStringFromInteger);}
catch (NumberFormatException e)
{// do processing for non numeric data}
```

Listing 5-5 (WrapperDemo.java) demonstrates some of these methods for the wrapper classes.

Listing 5-5: *WrapperDemo.java*

```
// Demo Data Type Class Methods
// WrapperDemo.java
public class WrapperDemo
{
    public static void main(String args[])
    {
    // create & display instances of Double, Float, Integer, and Long
    Double aDouble = new Double(123.456);
    Float aFloat = new Float(123.456F);
    Integer anInteger = new Integer (123);
    Long aLong = new Long(123456);
    System.out.println("aDouble =" + aDouble);
    System.out.println("aFloat =" + aFloat);
    System.out.println("anInteger =" + anInteger);
    System.out.println("aLong =" + aLong);
    // convert numeric to String & display
    String aStringFromDouble = new
        String(Double.toString(aDouble.doubleValue()));
    String aStringFromFloat = new
        String(Float.toString(aFloat.floatValue()));
    String aStringFromInteger = new
```

```
        String(Integer.toString(anInteger.intValue())));
String aStringFromLong = new String(Long.toString(aLong.longValue())));
System.out.println("aStringFromDouble =" + aStringFromDouble);
System.out.println("aStringFromFloat =" + aStringFromFloat);
System.out.println("aStringFromInteger =" + aStringFromInteger);
System.out.println("aStringFromLong =" + aStringFromLong);

// convert String to numeric & display
Double aDoubleFromString = Double.valueOf(aStringFromDouble);
Float aFloatFromString = Float.valueOf(aStringFromFloat);
Integer anIntegerFromString = Integer.valueOf(aStringFromInteger);
Long aLongFromString = Long.valueOf(aStringFromLong);
System.out.println("aDoubleFromString =" + aDoubleFromString);
System.out.println("aFloatFromString =" + aFloatFromString);
System.out.println("anIntegerFromString =" + anIntegerFromString);
System.out.println("aLongFromString =" + aLongFromString);

// do arithmetic with instances using instance methods
double d = aDouble.doubleValue() + aDoubleFromString.doubleValue();
System.out.println("d =" + d);
float f = aFloat.floatValue() + aFloatFromString.floatValue();
System.out.println("f =" + f);
int i = anInteger.intValue() + anIntegerFromString.intValue();
System.out.println("i =" + i);
long l = aLong.longValue() + aLongFromString.longValue();
System.out.println("l =" + l);
} // end main
} // end WrapperDemo.java
```

The output from the program is

```
aDouble =123.456
aFloat =123.456
anInteger =123
aLong =123456

aStringFromDouble =123.456
```

```
aStringFromFloat =123.456
aStringFromInteger =123
aStringFromLong =123456

aDoubleFromString =123.456
aFloatFromString =123.456
anIntegerFromString =123
aLongFromString =123456

d =246.912
f =246.912
i =246
l =246912
```

Arithmetic Operators

COBOL has the COMPUTE statement to do computation, plus individual statements for ADD, SUBTRACT, MULTIPLY, and DIVIDE. Java does computation using the **assignment statement,** which evaluates an **expression** on the right side of the assignment operator (=) and stores the result in the variable on the left side. An expression is simply some combination of operators, variables, and values that evaluate to a result. Note, unlike COBOL, Java expressions may evaluate to a Boolean value (true or false).

```
result = (expression);
```
———— the expression is evaluated and the result stored in the variable on the left side of the =

Java uses the basic arithmetic operators add, subtract, multiply, and divide (+, -, *, /), which are the same as those used in COBOL's COMPUTE statement. Some examples are

```
balance = balance - checkAmount;
interestCharged = loanBalance * interestRate;
```

> **COBOL Equivalent:**
> COMPUTE BALANCE = BALANCE - CHECK-AMOUNT
> COMPUTE INTEREST-CHARGED = LOAN-BALANCE * INTEREST-RATE

Java provides us with several additional arithmetic operators, as indicated in Table 5-4.

Table 5-4: *Java Arithmetic Operators*

Operator	Function	COBOL Equivalent
+	Add	+
-	Subtract	-
*	Multiply	*
/	Divide	/
%	Modulus	Mod function
i++	Post-increment	no direct equivalent
i--	Post-decrement	no direct equivalent
++i	Pre-increment	no direct equivalent
--i	Pre-decrement	no direct equivalent

The modulus operator returns the integer remainder of a division operation. For example, the expression 2%1 (that is, 2 / 1 = 2, remainder 0) returns 0, but 3%2 (that is, 3/2 = 1, remainder 1) returns 1.

The *increment/decrement* operators (i++, i--, ++i,--i) are inherited from the C++ language and have no direct COBOL equivalent, although we can do the same things with a little more code. These operators are merely coding shortcuts, but we explain them here because many Java programmers use them.

The Java language also has *assignment operators,* which are simply the arithmetic operators (+, -, *, /, %) combined with the assignment operator (=). Again, we can do the same thing in COBOL, but it requires a little more code. Table 5-5 illustrates these coding shortcuts.

As COBOL programmers, we generally shy away from coding shortcuts that reduce the clarity, and therefore the maintainability, of programs. As you become accustomed to these new techniques, however, they become more familiar and seem less cryptic.

Table 5-5: *Using Java Shortcut Code*

Java Code	Java Shortcut Code	COBOL Equivalent
i = i + 1;	i++;	COMPUTE I = I + 1
i = i – 1;	i--;	COMPUTE I = I – 1
i = j + 1;	i = ++j;	COMPUTE J = J + 1
i = j;		MOVE J TO I
i = j – 1;	i = --j;	COMPUTE J = J – 1
i = j;		MOVE J TO I
i = i + 2;	i += 2;	COMPUTE I = I + 2
i = i – 2;	i -= 2;	COMPUTE I = I – 2
i = i / 2;	i /= 2;	COMPUTE I = I / 2
i = i * 2;	i *= 2;	COMPUTE I = I * 2
i = i % 2;	i %= 2;	I = MOD(I, 2)

The Math Class

The Math class, a member of the java.lang package, provides several important computational methods. Some of the more popular methods are listed in Table 5-6. Note, those with an asterisk (*) have a corresponding COBOL function (ANSI-85). All the methods are static (class) methods, which means we do not create an instance of the Math class and we call the methods using the class name: **Math.random()**, for example.

Note the **round()** method returns a whole number, **round(double)** returns type long, and **round(float)** returns type int. This is significantly different than the way the COBOL ROUNDED clause works. COBOL rounds to the number of decimals contained in the result field picture clause.

Math also includes methods to do trigonometric and logarithm calculations if you are interested. In addition, it has two static constants:

Math.E contains the base of natural log *e*
Math.PI contains pi.

Table 5-6: *Selected Math Class Methods*

abs(x)	returns the absolute value of an argument
max(x,y)*	returns the greater of two values
min(x,y)*	returns the smaller of two values
pow(x,y)	returns the value of the first argument raised to the power of the second
random()*	returns a random number between 0 and 1
round(x)	returns the closest integer value to the argument
sqrt(x)*	returns the square root of a double value
floor(x)	returns truncated double value

We illustrate computation and the use of the <u>Math</u> class by writing code to compute the amount of a loan payment for the Community National Bank. If we know the original loan amount (BALANCE), the annual percentage interest rate (APR), and the loan duration expressed in number of months (MONTHS), we can calculate the monthly loan payment (PAYMENT) using the COBOL formula:

APR / 12 is the monthly rate

```
COMPUTE PAYMENT =
    (BALANCE * (APR / 12)) / (1 - 1 / (1 + APR / 12) ** MONTHS
```

In Java, we use the Math class and write

Math.pow (*x, y*) returns *x* raised to the *y* power

```
payment =
    (balance * (apr / 12))/(1 - 1/ Math.pow((1 + apr / 12), months));
```

Given the following data,

```
float balance = 1000F;
float apr = .08F;
int months = 6;
double payment = 0;
```

COBOL Equivalent:
```
01 BALANCE  PIC 9(5)V99 VALUE 1000.
01 APR      PIC V99     VALUE .08.
01 MONTHS   PIC 9(2)    VALUE 6.
01 PAYMENT  PIC 9(5)V99 VALUE ZEROS.
```

The output from the Java computation is

> 170.57724306813628

The output from the COBOL computation is

> 00170.57

If we wanted this value rounded to 170.58 in COBOL, of course, we simply use the ROUNDED option:

COMPUTE PAYMENT **ROUNDED** =
  (BALANCE * (APR/12)) / (1 – 1 / (1 + APR / 12) ** MONTHS.

The output from this COBOL computation is now:

> 00170.58

We can round the payment to 170.58 in Java, but it takes a little more effort. Remember the **round()** method in the Math class returns a whole number, not one with two decimals. To round in Java, we can use the following code:

1. Multiply by 100 to move the decimal 2 positions to the right:

   payment = payment * 100;

   > 170.57 ∧ 724306813628

2. Call **Math.round()** to round to a whole number. Note, because **round()** returns a whole value as data type long, we recast it to float:

   roundedPayment = (float) Math.round(payment);

   > 17058

3. Divide by 100 to move the decimal back to the left:

   roundedPayment = roundedPayment / 100;

   > 170 . 58

To simplify Java rounding, we can put this code in a method named **roundOff()** and then call it whenever we wish to have a value rounded to two decimal positions. We design this method to receive a double value, round it to 2 decimal positions, and return a float value. In fact, we use this method a little later in Chapter 7 when we develop a more complete amortization program for Community National Bank. A little exercise for you here is to rewrite **roundOff()** to accept and return long values.

```
// roundOff method                    ┌─ method returns a float value
static public float roundOff (double value)
{                                     └─ method receives a double value
    value = value * 100;        // move decimal 2 places to right
    // Math.round returns long - recast to float
    float roundedValue = (float) Math.round(value);
    roundedValue = roundedValue / 100;  // move decimal back left
    return roundedValue; // return roundedValue to calling program
}  // end roundOff
```

Listing 5-6 (MathClassDemo.java) demonstrates these computations.

Listing 5-6: *MathClassDemo.java*

```
// Demonstrate Use of Math class
// MathClassDemo.java
public class MathClassDemo
{
    public static void main(String args[])
    {  // declare variables
        float balance = 1000F;
        float apr = .08F;
        int months = 6;
        double payment;
        payment = (balance * (apr / 12))/ (1-1/Math.pow((1+ apr/12),months));
        System.out.println ("Payment = " + payment);
        System.out.println ("Rounded Payment = " + roundOff(payment));
    }  // end main
```

```
// roundOff method
static public float roundOff (double value)
{
    value = value * 100;      // move decimal 2 places to right
    // Math.round returns long - recast to float
    float roundedValue = (float) Math.round(value);
    roundedValue = roundedValue / 100;  // move decimal back to left
    return roundedValue;
} // end roundOff
} // end MathClassDemo
```

The output from the program is

```
Payment = 170.57724306813628
Rounded Payment = 170.58
```

The NumberFormat Class

COBOL uses an edit picture clause to format numeric data for display. This picture clause contains edit characters, such as $, Z, 0, to control the appearance of the edited value. Given the PAYMENT from the previous section, we format it to currency by coding an edit field (EDITED-PAYMENT) containing the appropriate edit characters and then move PAYMENT to EDITED-PAYMENT.

```
01 EDITED-PAYMENT   PIC $$,$$9.99.
MOVE PAYMENT TO EDITED-PAYMENT
DISPLAY "EDITED-PAYMENT =", EDITED-PAYMENT
```

The output is

```
EDITED-PAYMENT = $170.58
```

In keeping with the spirit of OO, however, Java uses methods in a class program, appropriately named NumberFormat, to format numerical data. The NumberFormat class is a member of the java.text package and it gives us several useful methods for formatting numerical data. Incidentally, this class also works for different countries by specifying locale. See the Java API Help documentation for the specifics. Here, we demonstrate two of these methods: one for currency and one for commas.

In the previous example, we had a payment value of 170.58. If we wish to have this value displayed in currency format (with a dollar sign $), we can use the NumberFormat class. Similarly, if we have another value, say 1234.56, which we wish to have displayed with a comma as 1,234.56, we again can use the NumberFormat class.

Two steps are required to convert our payment amount to currency ($170.58):

1. Create a *currency* instance of NumberFormat using the class method **getCurrencyInstance()**.

   NumberFormat currencyFormat = NumberFormat.getCurrencyInstance();

2. Call the **format()** method in the new instance to convert payment to a formatted String with a leading dollar sign:

   String formattedPayment = currencyFormat.format(payment);

   Variable holding the
   value 170.58

The String instance formattedPayment now contains $170.58.

We can also use NumberFormat to format numbers with commas, but without a dollar sign. Again, there are two steps:

1. Create an instance of NumberFormat using the class method **getInstance()**.

   NumberFormat numberFormat = NumberFormat.getInstance();

2. Call the **format()** method of the new instance to convert a number to a formatted String with commas inserted:

   We can use a variable
   or a literal value

   String formattedNumber = numberFormat.format(1234.56);

The String instance formattedNumber now contains 1,234.56.

Listing 5-7 (NumberFormatDemo.java) demonstrates several of the formatting methods in NumberFormat.

Listing 5-7: *NumberFormatDemo.java*

```java
// demonstrate methods in the NumberFormat class
// NumberFormatDemo.java

import java.text.*;

public class NumberFormatDemo
{
    public static void main(String args[])
    {
        // demonstrate currency format
        NumberFormat currencyFormat = NumberFormat.getCurrencyInstance();
        String currencyNumber = currencyFormat.format(123456.78);
        System.out.println ("currencyNumber = " + currencyNumber);

        // demonstrate comma format
        NumberFormat numberFormat = NumberFormat.getInstance();
        String commaNumber = numberFormat.format(123456.78);
        System.out.println ("commaNumber = " + commaNumber);

        // demonstrate percent format
        NumberFormat percentFormat = NumberFormat.getPercentInstance();
        String percentNumber = percentFormat.format(0.78);
        System.out.println ("percentNumber = " + percentNumber);

        // demonstrate decimal format
        DecimalFormat decimalFormat = new DecimalFormat("##,##0.00");
        String decimalNumber = decimalFormat.format(123456.7890);
        System.out.println ("decimalNumber = " + decimalNumber);
    } // end main
} // end NumberFormatDemo
```

The program output is

```
currencyNumber = $123,456.78
commaNumber = 123,456.78
percentNumber = 78%
decimalNumber = 123,456.79
```

Note, the decimal format forces rounding for us.

Summary of Key Points

1. Java uses *exceptions* as a tool to deal with errors and other important conditions that occur while our program is running. An exception is an instance that contains information about the condition that caused the exception to be created. We can use the existing Exception classes or define our own custom exceptions. We use the Java try-catch structure to execute code that can cause an exception.

2. Java has six numeric data types. Four of these (int, short, long and byte) contain whole numbers and two (float and double) allow decimal positions. We must explicitly *cast* to convert data types from one to another whenever truncation may occur.

3. In addition to the primitive data types, Java has classes for each of these. These classes are called *wrapper* classes because they wrap an instance around the data. These classes provide various methods to access and convert the data.

4. In addition to the standard add, subtract, multiply, and divide arithmetic operators, Java includes modulus, increment, decrement, and assignment operators.

5. The Math class extends Java's computation capability beyond the basic arithmetic operations. These methods include **pow()** to raise a value to a power, **round()** to return the closest integer value to the argument, and **floor()** to return a truncated value. Several of the Math class methods have similar COBOL intrinsic functions.

6. The NumberFormat class gives us tools to format numerical data by inserting commas and adding dollar signs.

Glossary

assignment operator one of the arithmetic operators combined with the equal sign (=); for example: +=

catch an exception using the *catch* block to intercept an exception that has been thrown.

custom exception Java has several standard exceptions. You can write a custom exception class for conditions unique to your program.

data type classes same as wrapper classes.

decrement operator Java has two decrement operators *pre-decrement* --i and *post-decrement* i--.

exception an instance that is created to signal a condition. The instance contains information about the condition.

expression a combination of operators, variables, and values that evaluates to a result.

increment operator Java has two increment operators *pre-increment* ++i and *post-increment* i++.

instance reference variable a variable that refers to or *points* to an object instance.

throw an exception the process of sending an exception instance is called *throwing* and uses the keyword *throw*.

type casting changing a data type.

wrapper classes Java classes for each of the primitive data types.

Chapter 6

Decision Making

Objectives
In this chapter you will study:
- Conditions
- Logical operators
- If-Then-Else Structure
- Case Structure
- Java switch
- Java break

In this chapter, you learn how to implement the selection and case structure using Java. You see how to write if and switch statements. Java and COBOL if statements are similar and, therefore, straightforward. However, switch is a distant cousin of the COBOL EVALUATE verb and has some similarities, but many important differences are discussed and illustrated in this chapter.

First, we examine the Java logical operators, conditions, and the **if** statement. This discussion includes the emulation of COBOL condition names using Java. Next we present the switch statement and explain its use. The chapter concludes with the development of a new method, **computeServiceCharge()**, for CheckingAccount. This method is first written using nested if statements and then is written again using switch.

123

The chapter assumes you understand the following:

COBOL

- Condition names
- Logical operators
- IF – Else – End-If
- Evaluate
- Continue

Java

- OO Concepts (Chapter 2)
- Java Program Structure (Chapter 3)
- Defining Data (Chapter 4)
- Computation (Chapter 5)

Service Charges at Community National Bank

The Community National Bank system computes a service charge for each checking account each month. The amount of the service charge is based on the type of account and the minimum balance in the account during the month.

CNB has three types of checking accounts: regular, business, and thrifty. The regular accounts are the most common and provide standard checking account services. The service charge for regular accounts is waived if the minimum balance is $500 or more, but is $5.00 otherwise. The service charge for business accounts is $6.00 if the minimum balance is $1,000 or more, $8.00 if the minimum balance is $500 to $999.99, and $10.00 if less than $500. Thrifty checking accounts are not charged a service fee—instead customers purchase their checks from the bank.

The decision rules for CNB are shown in Table 6–1. In this chapter, we design and write the Java code to compute the monthly service charge for each type of checking account.

Table 6-1. *CNB service charge calculations*

Type of Account	Minimum Balance	Service Charge
Regular	500.00 or more	none
	less than 500.00	5.00
Business	1,000.00 or more	6.00
	500.00 to 999.99	8.00
	less than 500.00	10.00
Thrifty	none	none

The If Statement

The COBOL IF statement evaluates a *condition* and then selects statements to execute depending on whether the condition is true or false. A COBOL condition is simply an expression that evaluates to either true or false. Java if statements look a lot like their COBOL counterpart, but Java programmers sometimes use the term *logical expression* instead of condition. A logical expression is a combination of logical operators, variables, and values that evaluate to a Boolean value—true or false.

Some of the Java logical operators are the same as COBOL, however, others are quite different. For example, Java's LESS THAN (<), LESS THAN OR EQUAL TO (<=), GREATER THAN (>), and GREATER THAN OR EQUAL TO (>=) operators are identical to COBOL's, although Java lacks the spelled-out versions we have in COBOL. Notably different are the EQUAL TO (==), OR (||), AND (&&), and NOT (!) operators used by Java.

NOTE

1. The Java EQUAL TO operator is two equal signs (==), not one (=).
2. The single symbol (=) is the Java assignment operator.
3. NOT EQUAL is denoted (!=) instead of (!==).
4. Java does not recognize the often-used (<>) to mean NOT EQUAL TO.

Table 6-2 recaps the Java logical operators.

Table 6-2. *Java logical operators*

Operator	Function
&&	AND
==	EQUAL TO
>	GREATER THAN
>=	GREATER THAN OR EQUAL TO
<	LESS THAN
<=	LESS THAN OR EQUAL TO
!	NOT
!=	NOT EQUAL TO
||	OR

Just like COBOL, the Java if statement evaluates a logical expression and then executes statements depending on whether the expression is true or false. The primary difference between the two is

1. Java requires the logical expression to be enclosed in parentheses.

2. A semicolon terminates the statement to be executed.

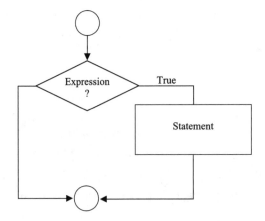

The structure of the Java if is

if (logical expression)
    statement;   Enclose the condition in parentheses

          Terminate with a semicolon

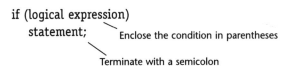

COBOL Equivalent:
IF condition
    statement
END-IF.

A Java example is

if (minimumBalance < 500)
    serviceCharge = 5.00F;

          F indicates a floating
          point value

COBOL Equivalent:
IF MINIMUM-BALANCE < 500
    MOVE 5.00 TO SERVICE-CHARGE
END-IF.

Using the ELSE Clause

We can also use the ELSE clause with Java, similar to COBOL:

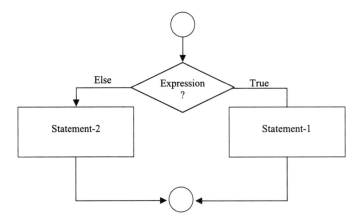

The structure of the Java if – else is

if (logical expression)
    statement-1;
else
    statement-2;

COBOL Equivalent:
IF condition
    Statement-1
ELSE
    Statement-2
END-IF.

A Java example is

```
if (minimumBalance < 500)
    serviceCharge = 5.00F;
else
    serviceCharge = 0.00F;
```

COBOL Equivalent:
```
IF MINIMUM-BALANCE < 500
    MOVE 5.00 TO SERVICE-CHARGE
ELSE
    MOVE 0.00 TO SERVICE-CHARGE
END-IF.
```

Also, like COBOL, Java can execute more than one statement based on a condition. When there is more than one statement to execute, we place the statements in a block using braces ({}). Notice the braces are needed only if you want to execute more than one statement.

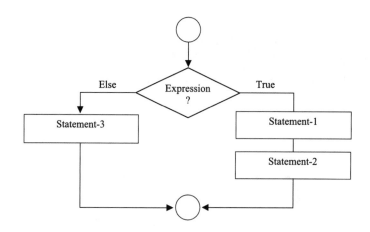

For example:

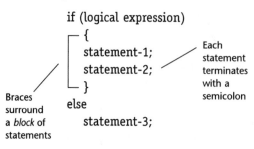

```
if (logical expression)
    {
    statement-1;
    statement-2;
    }
else
    statement-3;
```

Braces surround a *block* of statements

Each statement terminates with a semicolon

COBOL Equivalent:
```
IF condition
    statement-1
    statement-2
ELSE
    statement-3
END-IF.
```

Nested if Statements

Just like COBOL, we can write nested if statements using Java. Notice we do not place a semicolon after the Java expressions.

Like COBOL, the Java compiler ignores indentation. We use it to improve the readability of our code.

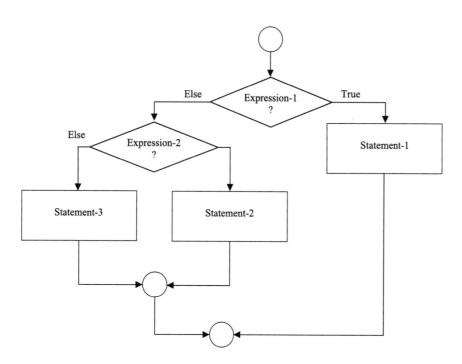

The structure of the Java nested if is

```
if (logical expression-1)
    statement-1;
else
    if (logical expression-2)
        statement-2;
    else
        statement-3;
```

COBOL Equivalent:
```
IF condition-1
    statement-1
ELSE
    IF condition-2
        statement-2
    ELSE
        statement-3
    END-IF
END-IF.
```

Writing Compound Conditions

We can also write compound conditions using Java's AND (&&) and OR (||) logical operators.

if (expression-1 && expression-2)
     statement;

> **COBOL Equivalent:**
> IF condition-1 AND condition-2
>   statement
> END-IF.

if (expression-1 || expression-2)
     statement;

> **COBOL Equivalent:**
> IF condition-1 OR condition-2
>   statement
> END-IF.

NOTE

1. Both COBOL and Java include the reserved word **CONTINUE**, however, they have completely different usage.

2. The COBOL **CONTINUE** is used in an **IF** statement to transfer control to the next scope terminator (**END-IF**).

3. The Java **continue** is used in loops (While, Do, and For) to terminate the current iteration and to begin the next. The Java continue is discussed more thoroughly in Chapter 7 on Looping.

Java's Conditional Operator

Java has a conditional operator, which enables us to write a simple if statement using shorthand. Its structure is

if expression true, store
this value in the variable

if expression false, store
this value in the variable

variable = logical expression ? value-1 : value-2;

The equivalent Java if statement is

```
if (logical expression)
    variable = value-1;
else
    variable = value-2;
```

For example, we could write the service charge logic for a regular account as:

```
serviceCharge = minimumBalance < 500 ? 5.00F : 0.00F;
```

instead of using the If-Else:

? follows the condition   : separates the two values

```
if (minimumBalance <  500)
    serviceCharge = 5.00F;
else
    serviceCharge = 0.00F;
```

Notice a question mark (?) follows the condition and a colon (:) separates the two values.

Use caution writing the conditional operator. Although it is a coding shortcut, it may be more difficult to read than the more familiar if statement.

Condition Names

Java does not have condition names like COBOL. We can use Boolean variables, however, to emulate condition names in some situations.

Let's assume the Community National Bank has assigned checking account type codes as follows:

Code	Account Type
1	regular account
2	business account
3	thrifty account

If we were writing in COBOL, we could code these condition names as:

```
05  ACCOUNT-TYPE    PIC 9(1).
    88  REGULAR-ACCOUNT     VALUE 1.
    88  BUSINESS-ACCOUNT    VALUE 2.
    88  THRIFTY-ACCOUNT     VALUE 3.
```

Recall that in the Java language, we declare variables and then either assign values at declaration time or assign values later. Also, recall that Boolean variables contain only true or false values.

For example, let's declare checking account type as integer:

int accountType;

Next, let's declare Boolean variables for each type of account:

boolean regularAccount, businessAccount, thriftyAccount;

Remember, this code does not assign values to these variables; it only declares them for later reference. Also, because these are Boolean variables, they may be assigned only true or false values

We then assign true or false values to these variables and interrogate them with the following Java code:

only one of these
variables will be
set to true—
the other two
will be false

```
regularAccount  = (accountType == 1);
businessAccount = (accountType == 2);
thriftyAccount  = (accountType == 3);
if (regularAccount)
    doSomething;
```

NOTE

1. COBOL condition names are set to *true* or *false* as values are stored in the field associated with the 88 level. The COBOL condition value is *dynamically* assigned.

2. Java DOES NOT automatically reassign values to Boolean operators as their related variables change values. The Boolean values must be explicitly reassigned each time a new value is stored in the related variable. In the previous code, each time a new value is stored in accountType, we must reassign values to the three Boolean variables: regularAccount, businessAccount, and thriftyAccount.

Computing the Service Charge with if Statements

Next, we develop the code to compute the service charge using nested if statements.

First, let's write the code in COBOL.

Listing 6-1: *COBOL service charge computation using IF statements*

```
05  ACCOUNT-TYPE  PIC 9(1).
    88  REGULAR-ACCOUNT     VALUE 1.
    88  BUSINESS-ACCOUNT    VALUE 2.
    88  THRIFTY-ACCOUNT     VALUE 3.
05  SERVICE-CHARGE     PIC 9(2)V99.
05  MINIMUM-BALANCE    PIC S9(5)V99.


COMPUTE-SERVICE-CHARGE.
  IF REGULAR-ACCOUNT
    IF MINIMUM-BALANCE < 500
        MOVE 5.00 TO SERVICE-CHARGE
    ELSE
        MOVE ZERO TO SERVICE-CHARGE
    END-IF
  ELSE
    IF BUSINESS-ACCOUNT
      IF MINIMUM-BALANCE < 500
          MOVE 10.00 TO SERVICE-CHARGE
      ELSE
          IF MINIMUM-BALANCE < 1000
              MOVE 8.00 TO SERVICE-CHARGE
          ELSE
              MOVE 6.00 TO SERVICE-CHARGE
          END-IF
      END-IF
    ELSE
        MOVE ZERO TO SERVICE-CHARGE
    END-IF
  END-IF.
```

Next, let's write the equivalent code using Java in the development of the **computeServiceCharge()** method. We first need to add the instance variable **accountType** to CheckingAccount. This new attribute is added to the class diagram shown in Figure 6-1.

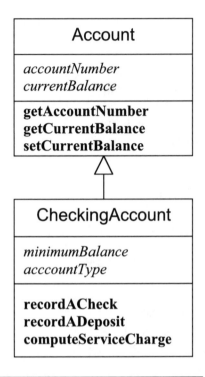

Figure 6-1. *Account and CheckingAccount with accountType*

The Java code for *accountType* is added to CheckingAccount.java immediately after the definition of minimumBalance:

```
public class CheckingAccount extends Account  // superclass is account
{ // class variable
    private float minimumBalance; // private limits access to this class
    protected int accountType;     // 1 is regular, 2 is business, 3 thrifty
```

Listing 6-2 shows the complete **computeServiceCharge()** using if statements.

Listing 6-2: *computeServiceCharge method using if statements*

```
1. public float computeServiceCharge ()
2. {
3.    float serviceCharge;
4.    // declare and assign values to the boolean variables
5.    boolean regularAccount  = (accountType == 1);
6.    boolean businessAccount = (accountType == 2);
7.    boolean thriftyAcount   = (accountType == 3);
8.    // compute the service charge
9.    if (regularAccount)
10.       if (minimumBalance < 500)
11.          serviceCharge = 5.00F;
12.       else
13.          serviceCharge = 0.00F;
14.    else
15.       if (businessAccount)
16.          if (minimumBalance < 500)
17.             serviceCharge = 10.00F;
18.          else
19.             if (minimumBalance < 1000)
20.                serviceCharge = 8.00F;
21.             else
22.                serviceCharge = 6.00F;
23.       else  // thrifty account
24.          serviceCharge = 0.00F;
25.    return serviceCharge;
26. } // end of computeServiceCharge
```

Comments:

1. This method is executed each time we want to compute the service charge for an account. Therefore, the assignment statements at lines 5 through 7 will be executed and one of the Boolean variables will be set to true, depending on the account type code contained in the variable accountType.

2. We could use logical expressions, for example(accountType = 1), instead of the Boolean variables.

3. The *F* at the end of lines 11, 13, 17, 20, 22, and 24 indicate the value is being placed in a floating-point variable.

4. Line 25 returns the computed service charge to the calling program.

5. Like COBOL, Java doesn't care at all whether we indent nested if statements, however, the indentation greatly improves the code's readability.

Case Structure: COBOL EVALUATE and Java switch

The case structure is a multiple-direction decision that can often replace nested if statements. The case structure is implemented in COBOL with the EVALUATE verb and in Java with the switch statement.

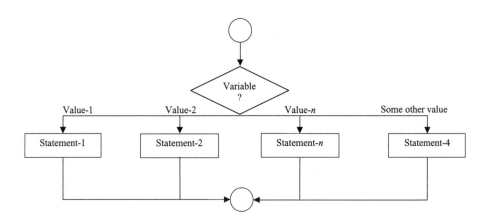

The general form of the Java switch is

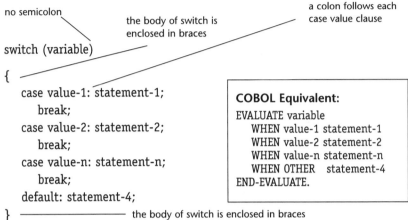

no semicolon

the body of switch is enclosed in braces

a colon follows each case value clause

```
switch (variable)
{
    case value-1: statement-1;
        break;
    case value-2: statement-2;
        break;
    case value-n: statement-n;
        break;
    default: statement-4;
}
```

the body of switch is enclosed in braces

> **COBOL Equivalent:**
> ```
> EVALUATE variable
>     WHEN value-1 statement-1
>     WHEN value-2 statement-2
>     WHEN value-n statement-n
>     WHEN OTHER   statement-4
> END-EVALUATE.
> ```

NOTE

The COBOL EVALUATE statement has some subtle, but important, differences from the Java switch statement:

1. COBOL can evaluate either a logical expression **(EVALUATE TRUE)** or the contents of a variable **(EVALUATE ACCOUNT-TYPE)**. Java can only evaluate the contents of a variable that must be type integer or character **(switch accountType)**.

2. When COBOL detects a matching value, the statements following the WHEN are executed and then control is transferred to the **END-EVALUATE** scope terminator. Java requires the use of the keyword **break** to transfer control to the end of the **switch** statement. If **break** is omitted, Java continues to execute **case** statements following the one where the match occurred.

3. The values we specify in the Java **switch** following the keyword **case** must be *ordinal*, meaning they must consist of ordinal data from a list, such as integers and letters of the alphabet. In contrast, we can write any logical expression following the WHEN in the COBOL EVALUATE statement.

Computing the Service Charge Using switch

Next, we develop the code to compute the service charge using the case structure.

First, let's write the code in COBOL.

Listing 6-3: *COBOL service charge computation using EVALUATE*

```
05  ACCOUNT-TYPE  PIC 9(1).
    88  REGULAR-ACCOUNT      VALUE 1.
    88  BUSINESS-ACCOUNT     VALUE 2.
    88  THRIFTY-ACCOUNT      VALUE 3.
05  SERVICE-CHARGE     PIC 9(2)V99.
05  MINIMUM-BALANCE·  PIC S9(5)V99.
COMPUTE-SERVICE-CHARGE.
    EVALUATE TRUE
        WHEN REGULAR-ACCOUNT
            IF MINIMUM-BALANCE < 500
                MOVE 5.00 TO SERVICE-CHARGE
            ELSE
                MOVE ZERO TO SERVICE-CHARGE
            END-IF
        WHEN BUSINESS-ACCOUNT
            IF MINIMUM-BALANCE < 500
                MOVE 10.00 TO SERVICE-CHARGE
            ELSE
                IF MINIMUM-BALANCE < 1000
                    MOVE 8.00 TO SERVICE-CHARGE
                ELSE
                    MOVE 6.00 TO SERVICE-CHARGE
                END-IF
            END-IF
        WHEN THRIFTY-ACCOUNT
            MOVE ZERO TO SERVICE-CHARGE
    END-EVALUATE.
```

Comments:

1. This code could be improved using nested **EVALUATE** statements:

```
COMPUTE-SERVICE-CHARGE.
    EVALUATE TRUE
    WHEN REGULAR-ACCOUNT
```

```
     EVALUATE MINIMUM-BALANCE
        WHEN < 500 MOVE 5.00 TO SERVICE-CHARGE
        WHEN OTHER MOVE ZERO TO SERVICE-CHARGE
     END-EVALUATE
   WHEN BUSINESS-ACCOUNT
     EVALUATE MINIMUM-BALANCE
        WHEN < 500  MOVE 10.00 TO SERVICE-CHARGE
        WHEN < 1000 MOVE 8.00 TO SERVICE-CHARGE
        WHEN OTHER  MOVE 6.00 TO SERVICE-CHARGE
   END-EVALUATE
   WHEN THRIFTY-ACCOUNT
     MOVE ZERO TO SERVICE-CHARGE
   END-EVALUATE
```

2. Although we can write nested switch statements in Java, we cannot use switch to test for relational conditions, such as (*minimumBalance* < 500). switch can only be used to test for specific ordinal values of an integer or character variable. switch does not provide us with relational expressions such as <, <=, > and >=.

Next, let's rewrite **computeServiceCharge()** using the Java switch statement:

Listing 6-4: *Java service charge computation using* switch

```
1. public float computeServiceCharge ()
2. {
3.    float serviceCharge;
4.    switch (accountType)
5.    {
6.      case 1: // regular account
7.        if (minimumBalance < 500)
8.            serviceCharge = 5.00F;
9.        else
10.           serviceCharge = 0.00F;
11.       break;
12.   case 2: // business account
13.     if (minimumBalance < 500)
```

```
14.         serviceCharge = 10.00F;
15.     else
16.         if (minimumBalance < 1000)
17.             serviceCharge = 8.00F;
18.         else
19.             serviceCharge = 6.00F;
20.     break;
21.     case 3:  // thrifty account
22.         serviceCharge = 0.00F;
23.     } // end of switch
24.     return serviceCharge;
25. }  // end computeServiceCharge
```

> **NOTE**
>
> The placement of the semicolon(;), colon (:), and braces ({}) is critical in the **switch** statement:
>
> **1.** There is NOT a semicolon following switch—see line 4
> **switch (accountType)**
>
> **2.** Each **case** terminates with a colon, not a semicolon
> **case 1 :**
>
> **3.** The body of the switch block is enclosed in braces

Comments:

1. Notice the braces ({ and }) at lines 5 and 23. These are required and indicate the boundaries of the switch block.

2. The break statements at lines 11 and 20 transfer execution to the end of the switch block at line 23.

3. As previously mentioned, we cannot replace the if statements here with nested switch statements. Java permits us to test only for specific ordinal values. For example, we cannot use switch with an expression like *"minimumBalance < 500"*.

4. Good programming practices would require us to code a default case to cover an account type other than 1, 2, or 3. To keep the examples brief, we have omitted the default here.

Summary of Key Points

1. The COBOL and Java logical operators have both similarities and differences:

Java	COBOL
&&	AND
==	EQUAL TO, =
>	GREATER THAN, >
>=	GREATER THAN OR EQUAL TO, >=
<	LESS THAN, <
<=	LESS THAN OR EQUAL TO, <=
!	NOT
!=	NOT EQUAL TO, NOT =, <>
||	OR

2. The COBOL and Java if statements are similar:

Java	COBOL
A. if (logical expression) statement;	IF condition statement END-IF.
B. if (logical expression) statement-1; else statement-2;	IF condition statement-1 ELSE statement-2 END-IF.
C. if (logical expression) {statement-1; statement-2;} else statement-3;	IF condition statement-1 statement-2 ELSE statement-3 END-IF.
D. if (logical expression-1) statement-1; else	IF condition -1 statement-1 ELSE

```
   if (logical expression-2)        IF condition -2
       statement-2;                      statement-2
   else                              ELSE
       statement-3;                      statement-3
                                     END-IF
                                   END-IF.
```

```
E.  if (expression-1 && expression-2)   IF condition -1
        statement;                          AND condition -2
                                                statement
                                        END-IF.
```

```
F.  if (expression-1 || expression-2)   IF condition -1
        statement;                          OR condition -2
                                                statement
                                        END-IF.
```

3. We can emulate COBOL condition names in Java
   ```
   regularAccount  = (accountType == 1);
   businessAccount = (accountType == 2);
   thriftyAccount  = (accountType == 3);
   if (regularAccount)
       doSomething;
   ```

4. Major differences exist between COBOL's EVALUATE and Java's switch statements

   A. COBOL can evaluate either a Boolean condition **(EVALUATE TRUE)** or the contents of a variable **(EVALUATE ACCOUNT-TYPE)**. Java can only evaluate the contents of a variable that must be type integer or character **(switch accountType)**.

   B. When COBOL detects a matching value, the statements following the WHEN are executed and then control is transferred to the END-EVALUATE scope terminator. Java requires the use of the keyword break to transfer control to the end of the switch statement. If break is omitted, Java continues to execute case statements following the one where the match occurred.

   C. The values we can specify in the Java switch following the keyword case must be ordinal. That is, they must consist of ordinal data from a list, such as integers and letters of the alphabet. In contrast, we can write any logical expression following the WHEN in the COBOL EVALUATE statement.

5. Java's conditional operator enables us to write abbreviated if statements. The shorthand code

serviceCharge = minimumBalance < 500 ? 5.00F : 0.00F;

can replace the If-Else:

```
if (minimumBalance <  500)
    serviceCharge = 5.00F;
else
    serviceCharge = 0.00F;
```

Glossary

Boolean variable a variable whose value is either *true* or *false*.

case structure a multiple-direction decision structure that can often replace nested if statements. Implemented in COBOL with the EVALUATE verb and in Java with the switch statement.

compound condition two conditions joined with the logical operators || (or) or && (and).

condition a logical expression.

condition name A COBOL condition name is the name of a condition defined as a level 88.

conditional operator a Java coding shortcut to writing simple if statement. Its format is: variable = logical expression ? value-1 : value-2;

logical expression an expression that evaluates to a Boolean value—true or false; a condition.

logical operator Java operators used in writing logical expressions (<, >, <=, >=, ==, &&, ||, !, !=)

Chapter 7

Loops

Objectives
In this chapter you will study:
- While Loop
- Do Loop
- For Loop
- Nested Loops
- Break Statement
- Continue Statement

This chapter shows you how to write Java loops. You learn how to write loops that mirror the familiar COBOL PERFORM statement, including the PERFORM-UNTIL, PERFORM-VARYING-UNTIL, and PERFORM-VARYING-UNTIL-AFTER. You will see that Java has three different types of loops: while, do, and for. We use each of these to duplicate the work done by the COBOL PERFORM statement. In addition, we review loops that test for the terminating condition at the beginning and at the end of the loop. We also demonstrate writing nested loops in Java.

The chapter begins with the simple COBOL PERFORM-UNTIL statement and shows you how to accomplish the same thing in Java. Then we work with the PERFORM-VARYING-UNTIL and, finally, the PER-FORM-VARYING-UNTIL-AFTER statement. Working programs are developed to illustrate the Java loop statements in action. At the end of the chapter, we design and develop a small program for the Community National Bank to compute a loan amortization, using some of the Java looping statements.

145

This chapter assumes you understand the following:

COBOL:

- Perform-Until
- Inline Perform (COBOL-85)
- Perform-Varying-Until
- Perform-Varying-Until-After
- With Test After (COBOL-85)

Java:

- OO Concepts (Chapter 2)
- Java Program Structure (Chapter 3)
- Defining Data (Chapter 4)
- Computation (Chapter 5)
- Decision Making (Chapter 6)

The Loop Structure

We write program loops to repeat a sequence of instructions. In COBOL, we use the PERFORM statement and its variations to construct loops. In Java, we have three different statements to choose from: while, do, and for. Regardless of the loop statement employed or the language used, for that matter, all loops are similar.

We write loops that test for the terminating condition either at the beginning of the loop (pre-test) or at the end of the loop (post-test). The main difference between pre-test and post-test loops is the post-test loop will always execute the loop statements at least once. The pre-test loop, however, will not execute the loop statements if the terminating condition is true when execution begins. The following flowcharts map these two general loop structures.

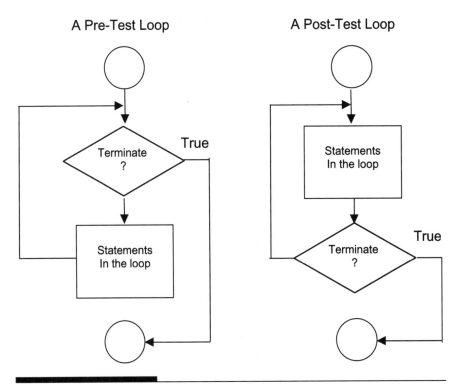

Figure 7-1. *Loop structures*

The COBOL PERFORM Statement

The COBOL language has several variations of the PERFORM used to code loops. The COBOL-74 PERFORM loop was always a pre-test. The following lists three of the more frequently used COBOL-74 PERFORM statements used to write loops:

```
COBOL-74
PERFORM paragraph_name number_of_times
PERFORM paragraph_name UNTIL terminate_condition
PERFORM paragraph_name VARYING variable-name
    FROM initial_value BY increment_value
        UNTIL terminate_condition
```

The paragraph_name referenced in these PERFORM statements contain the code to be executed in the loop. In other words, the paragraph referenced by paragraph_name contains the body of the loop.

COBOL-85 introduced the inline PERFORM and its corresponding scope terminator, END-PERFORM, which allows us to write a loop without the need for a separate paragraph. We simply sandwich the loop statements between the PERFORM and the END-PERFORM. COBOL-85 also gave us the option of specifying either a pre-test or a post-test loop structure by including the WITH TEST BEFORE (pre-test) or WITH TEST AFTER (post-test) clause. The WITH TEST BEFORE is the default.

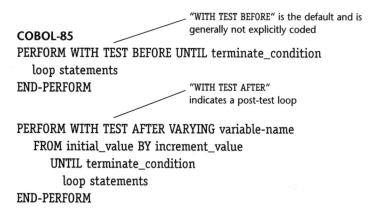

```
COBOL-85
PERFORM WITH TEST BEFORE UNTIL terminate_condition
    loop statements
END-PERFORM

PERFORM WITH TEST AFTER VARYING variable-name
    FROM initial_value BY increment_value
        UNTIL terminate_condition
            loop statements
END-PERFORM
```

"WITH TEST BEFORE" is the default and is generally not explicitly coded

"WITH TEST AFTER" indicates a post-test loop

We use the COBOL-85 PERFORM syntax for the remaining examples here.

The Java while Statement

The Java while statement is used to write pre-test loops, similar to the familiar COBOL PERFORM-UNTIL.

The basic structure of the while is

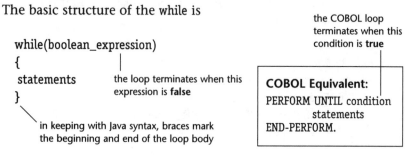

```
while(boolean_expression)
{
    statements
}
```

the loop terminates when this expression is **false**

in keeping with Java syntax, braces mark the beginning and end of the loop body

the COBOL loop terminates when this condition is **true**

COBOL Equivalent:
```
PERFORM UNTIL condition
    statements
END-PERFORM.
```

NOTE

1. The COBOL >, >=, < and <= operators are identical in Java.

2. However, the *equal to, not equal to, and, or,* and *not* operators are totally different:

Operator	COBOL	Java
Equal to	=	==
Not equal to	NOT =	!=
And	AND	&&
Or	OR	||
Not	NOT	!

To illustrate, let's use a while loop to print the numbers 1 through 5. First, we initialize our number to 1, and then we loop to print and increment the number. We want the loop to terminate after our number becomes greater than 5. The Java code is

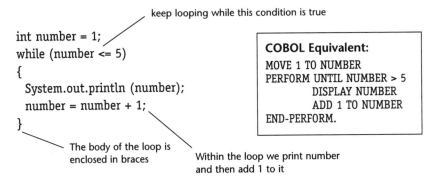

keep looping while this condition is true

```
int number = 1;
while (number <= 5)
{
    System.out.println (number);
    number = number + 1;
}
```

COBOL Equivalent:
```
MOVE 1 TO NUMBER
PERFORM UNTIL NUMBER > 5
        DISPLAY NUMBER
        ADD 1 TO NUMBER
END-PERFORM.
```

The body of the loop is enclosed in braces

Within the loop we print number and then add 1 to it

NOTE

If the braces are omitted, Java **assumes a one statement loop**. This example, without braces will create **an endless loop**, because the statement
    number = number + 1;
will not be part of the loop and number will not be incremented within the loop.

Another loop example is to determine the number of years it will take for the balance in a savings account to double in value, given a fixed rate of interest and assuming we make a fixed deposit at the end of every year. Let's first declare our variables and assign values. We use a beginning balance of $1,000, an annual interest rate of 5.0% and an annual deposit of $100.

```
// declare variables
float initialbalance = 1000F; // initial account balance
float annualDeposit = 100F; // amount of annual deposit
float apr = 0.05F;      // annual percentage rate of interest
float currentBalance;   // the running account balance
int numberOfYears;      // number of years to double in value
```

Before beginning the loop, we assign the initial account balance to currentBalance and initialize the numberOfYears variable to zero.

```
currentBalance = initialBalance;
numberOfYears = 0;
```

Then at the end of each year (each loop), we compute the interest earned during the year, add the interest to the current balance, and then add the annual deposit amount to the current balance. The statement to do this computation is

```
currentBalance = currentBalance * (1 + apr) + annualDeposit;
```

We then write the loop:

The loop terminates when currentBalance exceeds twice the initialBalance

Compute the new balance & increment numberOfYears

```
while (currentBalance <= (2 * initialBalance))
{
  currentBalance = currentBalance * (1 + apr) + annualDeposit;
  numberOfYears = numberOfYears + 1;
  System.out.println ("Year " + numberOfYears +
    Math.round (currentBalance));
}
```

The body of the loop is enclosed between braces

Print the year number and balance at end of each loop (year)

Note, the loop is a pre-test loop. It checks the terminating condition before executing the loop instructions. After the loop terminates, we print the numberOfYears and currentBalance.

```
System.out.print ("In " + numberOfYears + " years");
System.out.println ("The balance will be " +
    Math.round(currentBalance));
```

We have put this code together in a small program named WhileLoopDemo.java (see Listing 7-1).

Listing 7-1: *WhileLoopDemo.java*

```java
public class WhileLoopDemo
{
  public static void main (String args[])
  {
// we have an amount of money in an interest bearing account: initialBalance
// each year we make a fixed deposit to the account: annualDeposit
// the account earns at an annual rate of interest: apr
// how many years are required for our account to double in value: years

// declare variables
float initialBalance = 1000F;  // let's begin with $1,000 balance
float annualDeposit = 100F;   // then deposit $100 at end of each year
float apr = 0.05F;     // annual interest rate is 5%
float currentBalance;    // running balance

int numberOfYears;     // count the number of years

// initialize currentBalance and numberOfYears
currentBalance = initialBalance;
numberOfYears = 0;
System.out.println ("Output From while Loop"); // print headings
System.out.println ("Year    Balance");

// beginning of while loop
while (currentBalance <= (2 * initialBalance))
```

```
      {
        currentBalance = currentBalance * (1 + apr) + annualDeposit;
        numberOfYears = numberOfYears + 1;
        System.out.println (numberOfYears + "    " + Math.round(currentBalance));
      } // end of while loop

      System.out.print ("In " + numberOfYears + " years");
      System.out.println ("the balance will be " + Math.round(currentBalance));

    } // end of main method
  } // end of LoopDemo.java class program
```

The output from WhileLoopDemo.java is

```
Output From while Loop
Year       Balance
1          1150
2          1308
3          1473
4          1647
5          1829
6          2020
In 6 years the balance will be 2020
```

The Java do Statement

The Java do statement is used to write post-test loops. We use the COBOL-85 PERFORM WITH TEST AFTER clause to code COBOL post-test loops.

The basic structure of the do is

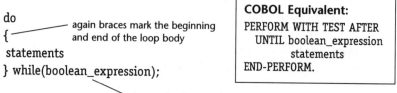

```
do                    ── again braces mark the beginning
{                        and end of the loop body
  statements
} while(boolean_expression);
```

the terminating condition is at the **end** of the do loop.
The loop terminates when this expression is **false**

> **COBOL Equivalent:**
> PERFORM WITH TEST AFTER
>   UNTIL boolean_expression
>   statements
> END-PERFORM.

The Java do loop is sometimes called a do-while loop because the while clause is written at the end of the loop. The do loop and while loop are similar except the while loop is pre-test and the do loop is post-test. Both terminate when the Boolean expression is false.

NOTE

1. Java loops terminate when the boolean_expression is **false**.
2. COBOL loops terminate when the boolean_expression is **true**.

We can use a do loop to print the numbers 1 through 5, just like we did before, and the code is quite similar. First, we initialize our number to 1, and then loop to print and increment the number. We want the loop to terminate when our number becomes greater than 5. The Java code is

```
int number = 1;          Within the loop we
do                       print number and
{                        then add 1 to it
    System.out.println (number);
    number = number + 1;
} while (number <= 5)
```

we write the while clause   keep looping while this
at the end of the do loop   condition is true

COBOL Equivalent:
```
MOVE 1 TO NUMBER
PERFORM WITH TEST AFTER
    UNTIL NUMBER > 5
        DISPLAY NUMBER
        ADD 1 TO NUMBER
END-PERFORM.
```

Note, the loop is a post-test loop. The condition is checked after the loop instructions. In this case, the loop would have executed at least once, regardless of the value of number.

When we place the while and do loops side by side (Figure 7-2) you can see their similarity. The only difference is the while loop has the while clause at the beginning and the do loop has do at the beginning and the while at the end. Notice the terminating condition and the statements within the loop are identical.

We can easily modify the previous program, WhileLoopDemo.java, to use the do statement. We name this modified program DoLoopDemo.java. We changed five lines (all boldface), but only two, the do and while statements, impact the program's execution.

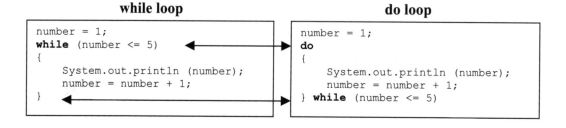

| while loop | do loop |

```
number = 1;
while (number <= 5)
{
    System.out.println (number);
    number = number + 1;
}
```

```
number = 1;
do
{
    System.out.println (number);
    number = number + 1;
} while (number <= 5)
```

Figure 7-2. *while loop and do loop*

Listing 7-2: *DoLoopDemo.java*

```
public class DoLoopDemo
{
    public static void main (String args[])
    {
    // we have an amount in an interest bearing account: initialBalance
    // each year we make a fixed deposit to the account: annualDeposit
    // the account earns at an annual rate of interest: apr
    // how many years are required for our account to double in value: years
    // declare variables
    float initialBalance = 1000F;  // let's begin with $1,000 balance
    float annualDeposit = 100F;   // then deposit $100 at end of each year
    float apr = 0.05F;     // annual interest rate is 5%
    float currentBalance;    // running balance   int numberOfYears;
    // count the number of years
    // initialize currentBalance and numberOfYears
    currentBalance = initialBalance;
    numberOfYears = 0;
    System.out.println ("Output From do Loop"); // print headings
    System.out.println ("Year    Balance");

    // beginning of do loop
    do
    {
```

```
    currentBalance = currentBalance * (1 + apr) + annualDeposit;
    numberOfYears = numberOfYears + 1;
    System.out.println (numberOfYears + "    " + Math.round(currentBalance));
} while (currentBalance <= (2 * initialBalance));  // end of do loop
System.out.print ("In " + numberOfYears + " years ");
System.out.println ("the balance will be " +
    Math.round(currentBalance));
} // end of main method
} // end of DoLoopDemo.java
```

The following shows the program's output, which is the same as the previous example.

DoLoopDemo.java Output

```
Output From do Loop
Year       Balance
1          1150
2          1308     .
3          1473
4          1647
5          1829
6          2020
In 6 years the balance will be 2020
```

The Java for Statement

So far we have used the Java while and do statements to write loops. These examples initialize a loop counter, such as number or numberOfYears, and the loop included a statement to increment the counter. When we use the while or do, we are responsible for initializing and incrementing any loop counter variables used. The COBOL counterpart of the Java while and do statements is the PERFORM-UNTIL.

In COBOL, we can use the PERFORM-VARYING-UNTIL statement to initialize and increment loop counters automatically for us. For example, let's again print 1 through 5, but this time let's use a PERFORM-VARYING-UNTIL statement.

```
PERFORM VARYING NUMBER FROM 1 BY 1
   UNTIL NUMBER > 5
   DISPLAY NUMBER
END-PERFORM.
```

This code represents a pre-test loop and is both simpler and shorter because we do not need the initialization statement (MOVE 1 TO NUMBER) or the increment statement (ADD 1 TO NUMBER).

We use the Java for loop to initialize and increment loop counters for us. It is a pre-test loop and its structure is

initialize the loop counter variable   The loop terminates when this expression is **false**   increment the variable

```
for (initialize_statement; boolean_expression; increment_statement)
{
   statements
}
```

semicolons are separators

braces mark the beginning and end of the loop body

COBOL Equivalent:
```
PERFORM VARYING variable-name FROM initial-value
   BY increment-value UNTIL condition
         statements
END-PERFORM.
```

We can use the for loop to once again print the numbers 1 through 5.

we can both declare & initialize number here   this is the same condition we used before   add 1 to number

```
for (int number = 1; number <= 5; number = number + 1)
{
     System.out.println (number);
}
```

COBOL Equivalent:
```
PERFORM VARYING number FROM 1 BY 1 UNTIL number > 5
         DISPLAY NUMBER
END-PERFORM.
```

1. If we declare the variable number in the for statement, its scope is limited to this loop.
2. We can choose to declare the variable outside the loop to give it method scope.

We have again modified WhileLoopDemo.java, this time to demonstrate the for statement. We name this modified program ForLoopDemo.java. We converted the while loop to a for loop and moved the initialize and increment statements into the for statement.

Listing 7-3: *ForLoopDemo.java*

```
public class ForLoopDemo
{
  public static void main (String args[])
  {
  // we have an amount in an interest bearing account: initialBalance
  // each year we make a fixed deposit to the account: annualDeposit
  // the account earns at an annual rate of interest: apr
  // how many years are required for our account to double in value: years
  // declare variables
  float initialBalance = 1000F; // let's begin with $1,000 balance
  float annualDeposit = 100F; // then deposit $100 at end of each year
  float apr = 0.05F;          // annual interest rate is 5%
  float currentBalance;       // running balance
  int numberOfYears;          // count the number of years

  // initialize currentBalance and numberOfYears
  currentBalance = initialBalance;
  System.out.println ("Output From for Loop"); // print headings
  System.out.println ("Year    Balance");

  // beginning of for loop
  for (numberOfYears = 0; currentBalance <= (2 * initialBalance);
    numberOfYears = numberOfYears + 1)
  {
```

```
    currentBalance = currentBalance * (1 + apr) + annualDeposit;
    System.out.println (numberOfYears + "   " +
       Math.round(currentBalance));
} // end of for loop

System.out.print ("In " + numberOfYears + " years ");
System.out.println ("the balance will be " + Math.round(currentBalance));
} // end of main method
} // end of ForLoopDemo.java
```

The output is the same as the previous two examples.

```
Output From for Loop
Year     Balance
1        1150
2        1308
3        1473
4        1647
5        1829
6        2020
In 6 years the balance will be 2020
```

Nested Loops

Like COBOL, we can write nested loops in Java. In COBOL, we can write a nested loop using two loop statements. For example:

```
PERFORM VARYING NUMBER1 FROM 1 BY 1 UNTIL NUMBER1 > 3
   PERFORM VARYING NUMBER2 FROM 1 BY 1 UNTIL NUMBER2 > 2
      DISPLAY NUMBER1, NUMBER2
   END-PERFORM
END-PERFORM.
```

This code executes the DISPLAY statement six times and prints:

Number1	Number2
1	1
1	2
2	1
2	2
3	1
3	2

We can rewrite this nested loop using the COBOL PERFORM-VARY-ING-AFTER statement, which simplifies the code a little:

```
PERFORM VARYING NUMBER1 FROM 1 BY 1 UNTIL NUMBER1 > 3
    AFTER NUMBER2 FROM 1 BY 1 UNTIL NUMBER2 > 2
        DISPLAY NUMBER1, NUMBER2
END-PERFORM.
```

The DISPLAY statement again executes six times and the output is the same as before.

Although Java does not have a counterpart to COBOL's PERFORM-VARYING-AFTER statement, we can certainly simulate it by writing a loop within a loop.

```
for (int number1 = 1; number1 <= 3; number1 = number1 + 1)
{
    for (int number2 = 1; number2 <= 2; number2 = number2 + 1)
    {
        System.out.println (number1 + "    " + number2);
    } // end of inner loop
} // end of outer loop
```

Similar to the COBOL example, this code executes the **println()** method six times and prints:

Number1	Number2
1	1
1	2
2	1
2	2
3	1
3	2

Remember, the scope of the variables declared in the loop is limited to the loop.

We can, of course, use any combination of while, do, and for statements to construct nested loops.

Java break and continue Statements

Java provides two statements to terminate prematurely or to skip a loop: break and continue. break immediately terminates a loop. continue terminates only the current iteration of the loop. The break and continue are typically used with an if statement, which tests for a condition that warrants the termination of the loop.

> **NOTE**
>
> 1. The Java continue and COBOL continue are totally different key words.
>
> 2. Java continue terminates the current loop iteration.
>
> 3. COBOL continue goes to the scope terminator in an IF statement.

To illustrate, we can print the numbers 1 through 5 as in previous examples, but here let's skip the number 3 by using the continue statement. This code will print 1, 2, 4, and 5.

```
int number = 1;
   while (number <=5)
      {
```

```
if (number == 3)              // don't print the number 3
{  number = number + 1;       // increment to avoid endless
                              // loop
      continue;               // continue skips to end of loop
} // end if
System.out.println (number);
number = number + 1;
} // end while
```

Now let's use the same code, but **stop** printing at 3 using the break.

```
int number = 1;
while (number <=5)
{
    if (number == 3)// stop loop at 3
        break;    // break terminates the loop
    System.out.println (number);
    number = number + 1;
} // end while
statements
```

This code will print only 1 and 2. The statement

```
if (number == 3)
break;
```

exits the loop when number reaches 3.

Producing a Loan Amortization Schedule

A loan amortization schedule gives us detailed payment information about a loan, such as the payment amount and the amount of interest and principal paid each month. In this section, we develop a method to compute and display a loan amortization schedule for Community National Bank.

If we know the original loan amount (balance), the annual percentage interest rate (apr), and the loan duration expressed in number of months (months), we can calculate the monthly loan payment using the formula we developed in Chapter 5:

apr / 12 is the
monthly rate

Math.pow (x, y) returns x
raised to the y power

payment = (balance * (apr / 12)/Math.pow ((1 – apr/12),months);

We can then use the **roundOff()** method also developed in Chapter 5 to round the payment amount to two decimal positions.

payment = roundOff(payment);

Next, knowing the monthly payment amount, we can then compute the interest and principal paid each month over the life of the loan. We write a while loop to loop once for each month. monthNumber is our loop counter and months is the duration of the loan.

while (monthNumber <= months)

The interest to be paid each month is simply the monthly interest rate applied to the remaining loan balance. Again, we round the interest.

interestPaid = roundOff (balance * apr / 12);

The portion of the payment applied to reducing the loan amount is the payment amount less the interest paid.

principalPaid = payment - interestPaid;

The new loan balance after the payment has been made is the previous balance, less the amount applied to principal.

balance = balance - principalPaid;

The complete program named Amortizer.java is shown in Listing 7-4.

Listing 7-4: *Amortizer.java*

```
import java.text.NumberFormat;
public class Amortizer
{
    public static void main (String args[])
    {
    // declare variables
```

```
float balance = 1000F;
float apr = .08F;
int months = 6;
float interestPaid = 0F;
float principalPaid = 0F;
float totalInterestPaid = 0F;
// compute payment
double doublePayment = (balance * (apr / 12))/ (1 - 1 / Math.pow ((1
  + apr/12), months));
float payment = (float) doublePayment;     // cast to float
payment = roundOff (payment);  // round to cents
// print heading
System.out.println ("Mo Payment  Interest  Principal Balance");

// beginning of while loop
int monthNumber = 1;
while (monthNumber <= months)
{
   interestPaid = roundOff (balance * apr / 12);
   totalInterestPaid = totalInterestPaid + interestPaid;
   if (monthNumber == months)
      payment = interestPaid + balance;  // adjust last payment
   principalPaid =  payment - interestPaid;
   balance = roundOff(balance - principalPaid);
   // print a line
   System.out.print ("  " + monthNumber);
   System.out.print ("   " + payment);
   System.out.print ("    " + interestPaid);
   System.out.print ("    " + principalPaid);
   System.out.println ("     " + balance);
   monthNumber = monthNumber + 1;
 } // end of while loop

 System.out.println ("Total Interest Paid " + roundOff(totalInterestPaid));
 } // end of main method

 // roundOff method
```

```
static public float roundOff (double value)
{
    value = value * 100;              // move decimal 2 places to right
    // Math.round returns long - recast to float
    float roundedValue = (float) Math.round(value);
    roundedValue = roundedValue / 100; // move decimal back to left
    return roundedValue;
} // end roundOff

} // end of Amortizer.java
```

The program output is shown in the following Figure 7-3.

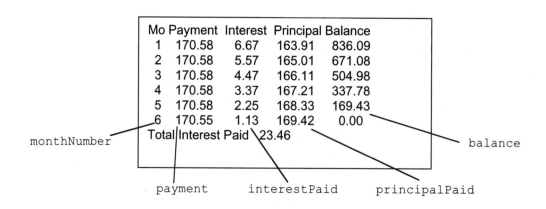

Figure 7-3. *Amortizer.java output*

A good exercise for you here is to convert Amortizer.java to a method and then write a Loan Processor program that calls the **amortizeLoan()** method. The method signature would be

public void amortizeLoan (float balance, float apr, int months)

Or, you could have the method return a value, say payment, if you wish.

Summary of Key Points

1. In general two types of loops exist: *pre-test* loops test for the terminating condition at the beginning of the loop and *post-test* loops test at the end of the loop.

2. Java has three loop statements: while, do, and for. while is a pre-test; do and for are post-test.

   - while(boolean_expression)   // loop while this is true
     ```
     {
         statements
     }
     ```
   - do
     ```
     {
         statements
     } while(boolean_expression) // loop while this is true
     ```
   - for (initialize; boolean_expression; increment)
     ```
     {                          // loop while this is true
         statements
     }
     ```

3. Java does not have a counterpart to COBOL's PERFORM-VARYING-AFTER statement, but we can simulate it by writing a loop within a loop using any of Java's looping statements.

   ```
   for (int number1 = 1; number1 <= 3; number1 = number1 + 1)
   {
       for (int number2 = 1; number2 <= 2; number2 = number2 + 1)
       {
           System.out.println (number1 + "     " + number2);
       } // end of inner loop
   } // end of outer loop
   ```

4. Java provides two statements to terminate a loop prematurely: break and continue. break immediately terminates a loop. continue terminates only the current iteration of the loop.

Glossary

post-test loop a loop whose terminating condition is tested at the end of the loop.

pre-test loop a loop whose terminating condition is tested at the beginning of the loop.

Chapter 8

Arrays

Objectives

In this chapter you will study:

- One-Dimensional Arrays
- Two-Dimensional Arrays
- Searching Arrays
- Passing Arrays as Arguments

This chapter shows you how to work with arrays. You learn how to define and manipulate both single and multidimensional arrays. In this chapter, as in others, we develop real working programs to illustrate using Java arrays.

COBOL uses the term single-level table; Java uses the term one-dimensional array.

In keeping with the spirit of Java, we use array and dimension here.

NOTE

This chapter begins with the declaration and population of one-dimensional arrays and then illustrates how to declare and populate two-dimensional arrays. The examples use both numeric and string data values. The chapter also describes how to search an array using Java and how to pass arrays as arguments to methods.

You will see that, although internally Java treats array processing somewhat differently than COBOL, to you the programmer, Java array handling looks a lot like COBOL table processing. Of course, we continue to point out significant differences between Java and COBOL, as well as pitfalls to avoid when writing Java from a COBOL programmer's perspective.

This chapter assumes you understand the following:

COBOL:

- Defining one- & two-level tables
- Initializing one- & two-level tables
- Table lookup techniques
- Using subscripts and indexes
- Perform-varying statement

Java:

- OO Concepts (Chapter 2)
- Java Program Structure (Chapter 3)
- Defining Data (Chapter 4)
- Decision Making (Chapter 6)
- Looping (Chapter 7)

Declaring One-Dimensional Arrays

We begin our discussion of one-dimensional arrays by looking at loan processing for the Community National Bank. Let's assume CNB wants to track the number of new loans made during each month for the calendar year. We can accomplish this by using a one-dimensional array with 12 elements—one element for each month.

In COBOL, we declare the array as:

```
01 LOAN-TABLE.                                    12 elements
   05 NUMBER-OF-LOANS  PIC 9(3)  OCCURS 12 TIMES.
```

Each element's name is NUMBER-OF-LOANS   Each element is PIC 9(3)

This code creates a 12-element array named LOAN-TABLE, with each element a PIC 9(3) field named NUMBER-OF-LOANS. We use the COBOL occurs clause to tell the compiler how many elements we want to have.

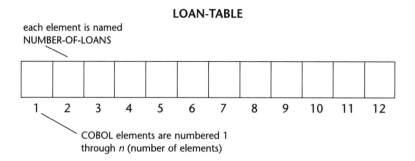

COBOL uses a subscript to indicate which element we wish to access. For example, to display the number of loans made in January, we write

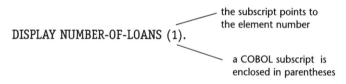

<table>
<tr><td></td><td>NOTE</td></tr>
</table>

1. COBOL makes a distinction between a *subscript* and an *index*. COBOL uses an index with the *SEARCH* verb.

2. Java does not use the term *subscript* but, instead, uses the term *index*. *Index* is used like the COBOL subscript—it specifies the element number of an array.

3. Here we use *subscript* when discussing COBOL and *index* when dealing with Java syntax.

The declaration of an array in Java looks quite similar to the variable declarations described in Chapter 4. Our loan array would be declared as:

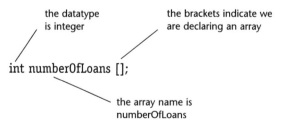

In fact, this statement does not reserve memory for our array. Notice we did not tell the Java compiler how many elements we needed. This statement simply tells Java we are going to create a variable named numberOfLoans and we will define it as an array more completely later.

To complete the array definition, we write

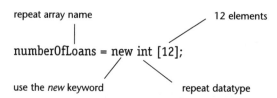

repeat array name   12 elements

numberOfLoans = new int [12];

use the *new* keyword   repeat datatype

This statement tells Java we want the array to have 12 elements. Note, we used two statements to declare the array.

If we prefer, we can combine these two statements into a single complete definition, but we repeat the datatype (int) and the brackets:

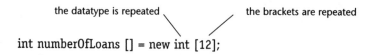

the datatype is repeated   the brackets are repeated

int numberOfLoans [] = new int [12];

The Java array appears as:

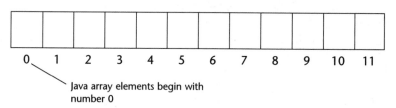

0   1   2   3   4   5   6   7   8   9   10   11

Java array elements begin with number 0

> **NOTE**
>
> 1. The element numbers for Java arrays begin with zero, not 1.
>
> 2. To keep us on our toes, in the array declaration Java allows us to put the brackets **before or after** the array name. Although both of the following formats are OK, we use the first because it is more similar to the COBOL syntax:
>
>   datatype arrayname [] = new datatype [number_of_elements];
>
>   or
>
>   datatype [] arrayname = new datatype [number_of_elements];
>
> 3. The *new* operator suggests we are creating an object **instance**, which is exactly what happens. This fact, however, has little impact on our array processing code. We point out those places where we need to be aware the array is actually an object instance.

Populating One-Dimensional Arrays

You can populate a COBOL array in two different ways: use the value clause in the Data Division or procedural statements in the Procedure Division to place values into the array. Here, the first example uses the value clause to establish values for the array.

```
01 NUMBER-OF-LOAN-VALUES.
    05  FILLER   PIC 9(3) VALUE 39.
    05  FILLER   PIC 9(3) VALUE 44.
    05  FILLER   PIC 9(3) VALUE 45.
    05  FILLER   PIC 9(3) VALUE 65.
    05  FILLER   PIC 9(3) VALUE 72.
    05  FILLER   PIC 9(3) VALUE 93.
    05  FILLER   PIC 9(3) VALUE 14.
    05  FILLER   PIC 9(3) VALUE 55.
    05  FILLER   PIC 9(3) VALUE 67.
    05  FILLER   PIC 9(3) VALUE 27.
    05  FILLER   PIC 9(3) VALUE 46.
    05  FILLER   PIC 9(3) VALUE 82.
01 LOAN-TABLE REDEFINES NUMBER-OF-LOAN-VALUES.
    05  NUMBER-OF-LOANS  PIC 9(3)  OCCURS 12 TIMES.
```

1. This example uses COBOL-78 syntax.

2. COBOL-85 (and COBOL–XX) lets us omit *filler*. We could write
PIC 9(3) VALUE 39.

3. The *redefines* clause allows multiple names and picture clauses to be assigned to the same data items.

To assign values to an array at execution time, we can write procedure division code:

```
MOVE 39 TO NUMBER-OF-LOANS(1)
MOVE 44 TO NUMBER-OF-LOANS(2)
..etc.
```

Regardless of the population technique, the populated array now appears as:

LOAN-TABLE

39	44	45	65	72	93	14	55	67	2	46	82
1	2	3	4	5	6	7	8	9	10	11	12

The statement:

```
DISPLAY NUMBER-OF-LOANS (3)
```

displays "45," the contents of the third element—the number of loans CNB made in March.

Similar to COBOL, we can populate Java arrays either at declaration time or with procedural statements. To declare and populate the array in a single statement, we write

```
int numberOfLoans [] = {39,44,45,65,72,93,14,55,67,27,46,82};
```

number of elements   values are enclosed in braces   don't forget
not specified   and separated by commas   the semicolon

Notice we omit the new operator and do not specify the number of elements when we declare and populate in the same statement. The Java compiler determines the number of elements from the data value list.

If we prefer to populate a Java array with assignment statements, we would write

remember, the first element in
a Java array is number 0!

```
numberOfLoans [0] = 39;
numberOfLoans [1] = 44;
. . etc.
```

To display the contents of an element, say the third one, using Java we can write

parentheses surround the argument being
passed to the method **println()**

remember, use brackets for
the index, not parentheses

```
System.out.println (numberOfLoans [2]);
```

an index value of 2 points to
the *third* element of the array

This will again print "45" from the third element of the array numberOfLoans.

Creating String Arrays

Let's assume we want an array containing the names of the months. In COBOL we would write

```
01  MONTH-NAME-VALUES.
    05  PIC X(36) VALUE 'JanFebMarAprMayJunJulAugSepOctNovDec'.
01  MONTH-NAME-TABLE REDEFINES MONTH-NAME-VALUES.
    05  MONTH-NAME PIC X(3) OCCURS 12 TIMES.
```

This creates a 12-element array with each element named MONTH-NAME:

MONTH-NAME-TABLE

Jan	Feb	Mar	Apr	May	Jun	Jul	Aug	Sep	Oct	Nov	Dec
1	2	3	4	5	6	7	8	9	10	11	12

To declare and populate this array using Java, we write

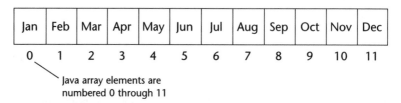

datatype is String

String monthNames [] = {"Jan","Feb","Mar","Apr","May","Jun",
"Jul","Aug","Sep","Oct","Nov","Dec"};

The Java array appears as:

Jan	Feb	Mar	Apr	May	Jun	Jul	Aug	Sep	Oct	Nov	Dec
0	1	2	3	4	5	6	7	8	9	10	11

Java array elements are
numbered 0 through 11

NOTE

1. Remember Java arrays are object instances.

2. The array instance has a public variable named length, which contains the number of elements in the array.

3. We can access this variable using the expression: arrayname.length. Notice the array length is the *number of elements* and not the number of bytes.

We have written a little Java program to illustrate the declaration and access of one-dimensional arrays. This program, named OneDimArrayDemo.java, creates the numberOfLoans array, the monthNames array, and then lists the number of loans by month for the year. The listing for OneDimArrayDemo.java is shown in Listing 8-1.

Listing 8-1: *OneDimArrayDemo.java*

```
1.  public class OneDimArrayDemo
2.  {
3.    public static void main (String args[])
4.    {
5.      // declare loan array & month name array
6.      int numberOfLoans [] = {39,44,45,65,72,93,14,55,67,27,46,82};
```

```
7.    String monthNames []{"Jan","Feb","Mar","Apr","May","Jun",
      "Jul","Aug","Sep","Oct","Nov","Dec"};
8.    int monthNumber; // monthNumber is the index
9.    // print month name & number of loans for the year
10.   monthNumber = 0; // index starts at 0 for January
11.   System.out.println ("Loans    Month");
12.   while (monthNumber < 12) // loop 12 times for 12 months
13.   {
14.     System.out.println (numberOfLoans [monthNumber] + "        "
        + monthNames [monthNumber]);
15.     monthNumber = monthNumber + 1;
16.   } // end of loop
17.   } // end of main method
18.   } // end of OneDimArrayDemo.java
```

This program has only one method—**main()**. This method, instead of being called by another program, executes when the program is loaded. The following describes how the program works.

1. Line 6 declares and populates the numberOfLoans array and line 7 the monthNames array.

2. Line 8 declares the index named monthNumber and line 10 initializes it to zero.

3. Note, we could have chosen to declare and initialize it in a single statement:
   int monthNumber = 0;

4. Line 11 prints a heading for the output.

5. Lines 12–16 define the loop that prints the contents of the two arrays. Note, the loop is executed 12 times. The first time it is executed, the index contains 0, the second time 1, the third time 2, and so forth.

6. Within the loop, line 14 prints an element from numberOfLoans and the corresponding element from monthNames. The specific element is determined by the contents of the index, monthNumber.

The output for OneDimArrayDemo.java looks like this:

Loans	Month
39	Jan
44	Feb
45	Mar
65	Apr
72	May
93	Jun
14	Jul
55	Aug
67	Sep
27	Oct
46	Nov
82	Dec

Declaring Two-Dimensional Arrays

A two-dimensional array consists of both rows and columns. To illustrate, let's assume the Community National Bank makes three different types of loans: auto loans, boat loans, and home loans. Also, let's assume CNB wishes to track the number of loans by type for each month. In other words, they want to know the number of auto, boat, and home loans that were made each month. We can use a two-dimensional array consisting of 3 rows and 12 columns. We assign row 1 to auto loans, row 2 to boat loans and row 3 to home loans. As before, each column represents a month. Our new array with 3 rows and 12 columns appears as:

	Jan	Feb	Mar	Apr	May	Jun	Jul	Aug	Sep	Oct	Nov	Dec
Auto Loans												
Boat Loans												
Home Loans												

In COBOL we define this table as:

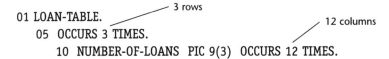

```
01 LOAN-TABLE.
   05  OCCURS 3 TIMES.
       10  NUMBER-OF-LOANS  PIC 9(3)  OCCURS 12 TIMES.
```

We then use two subscripts—one for row number and one for column number—to access a particular element in the array. To display the number of home loans in May (row 3, column 5), we would write

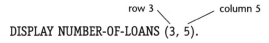

```
DISPLAY NUMBER-OF-LOANS (3, 5).
```

This statement displays the number of home loans made by CNB during May.

Declaring two-dimensional arrays in Java is easy—we simply write

```
int numberOfLoans [][];
```

two brackets are used for
a two-dimensional array

Remember, this format does not completely declare the array. We must also write

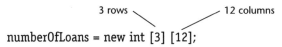

```
numberOfLoans = new int [3] [12];
```

to tell the compiler the number of rows and columns we want to have. Similar to the declaration of one-dimensional arrays, we can do all this in a single statement:

```
int numberOfLoans [] [] = new int [3] [12];
```

To display the number of Home loans in May, we would write the Java statement:

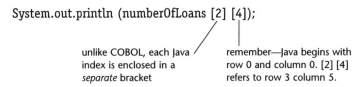

```
System.out.println (numberOfLoans [2] [4]);
```

unlike COBOL, each Java
index is enclosed in a
separate bracket

remember—Java begins with
row 0 and column 0. [2] [4]
refers to row 3 column 5.

> **NOTE**
>
> 1. Technically, Java does not have two-dimensional arrays, at least not like COBOL's two-level tables.
>
> 2. Remember, a Java array is really an instance.
>
> 3. A two-dimensional array is an array of arrays.
>
> 4. For our purposes here, we pretend we are simply working with two-dimensional arrays.

Populating Two-Dimensional Arrays

As before, we can populate a two-dimensional COBOL array either in the Data Division using VALUE clauses or using procedural statements in the Procedure Division.

```
01 LOAN-TABLE-VALUES.
    05  PIC X(36) VALUE '012023020021015012005009040020012026'.
    05  PIC X(36) VALUE '013010015025035041002016011001019031'.
    05  PIC X(36) VALUE '014011010019022040007030016006015025'.

01 LOAN-TABLE REDEFINES LOAN-TABLE-VALUES.
    05  OCCURS 3 TIMES.
        10  NUMBER-OF-LOANS  PIC 9(3)  OCCURS 12 TIMES.
```

The Java code to declare the two-dimensional array for number of loans is

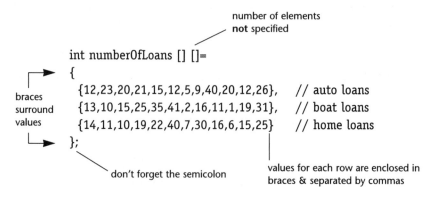

```
                                        number of elements
                                        not specified

            int numberOfLoans [] []=
      ┌──▶  {
braces      {12,23,20,21,15,12,5,9,40,20,12,26},    // auto loans
surround    {13,10,15,25,35,41,2,16,11,1,19,31},    // boat loans
values      {14,11,10,19,22,40,7,30,16,6,15,25}     // home loans
      └──▶  };
```

don't forget the semicolon

values for each row are enclosed in braces & separated by commas

The populated table appears as:

	Jan	Feb	Mar	Apr	May	Jun	Jul	Aug	Sep	Oct	Nov	Dec
Auto Loans	12	23	20	21	15	12	5	9	40	20	12	26
Boat Loans	13	10	15	25	35	41	2	16	11	1	19	31
Home Loans	14	11	10	19	22	40	7	30	16	6	15	25

We have written another small Java program here named TwoDimArrayDemo.java, shown in Listing 8–2, to illustrate the declaration, population, and access of two-dimensional arrays.

Listing 8-2: *TwoDimArrayDemo.java*

```
1.  public class TwoDimArrayDemo
2.  {
3.     public static void main (String args[])
4.     {
5.     int numberOfLoans [] []=
6.     {
7.     {12,23,20,21,15,12,5,9,40,20,12,26}, // auto loans in row 1
8.     {13,10,15,25,35,41,2,16,11,1,19,31}, // boat loans in row 2
9.     {14,11,10,19,22,40,7,30,16,6,15,25} // home loans in row 3
10.    };
11.    String monthNames [] = {"Jan","Feb","Mar","Apr","May","Jun","Jul",
       "Aug","Sep","Oct","Nov","Dec"};
12.    int typeOfLoan;   // row index
13.    int monthNumber;  // column index
14.    int numberOfLoansThisMonth;
15.    // print number of boat loans - row 2
16.    monthNumber = 0;
17.    System.out.println ("CNB Boat Loans");
18.    System.out.println ("Month   Number");
19.    while (monthNumber < 12) // loop 12 times
20.    {
```

```
21.    System.out.println (monthNames [monthNumber] + "     " +
22.    numberOfLoans [1] [monthNumber]);  // row index remains 1
23.    monthNumber = monthNumber + 1;
24.    } // end of loop to print boat loans
25.    // print the sum of each column (total loans for each month)
26.    monthNumber = 0;
27.    System.out.println ("CNB Total Loans");
28.    System.out.println ("Month   Number");
29.    while (monthNumber < 12)  // loop 12 times for 12 months
30.    {
31.      numberOfLoansThisMonth = 0;
32.      typeOfLoan = 0;
33.      while (typeOfLoan < 3)  // loop 3 times to sum this column
34.      {
35.        numberOfLoansThisMonth = numberOfLoansThisMonth +
         numberOfLoans [typeOfLoan] [monthNumber];
36.        typeOfLoan = typeOfLoan + 1;
37.      }   // end of row loop
38.      System.out.println (monthNames [monthNumber] + "     " +
         numberOfLoansThisMonth);
39.      monthNumber = monthNumber + 1;
40.    } // end of month loop
41. } // end of main method
42.} // end of TwoDimArrayDemo.java
```

Similar to OneDimArrayDemo.java, TwoDimArrayDemo.java has one method main that is executed when the program is loaded.

1. Lines 5–10 declare and populate the two-dimensional array numberOfLoans.

2. Line 11 populates the monthNames array.

3. Lines 12 and 13 declare the row index (typeOfLoan) and column index (monthNumber).

4. Line 14 declares the loan counter numberOfLoansThisMonth.

5. Lines 15–24 print the number of boat loans (row 2) for each month.

- Line 16 initializes the column index to 0.

- Lines 17 and 18 display a report heading.

- Lines 19–24 outline a loop that executes 12 times.

- Line 21 prints the month name and the number of boat loans for the month indicated by the index monthNumber.

- Line 23 increments the column index monthNumber. Note: the index for the row is held constant at 1 (that is, the 2nd row).

6. Lines 25–40 sum and print the total number of loans for each of the 12 months.

    - Line 26 reinitializes the column index monthNumber.

    - Lines 27 and 28 display the report heading.

    - Lines 29–40 outline a loop that executes 12 times.

        - Line 31 initializes the counter numberOfLoansThisMonth and line 32 initializes the row index typeOfLoan.

        - Lines 33–36 outline a loop that executes 3 times for each month (column)

            - Line 35 sums the numberOfLoansThisMonth

            - Line 36 increments the row index typeOfLoan.

        - Line 38 prints the month name and numberOfLoansThisMonth

        - Line 39 increments the column index monthNumber.

TwoDimArrayDemo.java Output

CNB Boat Loans	
Month	Number
Jan	13
Feb	10
Mar	15
Apr	25
May	35
Jun	41
Jul	2
Aug	16
Sep	11
Oct	1
Nov	19
Dec	31

CNB Total Loans	
Month	Number
Jan	39
Feb	44
Mar	45
Apr	65
May	72
Jun	93
Jul	14
Aug	55
Sep	67
Oct	27
Nov	46
Dec	82

A great exercise for you here is to rewrite one (or more) of the loops in TwoDimArrayDemo.java using the for statement.

Passing Arrays as Arguments

We can pass an entire array to a method by simply writing the array name as an argument in the statement calling the method. Or, if we wish, we can pass a single element by specifying the element as an argument. In fact, in the previous TwoDimArrayDemo.java, we pass an array element when we execute the statement:

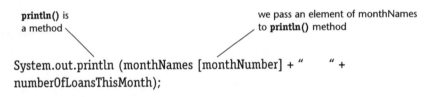

println() is a method

we pass an element of monthNames to **println()** method

```
System.out.println (monthNames [monthNumber] + "     " +
numberOfLoansThisMonth);
```

Two programs at the end of the next section demonstrate passing arrays to methods.

> **NOTE**
>
> 1. When we pass arguments to a method, the method gets a **copy** of the argument.
>
> 2. If we pass an object instance to a method, the method gets a copy of the instance reference variable, the pointer to the instance. The method has direct access to the instance through this reference variable.
>
> 3. Java arrays are object instances, which means when we pass an array to a method, the method gets a copy of the reference variable and, therefore, has direct access to the original array .
>
> 4. Passing a reference variable is called *passing by reference* because we pass a *reference to the data* instead of a *copy of the data.*

Searching Arrays

Just like COBOL, sometimes in a Java program we need to find a specific value in an array. In COBOL we call this searching process a table look up. COBOL also has the SEARCH verb that sometimes simplifies a table look up. Java, unfortunately, has no such facility and we must write the search the old-fashioned way.

The array search logic is essentially the same, regardless of the language being used. We look at each of the values in the array until we find the value we are seeking or we get to the end of the array. Specifically, we initialize an index to the beginning of the array and then loop until we find the desired value or we reach the end of the array.

To illustrate an array search, we have a 5-element array containing ZIP codes.

30309	40410	41515	65757	72701

The COBOL code to define this array is

```
01 ZIP-CODE-VALUES.
    05  PIC X(25) VALUE '3030940410415156575772701'.
01  ZIP-CODE-TABLE REDEFINES ZIP-CODE-VALUES.
    05  ZIP-CODE PIC X(5) OCCURS 5 TIMES.
```

To do the table look up, we define a program switch (FOUND-IT-SWITCH) to tell us if we find the value and we need a subscript (SUB). Let's assume ZIP-ARGUMENT contains the ZIP code we seek.

```
01 ZIP-ARGUMENT    PIC X(5).
01 FOUND-IT-SWITCH PIC X(3).
      88 FOUND-IT  VALUE 'YES'.
01 SUB       PIC 9(1).
```

Now, let's write the table look up in COBOL using an in-line PERFORM-VARYING.

```
MOVE 'NO' TO FOUND-IT-SWITCH
PERFORM VARYING SUB FROM 1 BY 1 UNTIL SUB > 5 OR FOUND-IT
    IF ZIP-ARGUMENT = ZIP-CODE (SUB) THEN
        MOVE 'YES' TO FOUND-IT-SWITCH
    END-IF
END-PERFORM
IF FOUND-IT THEN
    DISPLAY 'We found it!"
ELSE
    DISPLAY 'We did NOT find it!"
END-IF.
```

Next, we are going to write two little programs to illustrate an array search using Java. This example also demonstrates how to pass an array as an argument to a method.

The first program, FindZipCode.java in Listing 8-3, has one method named **findZip()**. This method receives two parameters from the calling program: zipToFind contains the ZIP code we are searching for and zipCode is an array containing an unknown number of ZIP codes. The method returns the Boolean variable foundIt to inform the calling program whether or not a matching ZIP code was found.

findZip()is called a static method. A static method is one not associated with a particular object instance. Instead, a static method provides a service for the class as a whole. Sometimes, we refer to a static method as a class method, as opposed to an instance method. Instance methods provide a service for an instance; class methods provide a service for a class. We wrote FindZipCode.java (see Listing 8–3) to find ZIP codes and, therefore, an instance of this class is meaningless in this context.

Listing 8-3: *FindZipCode.java*

```
1. public class FindZipCode
2. {
```

static indicates this · the first parameter is an integer · the 2nd parameter is an integer
is a class method · variable named zipToFind · array named zipCode

```
3.   public static boolean findZip (int zipToFind, int [] zipCode)
```
this method returns a
boolean value
```
4.     {
5.       int index = 0;
6.       boolean foundIt = false;
```

zipCode.length is the array size · && means "and." ! means "not"

```
7.       while (index < zipCode.length && !foundIt) // loop til found or end
8.       {
```
== means "equal to"
```
9.         if (zipToFind == zipCode [index]) // compare argument to element
10.          foundIt = true;    // set switch to true if we have a match
11.        else
12.          index = index + 1;   // else keep looking
13.      } // end of loop
14.      return foundIt;
15.   } // end of findZip method
16. } // end of FindZipCode.java
```

The second program, ZipCodeProcessor.java is listed in the following Listing 8–4. This program calls the **findZip()** method in FindZipCode.java.

Listing 8-4: *ZipCodeProcessor.java*

```
1. public class ZipCodeProcessor
2. {
3.   public static void main(String args[])
4.   {
5.     // declare & populate the array
```

```
6.    int zipCode [] ={30309,40410,41515,65757,72701};
7.    int zipArgument;
8.    boolean foundIt;
9.    zipArgument = 65757;  //  we should find this value
10.   // call findZip method & pass zipArgument and zipCode array
```

findZip() is a class method, therefore
we use the classname instead of an
instancename in the call

```
11.   foundIt = FindZipCode.findZip (zipArgument, zipCode);
12.   if (foundIt)
13.     System.out.println ("We found " + zipArgument);
14.   else
15.     System.out.println ("We did NOT find " + zipArgument);
16.   //  call findZip method again with a different argument
17.   zipArgument = 12345;  //  we should NOT find this value
18.   foundIt = FindZipCode.findZip (zipArgument, zipCode);
19.   if (foundIt)
20.     System.out.println ("We found " + zipArgument);
21.   else
22.     System.out.println ("We did NOT find " + zipArgument);
23.   } // end of main method
24. } // end of ZipCodeProcessor.java
```

We describe the execution of these programs line by line:

ZipCodeProcessor.java (Listing 8-4):

1. Line 6 declares and populates the array zipCode.

2. Line 7 declares the zipArgument and line 8 the Boolean variable foundIt.

3. Line 9 stores the ZIP code value 65757 into zipArgument.

4. Line 11 calls **findZip()** in FindZipCode.java, passing zipArgument containing 65757 and the array named zipCode containing 30309, 40410, 41515, 65757, 72701

FindZipCode.java (Listing 8-3):

5. Lines 5 and 6 initialize index to zero and foundIt to false.

6. Lines 7–13 outline the search loop. The statements inside the loop are executed until we find the ZIP code or reach the end of the table. Note, we use the public variable length contained in the array instance zipCode to determine the array size. This means **findZip()** can search an array of any size.

7. Line 9 compares the zipArgument to the contents of the array element referenced by index. The first time through the loop index contains zero (pointing to element 1), the second time it contains 1, and so forth. If the values are a match, foundIt is set to true and the loop terminates.

8. Line 12 increments index.

9. Line 14 returns foundIt to the calling program, ZipCodeProcessor.

ZipCodeProcessor.java (Listing 8-4):

10. Lines 12–15 print the results of the search.

11. Line 18 again calls findZip using a different ZIP code value.

Output from ZipCodeProcessor

```
We found 65757
We did NOT find 12345
```

Summary of Key Points

1. COBOL programmers use different array terminology than do Java programmers. Instead of "single-level table" and "subscript" Java programmers say "one-dimensional array" and "index."

2. We can declare an array without specifying the number of elements:

   int numberOfLoans [];

3. We can declare and populate a Java array with one statement:

   int numberOfLoans [] = {39,44,45,65,72,93,14,55,67,27,46,82};

4. Java array elements begin with index value 0, not 1.

5. Java uses brackets [ ] instead of parentheses ( ) when referencing an occurrence (element) within an array.

6. Java uses two sets of brackets for two-dimensional arrays.

7. We can create a Java array of any data type including String.

8. When working with two-dimensional arrays, Java row and column index values begin with 0, not 1.

9. We can pass an array element to a method by simply specifying the element.

10. A Java array is really an object instance. For the programmer, this raises two important issues. First, passing an array to a method makes the original array values available to the method. Second, we can access the public array instance variable arrayname.length to determine the number of elements in the array. Note, this variable contains the number of elements in the array, not the number of bytes.

11. The search logic in Java is similar to the COBOL table look up, only the syntax is different.

Glossary

class method a static method, a method that provides services for the class and not for a specific instance of the class.

index a variable containing a value that points to a specific element in a Java array. Java index values begin with 0 for the first element. In a two-dimensional array, the first index refers to the row and the second to the column, relative to zero.

instance method a method that provides services for a specific instance of the class.

one-dimensional array an array that has only one dimension, a row of elements. A Java array is really an instance and is referenced with an instance reference variable.

passing by reference passing a reference variable as an argument to a method is called *passing by reference* because we pass a *reference to the data* instead of a *copy of the data*. Note, when a method receives a reference variable, it has access to the instance referenced by the variable.

static method a class method, a method that provides services for the class and not for a specific instance of the class.

subscript a COBOL term corresponding to a Java index. It points to an element in an array.

two-dimensional array an array that has only two dimensions, elements arranged into rows and columns. A Java array is really an instance and is referenced with an instance reference variable.

Chapter 9

Data Access

Objectives

In this chapter you will study:

- Object Persistence
- Sequential File Access
- SQL Database Access
- Object Serialization
- Network Access

This chapter introduces you to Java data access techniques using classes supplied in three packages: java.io, java.sql, and java.net. You are, undoubtedly, familiar with reading and writing files using COBOL. Java uses a somewhat different approach and, therefore, you will not find the clear parallels between COBOL and Java in this chapter that you have seen in the previous chapters.

Here we develop programs to demonstrate sequential file I-O and database access. In addition, we demonstrate a technique called *Object Serialization* used by Java to store intact object instances in files for later retrieval. Although a demonstration of network access is beyond the scope of this book, we do present an overview.

The chapter begins with a brief description of the I-O classes contained in the java.io package and their hierarchy. Then a relatively simple sequential file I-O demonstration is presented. Next, we repeat the example using a relational database. Object Persistence is then discussed and illustrated using Java's Object Serialization classes. The chapter concludes with a discussion of network access using classes in the java.net package.

191

This chapter assumes you understand the following:

Java:

- OO Concepts (Chapter 2)

- Java Program Structure (Chapter 3)

- Defining Data (Chapter 4)

- Decision Making (Chapter 6)

- Looping (Chapter 7)

- Arrays (Chapter 8)

Java's I-O Class Library (java.io)

The basic purpose of the classes contained in the java.io package is to provide tools to input and output data. This data can be going to any output device or coming from any input device. These classes take care of reading, writing, converting, and parsing data for our programs.

Java uses the term *data stream* to refer to any input or output data. A Java stream is simply a flow of bytes of data, either into or out of a program. A program reads data from an *input stream* and writes data to an *output stream*, regardless of the data source or destination. This abstraction keeps our code device independent—we don't worry about the particular input-output (I-O) device we are using. We simply refer to the appropriate stream.

Java actually has two kinds of streams: *byte streams* store data in Unicode (2 bytes per character) format, and *character stream* data is stored in the native format of the system where the data is being used. Character streams are automatically converted back to Unicode when read by our program.

Using the stream concept, we can have data I-O without being particularly concerned about the physical device the data is flowing from or to. Remember, Java programs are designed to be highly portable and are intended to run on a variety of platforms. We want to avoid having our program code being device dependent.

A partial list of the java.io class hierarchy is shown in Figure 9–1.

File (instances represent physical files)
InputStream (superclass for *byte* input streams)
    FileInputStream (reads an input stream)
    ObjectInputStream (reads object instances from a file)
OutputStream (superclass for *byte* output streams)
    FileOutputStream (writes an output stream)
    ObjectOutputStream (writes object instances to a file)
        RandomAccessFile (provides random file access)
Reader (superclass for *character* input streams)
    InputStreamReader
    FileReader
StreamTokenizer (parses text files into data items (tokens))
Writer (superclass for *character* output streams)
    PrintWriter

Figure 9–1. *Partial java.io Class Hierarchy*

Object Persistence

Until now we have ignored the issue of storing objects for later retrieval. We created objects and worked with them but, conveniently, avoided the problem of keeping them for future use. For example, we created instances of <u>Customer</u> and <u>Account</u>, but these instances disappeared when our programs stopped running. In the real world, we obviously need object instances to be stored for subsequent processing.

A *persistent* object is one with a life longer than the running of the program that creates it. In contrast, a *transient* object lives only as long as the program that created it is executing. In most applications, we need persistent objects, although until now we have worked only with transient object instances.

Numerous options exist for storing object instances or, at least, the data contained in the instances. For example, we can write the data to a sequential file, store it in a relational database, or use a Java technique called Object Serialization to store complete, intact object instances. In the following sections, we demonstrate all three approaches.

Sequential File I-O

If we wish to store the Customer data in a COBOL sequential file, we first define the file:

```
FD  CUSTOMER-FILE.
01  CUSTOMER-RECORD.
    05  CUSTOMER-NAME  PIC X(25).
    05  SS-NO          PIC X(9).
    05  ADDRESS        PIC X(35).
    05  PHONE-NUMBER   PIC X(10).
```

Then write code to create the file

```
OPEN OUTPUT CUSTOMER-FILE
..
..
WRITE CUSTOMER-RECORD
..
..
CLOSE CUSTOMER-FILE
```

To read the data, we would write:

```
OPEN INPUT CUSTOMER-FILE
..
..
READ CUSTOMER-FILE
    AT END MOVE "YES" TO EOF-SW
END-READ
..
..
CLOSE CUSTOMER-FILE
```

Just like COBOL, we can store Java data in a sequential file. The following example illustrates one approach by writing customer data to a text file named "Customer.txt" and then reading the values back in and displaying them.

The steps to write to a text file are

1. Create an instance of the <u>File</u> class containing the filespec for our file:

File aFile = new File ("filespec");

2. Create an instance of <u>FileOutputStream</u> using the <u>File</u> instance created in Step 1:

FileOutputStream fo = new FileOutputStream (aFile);

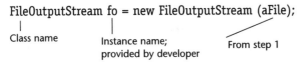

3. Create an instance of <u>PrintStream</u> using the FileOutputStream instance created in Step 2:

PrintStream ps = new PrintStream(fo);

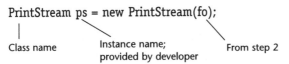

4. Call the **println()** method of the PrintStream instance to write a data item. The argument is the variable name of the data item we wish to write

ps.println(variable_name);

The steps to read data from a text file are similar:

1. Create an instance of the <u>File</u> class containing the filespec for our file:

File aFile = new File ("filespec");

2. Create an instance of <u>FileInputStream</u>, using the <u>File</u> instance created in Step 1:

FileInputStream fi = new FileInputStream (aFile);

3. Create an instance of <u>DataInputStream</u> using the FileInputStream instance created in Step 2:

DataInputStream i = new DataInputStream(fi);

4. Call the **readLine()** method of the <u>DataInputStream</u> instance:

variable_name = i.readline();

Here, we illustrate sequential file I-O by writing customer data to a text file and then reading the values back in and displaying them.

To write the program named SequentialFileDemo.java, we first import the classes from the java.io package:

import java.io.*;

Then we create an instance of <u>File</u>, which identifies the file we will use

```
// create a File instance for Customer.txt
File customerFile = new File ("C:/Customers/Customer.txt");
```

Notice we use the forward slash "/" instead of the backward slash "\." Java uses the backward slash as an escape character, which is used to indicate special characters, such as new line "\n" and backspace "\b." The forward slash "/" is converted into whatever the system running the program needs. For example, the program here was written and executed on a Windows machine, but will work equally well on a UNIX system.

Next we create and populate the attributes for <u>Customer</u>:

```
// data for the output file
String name = "Jed Muzzy";
String ssNo = "499444471";
String address = "P.O. Box 1881, Great Falls, MT 59601";
String phoneNumber = "None";
```

Now write the attribute values to customerFile. Note, we use the try–catch structure because **println()** can throw an IOException.

```
try
{
    FileOutputStream fo = new FileOutputStream (customerFile);
    PrintStream ps = new PrintStream(fo);
    ps.println(name);
    ps.println(ssNo);
    ps.println(address);
    ps.println(phoneNumber);
```

```
   }
catch (Exception event)
   {System.out.println ("I/O error during write to CustomerFile");}
```

Then we read the data back and display it. We again use try–catch because **readLine()** can also throw an IOException.

```
// now read it back
try
{
   FileInputStream fi = new FileInputStream (customerFile);
   DataInputStream i = new DataInputStream(fi);
   name = i.readLine();
   ssNo = i.readLine();
   address = i.readLine();
   phoneNumber = i.readLine();
   System.out.println ("Name: " + name);
   System.out.println ("SS No: " + ssNo);
   System.out.println ("Address: " + address);
   System.out.println ("Phone: " + phoneNumber);
}
catch (Exception event)
   {System.out.println ("I/O error during read from CustomerFile");}
```

The program output is

```
Name: Jed Muzzy
SS No: 499444471
Address: P.O. Box 1881, Great Falls, MT 59601
Phone: None
```

The complete program listing for SequentialFileDemo.java is shown in Listing 9-1.

Listing 9-1: *SequentialFileDemo.java*

```java
import java.io.*;
public class FileDemo
{
    public static void main(String args[])
    {
    // data for the output file
    String name = "Jed Muzzy";
    String ssNo = "499444471";
    String address = "P.O. Box 1881, Great Falls, MT 59601";
    String phoneNumber = "None";

    // create a text file containing Customer attributes
    File customerFile = new File ("C:/Customers/Customer.txt");
    try
    {
        FileOutputStream fo = new FileOutputStream (customerFile);
        PrintStream ps = new PrintStream(fo);
        ps.println(name);
        ps.println(ssNo);
        ps.println(address);
        ps.println(phoneNumber);
    }
    catch (Exception event)
        {System.out.println ("I/O error during write to CustomerFile");}

    // now, read it back in
    try
    {
        FileInputStream fi = new FileInputStream (customerFile);
        DataInputStream i = new DataInputStream(fi);
        name = i.readLine();
        ssNo = i.readLine();
        address = i.readLine();
        phoneNumber = i.readLine();
        System.out.println ("Name: " + name);
```

```
        System.out.println ("SS No: " + ssNo);
        System.out.println ("Address: " + address);
        System.out.println ("Phone: " + phoneNumber);
    }
    catch (Exception event)
        {System.out.println ("I/O error during read from CustomerFile");}
    } // end main
} // end SequentialFileDemo.java
```

Note two important points concerning this example. First, the example really does nothing more than write some data to secondary storage and then read it back. To use this storage technique with our <u>Customer</u> class, we would need to write methods to send and retrieve the attribute values being stored. Second, a <u>Customer</u> instance is not being stored—only the values of the attributes of a particular <u>Customer</u> instance are stored. To use the information, the data would have to be retrieved and inserted into a "blank" <u>Customer</u> instance. Using sequential files, as previously illustrated, would require the follow conceptual steps for proper OO programming:

To store data:

1. Accept input from user (or other sources)

2. Create a <u>Customer</u> instance and populate the instance with data from input source

3. Send a message to the class handling data management for <u>Customer</u> requesting storage of the data; the message should contain the attribute values to be stored.

To retrieve data:

1. Create a <u>Customer</u> instance

2. Send a message to the class handling data management for <u>Customer</u> requesting the data; the message should return the attribute values for the instance

3. Populate the blank <u>Customer</u> instance with the retrieved values.

Database Access

Today, many organizations use relational databases to store data. A relational database contains data stored in tables consisting of rows and columns. Each column is a field or data item and each row is a record or entity. A table for customers would have four columns: Name, SS No., Address, and Phone. The table will have a separate row for each customer. (See Figure 9-2, Customer Database Table.)

We can have multiple tables that are related. For example, at Community National we could have a table for customers and another for checking accounts. These tables would be connected with a relationship (that is, a common key field). For example, we could add the customer's SSNo to the Account table and then we could find the owner of an Account or all the accounts owned by a particular Customer.

Structured Query Language (SQL) is a standardized (ANSI 1986 & 1992) database language with widespread acceptance and use. SQL provides a set of English-like statements to access and manipulate data in a relational database. The SQL Select statement is used to retrieve data. We simply write the name of the columns we want retrieved. For example, to retrieve all four Customer fields, we write

Select Name, SSNo, Address, Phone from Customer

We now demonstrate this Select in two examples: one with COBOL, the other with Java.

In the following COBOL example (Listing 9-2), the data from a relational database table (as shown in Figure 9-2) is extracted and displayed. Basically, SQL is "embedded" in traditional COBOL code using syntax specific to database operations. Note: the syntax may vary slightly due to the type of database and compiler used.

Listing 9-2: *COBOL SQL example*

```
Identification Division.
...
Data Division.
Working-Storage Section.
Detail-line
```

```
05  DL-Name    PIC X(20).
05  DL-SSN     PIC X(9).
05  DL-Address PIC X(40).
05  DL-Phone   PIC X(13).
*
    EXEC SQL BEGIN DECLARE SECTION END-EXEC.
*  This begins the section which will hold the
*  variables from the table (we'll call them host variables)
01  HV-Name    PIC X(20).
01  HV-SSN     PIC X(9).
01  HV-Address PIC X(40).
01  HV-Phone   PIC X(13).
*
EXEC SQL END DECLARE SECTION END-EXEC.
*  End of the variable section
*
   EXEC SQL INCLUDE SQLCA END-EXEC.
PROCEDURE DIVISION.
MAIN-CONTROL.
*
   EXEC SQL DECLARE C CURSOR FOR
     SELECT NAME, SSN, ADDRESS, PHONE FROM CUSTOMER
   END-EXEC.
*  A 'cursor' is used to hold a set of data from the
*  the table; holds multiple rows
*
*  Open the cursor
     EXEC SQL OPEN C END-EXEC.
*  Now, read the data from the cursor and display it
*
   PERFORM UNTIL SQLCODE NOT = 0
     EXEC SQL FETCH C
     INTO :HV-NAME, :HV-SSN, :HV-ADDRESS, :HV-PHONE
     END-EXEC
     MOVE HV-NAME TO DL-NAME
     MOVE HV-SSN TO DL-SSN
     MOVE HV-ADDRESS TO DL-ADDRESS
```

```
        MOVE HV-PHONE TO DL-PHONE
        DISPLAY DETAIL-LINE
        END-PERFORM.
    *
        EXEC SQL CLOSE C END-EXEC.
        STOP RUN.
```

Fortunately, Java provides facilities for easy database access. The Java database connectivity (JDBC) class program library is contained in the java.sql package. This package provides classes and methods that enable us to write programs to access relational databases using SQL. JDBC is both platform and database independent and is intended to provide a seamless interface to any SQL relational database. This includes remote as well as local databases. (Additional JDBC information is at http://java.sun.com/products/jdbc.)

We use four java.sql classes to access relational databases:

1. <u>DriverManager</u>—creates and maintains database connections.

2. <u>Connection</u>—represents each database connection.

3. <u>Statement</u>—executes SQL statements.

4. <u>ResultSet</u>—contains data that is retrieved from the database.

An exception class named SQLException also exists, which is used to contain error messages and vendor-specific codes resulting from the execution of SQL statements. A single SQL statement can generate multiple SQLException instances and we should access them all.

To demonstrate Java database access, we first create a simple database containing one table: Customer. This example uses Microsoft Access, but it could be any SQL relational database. First, we create a Table that contains our four columns: Name, SSNo, Address, and Phone. Here, the table is populated with our customer, Jed Muzzy, as shown in Figure 9-2.

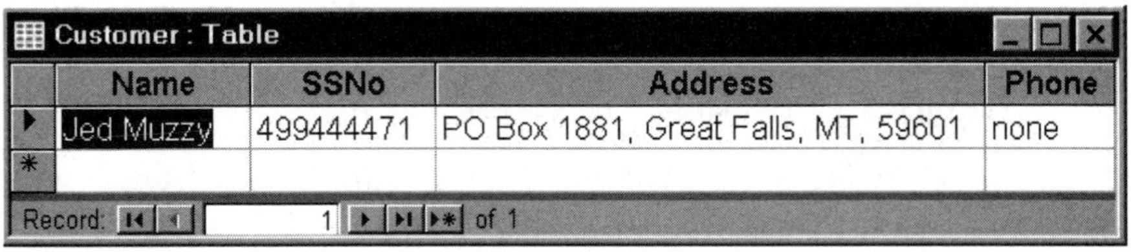

Figure 9–2. *Customer Database Table*

Let's write a small Java program named DataBaseDemo.java to retrieve the Customer data using the JDBC SQL interface tools. First, we tell the Java compiler to import the SQL package:

```
import java.sql.*;
```

Then we declare variables to contain the retrieved data:

```
// declare variables for the data
String name, ssNo, address, phoneNumber;
```

JDBC uses a Uniform Resource Locator (URL) to identify databases. We define a String variable to contain the URL database identification:

```
// declare url for the database
String url = "jdbc:odbc:Customers";  // The DB name is "Customers"
```

The use of ODBC in the previous string is based on the type of database we are using for this particular example, MS-Access. Open Database Connectivity (ODBC) is a Microsoft-sponsored standard for database connectivity. Other database types may require a different set of drivers.

We also define a String variable to contain the SQL Select statement we will execute to retrieve the customer data:

```
// define the SQL query statement
String sqlQuery = "SELECT Name, SSNo, Address, Phone FROM Customer";
```

The statements to establish a database connection and retrieve data can throw an exception, therefore, we use the try-catch structure for this code. Our database example is running on a MS Windows system and we first load the appropriate driver using the class method **forName()**.

```
try
{  // load the jdbc - odbc bridge driver for MS-Windows
   Class.forName("sun.jdbc.odbc.JdbcOdbcDriver");
```

We next create a connection instance using the **getConection()** method in the <u>DriverManager</u> class. "JavaDemo" is the ID and "JavaIsFun" is the password required to access the database.

```
// create connection instance
Connection aConnection =
DriverManager.getConnection(url, "JavaDemo", "JavaIsFun");
```

Then we call the connection method **createStatement()** to create a Statement object instance to execute the SQL code:

```
// create statement object instance
Statement aStatement = aConnection.createStatement();
```

Finally, we execute the SQL statement contained in sqlQuery by calling **executeQuery()**. The data returned is contained in the ResultSet instance named rs.

```
// execute the SQL query statement
ResultSet rs = aStatement.executeQuery(sqlQuery);
```

Following the successful execution of the SQL Select statement, the ResultSet instance, rs, contains the data arranged in rows, one row per customer. The method **next()** moves a logical pointer to the next row of data and returns a Boolean value true or false indicating if more data exists.

```
// get first row of data
boolean more = rs.next();
```

Once we have a pointer to a row of data, we then call the ResultSet instance method **getString()** to retrieve data from a specific column (here all of our data is String, but there are additional methods for other data types, such as **getFloat()**, **getInt()**, and so forth).

Although, in this example, we have only one row of data (one customer), we have written a loop that will process multiple rows. A good exercise here is to create your own Customer database with several customers and then use DataBaseDemo.java to retrieve and list all of them for you.

```
while (more) // loop while there are rows of data
{
  // extract the data & display
  name = rs.getString(1);
  ssNo = rs.getString(2);
  address = rs.getString(3);
  phoneNumber = rs.getString(4);
  System.out.println("Name: " + name);
  System.out.println("SS No: " + ssNo);
  System.out.println("Address: " + address);
  System.out.println("Phone: " + phoneNumber);

  // get next row
  more = rs.next();
} // end while loop
```

We then close the connection and end the try block:

```
rs.close();   // close everything
aStatement.close();
aConnection.close();
} // end try
```

The first catch block used in this example traps the
ClassNotFoundException, which will be thrown if the appropriate driver
is not loaded.

```
catch (ClassNotFoundException e)
  {System.out.println("Exception caught "+ e);}
```

The second catch block traps errors encountered during the SQL
execution. As we previously indicated, a single SQL statement can result
in multiple exceptions being thrown. Here we write a loop to identify all
of those that may be thrown.

```
catch (SQLException e)
{ while (e != null) // we can have multiple exceptions
  {  System.out.println("SQLException caught "+ e);
   e = e.getNextException();
  } // end while loop
```

} // end catch

The program output is the same as before:

```
Name: Jed Muzzy
SS No: 499444471
Address: P.O. Box 1881, Great Falls, MT 59601
Phone: None
```

The complete program is provided in Listing 9-3.

Listing 9-3: *DatabaseDemo.java*

```java
// Demonstrate SQL Database Access
// DataBaseDemo.java
import java.sql.*;
public class DataBaseDemo
{
    public static void main(String args[])
    {
    // declare variables for the data
    String name, ssNo, address, phoneNumber;
    // declare url for the database
    String url = "jdbc:odbc:Customers";  // The dB name is "Customers"
    // define the SQL query statement
    String sqlQuery = "SELECT Name, SSNo, Address, Phone FROM
    Customer";
    try
    {   // load the jdbc - odbc bridge driver for Windows-95
        Class.forName("sun.jdbc.odbc.JdbcOdbcDriver");
        // create connection instance
        // "JavaDemo" is ID & "JavaIsFun" is password
        Connection aConnection =
            DriverManager.getConnection(url, "JavaDemo", "JavaIsFun");
        // create statement object instance
        Statement aStatement = aConnection.createStatement();
        // execute the SQL query statement
        ResultSet rs = aStatement.executeQuery(sqlQuery);
```

```
            // get first row
            boolean more = rs.next();
            while (more) // loop while there are rows of data
            {  // extract the data & display
                name = rs.getString(1);
                ssNo = rs.getString(2);
                address = rs.getString(3);
                phoneNumber = rs.getString(4);
                System.out.println("Name: " + name);
                System.out.println("SS No: " + ssNo);
                System.out.println("Address: " + address);
                System.out.println("Phone: " + phoneNumber);

                // get next row
                more = rs.next();
            } // end while loop
            rs.close();      // close everything
            aStatement.close();
            aConnection.close();
            } // end try

        catch (ClassNotFoundException e)
            {System.out.println("Exception caught "+ e);}
        catch (SQLException e)
        {  while (e != null) // we can have multiple exceptions
            {  System.out.println("SQLException caught "+ e);
            e = e.getNextException();
            } // end while loop
        } // end catch
        } // end main} // end DataBaseDemo.java
```

Object Serialization

In the previous two sections, we used sequential files and relational databases to accomplish object persistence. Note, however, in reality only
the values of the object's attributes were being stored. The actual object

was not stored. In this section, we illustrate a convenient technique called Object Serialization to store whole objects (not just attributes) for future access. Object serialization is a Java technique available with JDK used to store object instances in a file with all their relevant information, so we can retrieve them in the same state as when they were stored. This means the retrieved instances have all their original attribute values, methods, and relationships. We cannot distinguish between a newly created instance and one that has been retrieved using object serialization. This is in sharp contrast to storing only the attribute values of instances. Object serialization stores complete, intact object instances.

The steps to store an object instance are

1. Create an instance of the File class containing the filespec for our file:

   File aFile = new File ("filespec");

2. Create an instance of <u>FileOutputStream</u> using the File instance created in Step 1:

   FileOutputStream fo = new FileOutputStream (aFile);

3. Create an instance of <u>ObjectOutputStream</u> using the FileOutputStream instance created in Step 2:

   ObjectOutputStream o = new ObjectOutputStream(fo);

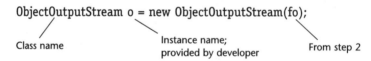

   Class name   Instance name; provided by developer   From step 2

4. Call the **writeObject()** method of the <u>ObjectOutputStream</u> instance. The arguments are the reference variables for the instances we wish to store:

   o.writeObject(object_reference_variables);

> **NOTE**   The first two steps are the same as the sequential file process illustrated earlier.

The steps to retrieve an object instance are similar:

1. Create an instance of the File class containing the filespec for our file:

File aFile = new File ("filespec");

2. Create an instance of <u>FileInputStream</u>, using the File instance created in Step 1:

FileInputStream fi = new FileInputStream (aFile);

3. Create an instance of <u>ObjectInputStream</u> using the <u>FileInputStream</u> instance created in Step 2

ObjectInputStream i = new ObjectInputStream(fi);

4. Call the **readObject()** method of the <u>ObjectInputStream</u> instance:

object_reference_variable = i.readObject();
object_reference_variable refers to the instance being retrieved.

The first two steps are the same as the sequential file process illustrated earlier.	**NOTE**

We can store any number of instances using this technique. Also, the instances do not have to be from the same class. For example, we could store both <u>Customer</u> and <u>CheckingAccount</u> instances in the same file.

Here we illustrate object persistence using object serialization by creating an instance of our Customer class, writing it to a file, and then retrieving it and displaying the attribute values. We use the existing class program Customer.java from Chapter 3, but we implement the Serializable interface.

public class Customer implements java.io.Serializable

We then write a new class program, named ObjectSerializationDemo.java to create, store, and retrieve the Customer instance. This new program is patterned closely after the previous CustomerProcessor.java program. Remember, however, the object instances previously created by CustomerProcessor.java had a short life—they expired when the program terminated. The instances created here in this example are persistent. They reside in a file named "Customer.dat" and are available for retrieval whenever needed.

To write ObjectSerializationDemo.java, we first import the classes from the java.io package needed for serialization:

import java.io.*;

Then we create an instance of <u>File</u>, which identifies the specific file we will use:

```
// create a File instance for Customer.dat
   File customerFile = new File ("C:/Customers/Customer.dat");
```

Next we create a customer instance using a reference variable named aCustomer:

```
// create a customer instance
String name = "Jed Muzzy";
String ssNo = "499444471";
String address = "P.O. Box 1881, Great Falls, MT 59601";
String phoneNumber = "None";
Customer aCustomer =  new Customer(name, ssNo, address, phoneNumber);
```

Now, let's write the instance to *customerFile*. Note, we must use the try–catch structure because the method **writeObject()** can throw an IOException. Java will not compile our program unless we make provision to handle the exception.

```
try
{
   FileOutputStream fo = new FileOutputStream (customerFile);
   ObjectOutputStream o = new ObjectOutputStream (fo);
   o.writeObject(aCustomer);                    // write the instance
}
catch (IOException event)
{System.out.println ("I/O error during write to customerFile");}
```

Then we read the instance back and display the attribute values, but this time, we use a different reference variable, aNewCustomer. We again must use try–catch because **writeObject()** can also throw an IOException.

```
try
{
   FileInputStream fi = new FileInputStream (customerFile);
   ObjectInputStream i = new ObjectInputStream (fi);
   Customer aNewCustomer = (Customer) i.readObject();// read instance
```

```
    // then display the attributes from retrieved customer instance
    System.out.println ("Name: " + aNewCustomer.getName());
    System.out.println ("SS No: " + aNewCustomer.getSSNo());
    System.out.println ("Address: " + aNewCustomer.getAddress());
    System.out.println ("Phone: " + aNewCustomer.getPhoneNumber());
  }
catch (IOException event)
{System.out.println ("I/O error during read from customerFile");}
```

The program output is exactly the same as the previous two examples:

```
Name: Jed Muzzy
SS No: 499444471
Address: P.O. Box 1881, Great Falls, MT 59601
Phone: None
```

The complete program for ObjectSerializationDemo.java is shown in Listing 9-4.

Listing 9-4: *ObjectSerializationDemo.java*

```
// Demonstrate Object Persistence using Serialization
//
// ObjectSerializationDemo.java
import java.io.*;
public class ObjectSerializationDemo
{
public static void main (String args[])
{
  // create a File instance for Customer.dat
  File customerFile = new File ("C:/Customers/Customer.dat");
  // create a customer instance
  String name = "Jed Muzzy";
  String ssNo = "499444471";
  String address = "P.O. Box 1881, Great Falls, MT 59601";
  String phoneNumber = "None";
  Customer aCustomer = new Customer(name,ssNo,address,phoneNumber);
```

```java
Customer aNewCustomer;
// and store it in "Customer.dat"
try
{
   FileOutputStream fo = new FileOutputStream (customerFile);
   ObjectOutputStream o = new ObjectOutputStream (fo);
   o.writeObject(aCustomer);  // write the instance
}
catch (Exception event)
{System.out.println ("I/O error during write to CustomerFile");}

// now read it back
try
{
   FileInputStream fi = new FileInputStream (customerFile);
   ObjectInputStream i = new ObjectInputStream (fi);
   // read an instance and cast it to type Customer
   aNewCustomer = (Customer) i.readObject(); // read the instance
   // display the attributes from retrieved customer instances
   System.out.println ("Name: " + aNewCustomer.getName());
   System.out.println ("SS No: " + aNewCustomer.getSSNo());
   System.out.println ("Address: " + aNewCustomer.getAddress());
   System.out.println ("Phone:" + aNewCustomer.getPhoneNumber());
}
catch (Exception event)
   {System.out.println ("I/O error during read customerFile");}
} // end main
} // end of ObjectSerializationDemo.java
```

Network Access

Classes in the java.net package provide us with a rich set of tools for accessing systems connected to a network, either an intranet or the Internet. Java's network communications is based on the client-server computing model.

Java, like most communications programs, uses the *socket* concept to provide network connections. The <u>Socket</u> class in the java.net package is used in network communication. A Socket instance is an interface to a communications link between a client and server. Java programs read and write data to an instance of the <u>Socket</u> class, but they use an input or output stream to do so.

The server attaches a <u>Socket</u> instance to a communications port and waits to receive a client request. The client program uses a <u>Socket</u> instance to establish communication with the server program and then reads and writes data through the <u>Socket</u> instance using one of the I-O streams previously discussed.

World Wide Web access is also provided by classes in java.net. We connect to a URL using an instance of the URL class containing the URL access information. We then create an instance of <u>DataInputStream</u> from the java.io package and use the **readLine()** method to input data from the URL.

If we wish to both read and write to the URL, we also need to create an instance of URLConnection and then create both <u>DataInputStream</u> and <u>DataOutputStream</u> instances to read and write data.

Summary of Key Points

1. The java.io package contains classes to do input and output. A Java *stream* is simply a flow of bytes of data, either into or out of our program. Our program reads data from an *input stream* and writes data to an *output stream* instead of a physical device.

2. Java uses two kinds of streams: *byte streams* store data in Unicode (2 bytes per character) format and *character stream* data is stored in the native format of the machine being used.

3. A *persistent* object instance is an instance stored in a file that can be retrieved for later processing. A *transient* instance is one that exists only while the program is running. When the program terminates, the instance is erased from memory.

4. Objects can be stored a variety of common ways, including sequential files and relational databases, among others. However, these traditional data storage methods only store the attributes of the objects. Object serialization, a technique provide by Java, allows for true object persistence.

5. Java accesses relational databases using classes in the java.sql package.

6. *Object Serialization* is a technique to store object instances in a file. We use the ObjectOutputStream class to store the instances and the ObjectInputStream class to retrieve them. Object instances stored using this technique appear **exactly the same** when they are retrieved as when they were stored.

7. Classes in the java.net package enable us to access systems connected to a network, either an intranet or the Internet.

Glossary

byte stream a flow of data in Unicode format.

character stream a flow of data in the system's native format, automatically converted back to Unicode when it comes into our program.

object persistence the technique of storing object instances, or their attribute values, so they may be reconstructed at a later time.

object serialization a Java technique (introduced with JDK 1.1) used to store complete instances in a file. These instances can then be retrieved intact as if they were just created.

persistent instance an instance that exists longer than the execution of the program, an instance, or its data stored in a file.

socket an instance of the <u>Socket</u> class is used to establish communication between a client and a server.

sql Structured Query Language, a standardized (ANSI) database language. Java uses classes in the java.sql package to execute sql statements.

stream a flow of data either into or out of a program.

transient instance an instance that is erased when the program terminates.

Chapter 10

Graphical User Interfaces

Objectives

In this chapter you will study:

- Designing & Writing GUI Programs
- Java's Abstract Windowing Toolkit (AWT)
- Event-driven programming
- Creating & displaying Windows
- Adding Buttons to Windows
- Using TextFields, Labels, & Panels
- Adding Menus to Windows
- Writing Applets

This chapter introduces you to writing graphical user interfaces (GUIs) using classes in the Java Abstract Windowing Toolkit (AWT) package. The material presented here does not have a direct COBOL counterpart, nonetheless, having an overview of the GUI capabilities of the Java AWT is important, especially because it clearly demonstrates the relationships between GUI and Problem Domain classes.

The chapter begins with a brief description of Java's AWT and event-driven programming. Then we illustrate how to display and close a Java window. Next we add push buttons, labels, and text fields to the window to create a functioning GUI program to input new customer information for the Community National Bank. Then we add drop-down menus to the program. The chapter concludes with the creation of an Applet to enter new customer information for the bank.

This chapter assumes you understand the following:

Java:

- OO Concepts (Chapter 2)

- Java Program Structure (Chapter 3)

- Defining Data (Chapter 4)

- Computation (Chapter 5)

- Decision Making (Chapter 6)

- Looping (Chapter 7)

Java's Abstract Windowing Toolkit

Java provides several nice tools to assist us in writing graphical user interfaces (GUIs). Java GUI applications use classes supplied in the Java.awt class library, called a *package,* to display and interact with GUI components. AWT is the Abstract Windowing Toolkit and supports cross platform GUI implementation. Java's AWT consists of approximately 50 class programs. In this section, however, we work with only a few of these. Some of the more common GUI components of the AWT include frames (windows), push buttons, menu bars, labels, and text fields.

Figure 10-1 shows the hierarchy of some of the AWT classes. Those shown in **boldface** are those we work with in this chapter.

Before we can write a GUI program, however, we need to understand the basics of event-driven programming and event handling. Although you may have written event-driven programs using other languages, Java's approach is somewhat different. Remember, Java *is OO.*

Event-Driven Programming

GUI programming requires that our program interact with the user by responding to user initiated events, such as key presses or mouse clicks.

A GUI event is really a signal from some GUI component such as a window, button, or menu selection the user has clicked. The particular

Component (everything GUI is a component)
    Button
    Container
        Window
            Frame (our GUI applications *extend* this class)
        Panel (invisible container for other GUI components)
            Applet (applets execute within a browser program)
        Label (used to display data)
        TextComponent
            TextField (used to display & enter data)

        MenuComponent
        MenuBar
        Menu
        MenuItem

LayoutManager (positions GUI components in our frame)

Figure 10-1. *Partial AWT Class Hierarchy*

GUI component having the event is called the ***source object***—it is the source of the event. In this chapter, we detect events from three source objects: frames (windows), buttons, and menu items.

The event information is stored in an object instance created by Java. Java has different event classes, each tailored to the specific type of event. Here we work with the WindowEvent and ActionEvent classes. WindowEvent, as the name suggests, is used for window events, such as closing a window. ActionEvent is used for button and menu item click events.

A GUI program deals with events by first ***registering*** for the specific events it wants to deal with ***listening*** for those events to occur, and, finally, ***handling*** those events in a method.

1. Registering: Our program notifies the GUI component (window or button) that we wish to be informed about an event. We notify the component by invoking a ***registration method*** for the component. The registration method for window events is **addWindowEventListener()** and for button and menu item events, it is **addActionEventListener()**.

2. Listening: Our program becomes a *listener object* for events that occur to the source object. The source object notifies us when an event occurs by calling a specific method in our program.

3. Handling: We write an *event handler method* to deal with an event. Java calls this method whenever the source object detects an event for which we have registered. The event handler method for button clicks is **actionPerformed()** and the method for closing a window is **windowClosing()**. We demonstrate the use of both of these methods shortly.

Displaying & Closing a Window

Our first GUI program illustrates how to create and display a window and then how to respond to a window event—closing the window.

To create a window, we write a class program that is a subclass (extends) the Frame class. Let's name this program MyWindow.java and describe it line by line. This program begins with two import statements:

```
import java.awt.*;
import java.awt.event.*;
```

These statements simply tell the Java compiler we will use classes contained in the java.awt and java.awt.event class libraries. Java calls these libraries *packages*. We write import statements to make classes in packages available to our program.

Next, is the class header:

```
public class MyWindow extends Frame implements WindowListener
```

This header indicates MyWindow is a subclass of Frame and it *implements* an *Interface* named WindowListener.

An interface is a program quite similar to a class program. In fact, Java uses interfaces to skirt some of the sticky problems associated with multiple inheritance. Some important differences exist between a class and an interface, however:

1. We use keyword interface instead of class in class header

2. All interface methods are public and abstract

3. All variables are public, static, final (constants)

4. To inherit from an interface, we write

implements interface_name

instead of, or in addition to,

extends class_name

For example:

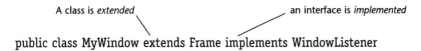

A class is *extended*   an interface is *implemented*

public class MyWindow extends Frame implements WindowListener

This header specifies that our program, MyWindow.java, inherit methods and attributes from the Frame class and *from* the WindowListener interface. Note from Figure 10-1, Frame is a subclass of Window, Container, and Component. The class hierarchy appears in Figure 10-2.

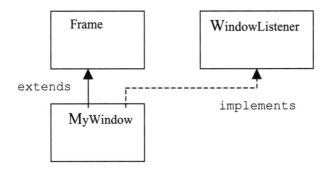

Figure 10-2. *MyWindow Hierarchy*

Next we declare a reference variable for our window object instance. Note, we declare it static because it is a class variable.

```
static MyWindow aWindow; // reference variable for window instance
```

The main method appears next. **main()** is called by Java when our program is loaded.

```
public static void main(String args[]) // main method called first
{
    aWindow = new MyWindow(); //create instance-call constructor
    myWindow.setSize(300,150); // pixels wide x pixels high
    myWindow.setTitle("A Title for My Window"); // place title
    myWindow.show();          // display the window
} // end of main
```

The methods **setSize()**, **setTitle()**, and **show()** are all inherited from the <u>Frame</u> class.

Then comes the constructor method. The constructor is called when Java executes

```
aWindow = new MyWindow()
```

in the previous main method.

```
public  MyWindow ()       // constructor method
{ addWindowListener(this); // register as listener for window events
} // end of constructor
```

Here we invoke the inherited method **addWindowListener()** using the keyword *this* as an argument. this refers to the current object instance, which is the newly created instance of <u>MyWindow</u>.

Notice we are registering the window instance as a listener for window events occurring to the window. In other words, the window instance listens for its own events. A listener object and source object can be, and often are, the same objects.

Following the constructor, we have seven event handler methods. Because we implemented the <u>WindowListener</u> interface, we are required to include all seven methods. Notice, however, the only one that does anything is **windowClosing()**, which terminates the program.

```
public void windowClosing(WindowEvent event)
{ System.exit(0);    // terminate this program
} // end of windowClosing
public void windowClosed(WindowEvent event)
{}
public void windowDeiconified(WindowEvent event)
{}
public void windowIconified(WindowEvent event)
{}
public void windowActivated(WindowEvent event)
{}
public void windowDeactivated(WindowEvent event)
{}
public void windowOpened(WindowEvent event)
{}
```

The complete program is shown in Listing 10-1.

Listing 10-1: *MyWindow.java*

```
import java.awt.*;
import java.awt.event.*;
public class MyWindow extends Frame implements WindowListener
{
  static MyWindow aWindow;       // reference variable for window instance
  public static void main(String args[]) // main method called first
  {
      aWindow = new MyWindow();  // create instance & call constructor
      aWindow.setSize(300,150);    // pixels wide x pixels high
      aWindow.setTitle("A Title for My Window"); // place title
      aWindow.show();               // display the window
  } // end of main
  public  MyWindow ()        //  constructor method
  { addWindowListener(this); // register as listener for window events
  } // end of constructor - both a source object & a listener object
  // The following 7 methods are required because we implemented
  //   the WindowListener interface
```

```
//  When a window event occurs, Java calls the appropriate handler
//  method below.  windowClosing is the only one we have code for.
public void windowClosing(WindowEvent event)
{ System.exit(0);       // terminate this program
} // end of windowClosing
public void windowClosed(WindowEvent event)
{}
public void windowDeiconified(WindowEvent event)
{}
public void windowIconified(WindowEvent event)
{}
public void windowActivated(WindowEvent event)
{}
public void windowDeactivated(WindowEvent event)
{}
public void windowOpened(WindowEvent event)
{}
} // end of MyWindow.java
```

The following seven steps recap the execution steps of MyWindow.java.

1. The **main()** method is called by Java when the program is loaded.

2. Next, **main()** creates an instance of <u>MyWindow</u> using reference variable aWindow and Java automatically calls the constructor method.

3. The constructor calls (inherited) **addWindowListener()** method to register the new instance of MyWindow (this) as a listener for window events.

4. The main method resumes execution to set window size & title and to display window.

5. The user clicks close window icon.

6. Java calls the **windowClosing** method.

7. The **windowClosing** method terminates the program.

The window displayed by MyWindow.java is shown in Figure 10-3.

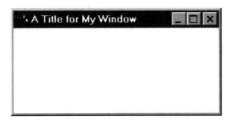

Figure 10-3. *The window displayed by MyWindow.java*

Adding a Button to a Window

Next, we develop a small program to illustrate how to add a button to a window and how to respond to a button click event. Before we start writing the program, however, we need to mention briefly how Java arranges GUI components within a window.

Java uses class programs called *layout managers* to determine where GUI components are to be placed in a window. This enables us to write GUI code without worrying about the resolution setting of the screen or even about the platform being used, for that matter. Remember, we are writing programs that will run on any platform. The layout manager worries about the implementation details for us. All we need do is decide which layout manager to use and then tell that manager, in general, how to arrange our GUI components placed in the window.

The AWT has five layout manager classes to determine the location and size of the various components we place in a window. In this chapter, however, we need to use only three of them: FlowLayout, BorderLayout, and GridLayout.

1. FlowLayout places components in successive rows. This is the default manager for the Panel & Applet classes.

2. <u>BorderLayout</u> places components in the borders & center (north, south, east, west, and center). This is the default manager for the Frame class.

3. <u>CardLayout</u> places components on top of each other (like a deck of cards).

4. <u>GridLayout</u> arranges components in a rectangular grid. We specify the number of rows and columns.

5. <u>GridBagLayout</u> is more complex than <u>GridLayout,</u> but it gives us more options.

Our second GUI program is named MyWindowWithAButton.java and we design it to inherit the methods from our previous program MyWindow.java. This eliminates the need to rewrite the event registration and event handling methods, once again demonstrating the benefits of inheritance in OO programming.

We begin the new program with the same two import statements:

```
import java.awt.*;
import java.awt.event.*;
```

The class header specifies the new program name <u>MyWindowWithAButton</u> and indicates our superclass now is <u>MyWindow</u>. Note, here we write implements ActionListener instead of implements <u>WindowListener</u> because the event handler methods for the button are in <u>ActionListener</u> and *not* in <u>WindowListener</u>.

```
public class MyWindowWithAButton extends MyWindow implements
ActionListener
```

The hierarchy for MyWindowWithAButton is shown in Figure 10-4.
Next, we declare reference variables for both the window and the button.

```
static MyWindowWithAButton aWindow;   // window reference variable
static Button aButton;        // button reference variable
```

Java calls the **main()** method when our program is loaded. Its job is to create object instances of the window and button, size and title the window, and then display the window with the button.

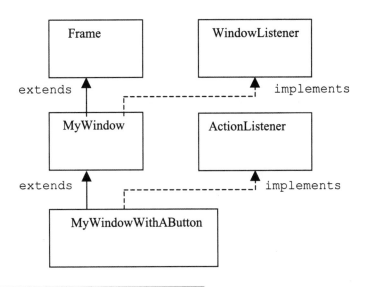

Figure 10-4. *MyWindowWithAButton hierarchy*

```
public static void main(String args[])  // main method called first
{
  aWindow = new MyWindowWithAButton(); // create window instance
  aWindow.setSize(400,100);        // pixels wide x pixels high
  aWindow.setTitle("A Title for My Window With My Button");
  myWindow.show();                 // display the window
} // end of main method
```

The first statement in main creates the window instance and calls the constructor method. Incidentally, the constructor in the superclass, in our case MyWindow.java, is *automatically* called when we create an object instance of MyWindowWithAButton.java, the subclass. The constructor in MyWindow.java registers MyWindow as a window event listener.

```
public  MyWindowWithAButton ()     // constructor method
{
  setLayout(new FlowLayout());     // arrange components
  aButton = new Button ("Click Me!"); // create button instance
```

```
add(aButton);               // add button to window
aButton.addActionListener(this);    // register as listener
} // end constructor
```

The constructor for MyWindowWithAButton then does six things:

1. Creates an instance of MyWindowWithAButton.

2. Invokes the constructor in MyWindow.java to register as a listener for window events.

3. Selects a layout manager, FlowLayout.

4. Creates a button instance.

5. Adds the new button instance to the window.

6. Registers our program as a listener for button events.

The statement:

```
setLayout(new FlowLayout());
```

calls the method **setLayout()**, inherited from the Component class, to set the FlowLayout manager for our window. FlowLayout simply places GUI components from left to right in rows. The inherited method **add()** attaches the new button instance to the window.

After the constructors are executed, we resume execution of the statements in **main()**. These statements again set the window size, set the title, and display the window, similar to the main method in MyWindow.java.

Finally, we add a handler method to respond to a button click event. The method

```
public void actionPerformed(ActionEvent event)
```

is called when the button is clicked. The parameter event is an instance reference variable of type ActionEvent.

We then see if the event source is our button and display a message if it is.

```
if (event.getSource() == myButton) // if event source is our button
    System.out.println ("I've Been Clicked!");
```

The complete program is shown in Listing 10-2.

Listing 10-2: *MyWindowWithAButton.java*

```java
import java.awt.*;
import java.awt.event.*;
public class MyWindowWithAButton extends MyWindow implements
ActionListener
{
  static MyWindowWithAButton aWindow;    // window reference variable
  static Button aButton;                 // button reference variable
  public static void main(String args[])  // main method called first
  {
     aWindow = new MyWindowWithAButton();   // create window instance
     aWindow.setSize(400,100);        // pixels wide x pixels high
     aWindow.setTitle("A Title for My Window With My Button");
     aWindow.show();                  // display the window
  } // end of main method
  public  MyWindowWithAButton ()        // constructor method
  {
     setLayout(new FlowLayout());       // arrange components
     aButton = new Button ("Click Me!");   // create button instance
     add(aButton);              // add button to window
     aButton.addActionListener(this);     // register as listener
  } // end constructor
  // this is the event handler method for button click
  public void actionPerformed(ActionEvent event)
  {
     if (event.getSource() == aButton)   // if event source is our button
       System.out.println ("I've Been Clicked!");
  } // end of actionPerformed
} // end of MyWindowWithAButton.java
```

A step-by-step explanation of the execution of MyWindowWithAButton follows:

1. The **main()** method is called by Java when the program is loaded.

2. Next, **main()** creates an instance of MyWindowWithAButton using the reference variable aWindow.

3. The constructor method in the superclass <u>MyWindow</u> is automatically called.

4. <u>MyWindow</u> constructor calls the inherited **addWindowListener** method to register the new instance of MyWindowWithAButton (this) as a listener for window events.

5. MyWindowWithAButton constructor then resumes execution.

6. We select FlowLayout as the layout manager to position our button in the window.

7. Create an instance of Button named myButton with title "Click Me".

8. Call inherited method **add()** to add the new button instance to the window.

9. Call the Button method **addActionListener()** to register as a listener for button events.

10. The main method resumes execution to set window size & title and to display window.

11. The user clicks button and Java calls **actionPerformed()** method.

12. The method **actionPerformed()** displays "I've Been Clicked".

13. The user clicks close window icon.

14. Java calls **windowClosing()** method inherited from <u>MyWindow</u>.

15. The **windowClosing()** method terminates the program.

The window displayed appears as (Figure 10-5):

Figure 10-5. *A window with a button*

When the button is clicked, the program displays:

I've Been Clicked!

Notice we can close the window the same as before. The **windowClosing()** method is inherited from MyWindow.java.

Adding Labels, TextFields, and Panels to a Window

In this section, we develop a program named NewCustomerWindow.java that uses a window to input new customer information for the Community National Bank. The new customer information is then used to create a Customer instance, using the Customer class program we developed in Chapter 3. In fact, the NewCustomerWindow.java program is quite similar to CustomerProcessor.java used in Chapter 3.

First, we create a window and then we add <u>Labels</u>, <u>TextFields</u>, and <u>Buttons</u> to construct the desired GUI.

The Label class (refer to Figure 10-1) is used to place text on a window. We can place the text when we create the label instance or later using the **setText()** method. The <u>TextField</u> class is similar to <u>Label</u> except, in addition to displaying data, the user can type text into the <u>TextField</u> instance and we can retrieve this text using the **getText()** method.

The window created by NewCustomerWindow.java appears as (Figure 10-6):

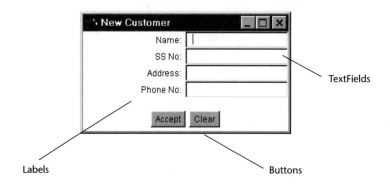

Figure 10-6. *New Customer Window*

As you can see, we use four <u>Labels</u>, four <u>TextFields</u>, and two <u>Buttons</u>. What you cannot see, however, is we have two *Panels.* The Panel class is an invisible subclass of <u>Component </u>that we place in a window to hold other GUI components, such as <u>Labels</u>, <u>TextFields</u>, and <u>Buttons</u>. Figure 10-7 shows the New Customer Window with the Panels indicated.

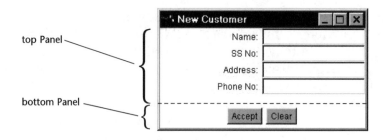

Figure 10-7. *Panels in New Customer Window*

We begin NewCustomerWindow.java similar to MyWindowWithAButton.java. First, we have the same two import statements:

```
import java.awt.*;
import java.awt.event.*;
```

The class header specifies the new program name NewCustomerWindow, which is, again, a subclass of MyWindow. NewCustomerWindow also implements the interface ActionListener because it will also listen for Button events.

```
public class NewCustomerWindow extends MyWindow implements
ActionListener
```

Next, we declare reference variables for the Buttons, TextFields, and the two panels. Note, we do not declare variables for the Label instances because we do not need to refer to them.

```
// reference variables for GUI components
Button btAccept, btClear;              // buttons
TextField tfName, tfSSNo, tfAddress tfPhoneNumber; // text fields
Panel pTop, pBottom;              // panels
```

Then we declare the variables to hold the customer information:

```
// customer attribute definitions
String name, ssNo, address, phoneNumber;
```

When our program is loaded, Java calls the **main()** method, which creates an instance of NewCustomerWindow, calls the constructor method, and then establishes the new window's size and displays it:

```
public static void main(String args[])
{
   NewCustomerWindow aWindow = new NewCustomerWindow();
   aWindow.setSize(300,170);              // pixels wide x pixels high
   aWindow.show();          // display the window
} // end of main method
```

The constructor method creates all the GUI components for the window. First, we set the window's title and then we create the two Panel instances we will use:

```
public NewCustomerWindow ()   // constructor method
{
  setTitle("New Customer");    // place title
  pTop = new Panel();          // make two panels for the window
  pBottom = new Panel();
```

Next, we create the Label and TextField instances and place them in the top Panel instance, using the <u>GridLayout</u> manager with four rows and two columns.

```
// place labels & textfields in top panel
pTop.setLayout(new GridLayout(4, 2));     // 4 rows & 2 cols
pTop.add(new Label("Name:  ", Label.RIGHT)); // Right justify text
pTop.add(tfName = new TextField());
pTop.add(new Label("SS No:  ", Label.RIGHT));
pTop.add(tfSSNo = new TextField());
pTop.add(new Label("Address:  ", Label.RIGHT));
pTop.add(tfAddress = new TextField());
pTop.add(new Label("Phone No:  ", Label.RIGHT));
pTop.add(tfPhoneNumber = new TextField());
```

Then we create the Button instances and place them in the bottom Panel instance, using <u>FlowLayout</u> manager.

```
// create & place the buttons in bottom panel
  pBottom.setLayout(new FlowLayout());
  pBottom.add(btAccept = new Button("Accept"));
  pBottom.add(btClear = new Button("Clear"));
```

Next, we place the two Panel instances in the window frame, using BorderLayout manager.

```
// place panels in the frame
setLayout(new BorderLayout());
add("North", pTop);
add("South", pBottom);
```

And, finally, we register the <u>NewCustomerWindow</u> instance as a listener for Button events:

```
btAccept.addActionListener(this); // listen for Button Events
```

```
btClear.addActionListener(this);
```

Now we write the code to handle button click events. First, we detect the event and then we call the appropriate method:

```
// event handler method for button clicks
public void actionPerformed(ActionEvent event)
{
    if (event.getSource() == btAccept) // if source is accept button
        accept();
    if (event.getSource() == btClear)  // if source is clear button
        clear();
} // end of actionPerformed
```

We have written a separate method for each button click. The method **accept()** gets the new customer data from the <u>TextFields</u>, creates an instance of the Customer class using this data, and then retrieves and displays the attribute values from the newly created instance. We use the TextField **getText()** method to get the customer's name, SS number, address, and phone number from the <u>TextFields</u>.

```
private void accept()
    {
    name = tfName.getText();  // get data from textfields
    ssNo = tfSSNo.getText();
    address = tfAddress.getText();
    phoneNumber = tfPhoneNumber.getText();
```

Then we call the constructor method in the <u>Customer</u> class to create the instance.

```
// create an account instance
Customer aCustomer =  new Customer(name, ssNo, address, phoneNumber);
```

and display the attribute values obtained from the accessor methods in <u>Customer</u>.

```
// retrieve and display customer information
System.out.println ("Name: " + aCustomer.getName());
System.out.println ("SS No: " + aCustomer.getSSNo());
System.out.println ("Address: " + aCustomer.getAddress());
```

```
    System.out.println ("Phone: " + aCustomer.getPhoneNumber());
} // end accept method
```

The **clear()** method simply uses the <u>TextField</u> **setText()** method to store spaces in the TextFields.

```
private void clear()
{
  tfName.setText(" ");
  tfSSNo.setText(" ");
  tfAddress.setText(" ");
  tfPhoneNumber.setText(" ");
} // end of clear method
```

When we enter the information shown in Figure 10-8, the program creates a Customer instance and displays the output shown in the following.

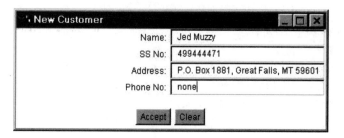

Figure 10-8. *Entering New Customer Information*

The program output looks like this:

```
Name: Jed Muzzy
SS No: 499444471
Address: P.O. Box 1881, Great Falls, MT  59601
Phone: none
```

The complete program for <u>NewCustomerWindow</u> is shown in Listing 10-3.

Listing 10-3: *NewCustomerWindow.java*

```java
import java.awt.*;
import java.awt.event.*;
public class NewCustomerWindow extends MyWindow implements
ActionListener
{
  // reference variables for GUI components
  Button btAccept, btClear;              // buttons
  TextField tfName, tfSSNo, tfAddress, tfPhoneNumber;   // text fields
  Panel pTop, pBottom;                   // panels
  // customer attribute definitions
  String name, ssNo, address, phoneNumber;
public static void main(String args[])  // main method called first
{
  NewCustomerWindow aWindow = new NewCustomerWindow();
  aWindow.setSize(300,170);    // pixels wide x pixels high
  aWindow.show();              // display the window
} // end of main method
public NewCustomerWindow () //  constructor method
{
  setTitle("New Customer"); // place title
  pTop = new Panel();  // make two panels for the window
  pBottom = new Panel();
  // place labels & textfields in top panel
  pTop.setLayout(new GridLayout(4, 2));     // 4 rows & 2 cols
  pTop.add(new Label("Name: ", Label.RIGHT)); // Right justify the text
  pTop.add(tfName = new TextField());
  pTop.add(new Label("SS No: ", Label.RIGHT));
  pTop.add(tfSSNo = new TextField());
  pTop.add(new Label("Address: ", Label.RIGHT));
  pTop.add(tfAddress = new TextField());
  pTop.add(new Label("Phone No: ", Label.RIGHT));
  pTop.add(tfPhoneNumber = new TextField());
```

```
  // create & place the buttons in bottom panel
  pBottom.setLayout(new FlowLayout());
  pBottom.add(btAccept = new Button("Accept"));
  pBottom.add(btClear = new Button("Clear"));
  // place panels in the window
  setLayout(new BorderLayout());
  add("North", pTop);
  add("South", pBottom);
  btAccept.addActionListener(this);   // listen for Button Events
  btClear.addActionListener(this);
} // end of constructor method
  // event handler method for button clicks
public void actionPerformed(ActionEvent event)
{
  if (event.getSource() == btAccept) // if source is accept button
    accept();
  if (event.getSource() == btClear)  // if source is clear button
    clear();
} // end of actionPerformed
private void accept()
{
  name = tfName.getText(); // get data from textfields
  ssNo = tfSSNo.getText();
  address = tfAddress.getText();
  phoneNumber = tfPhoneNumber.getText();
  // create a customer instance
    Customer aCustomer =   new Customer(name, ssNo, address,
phoneNumber);
  // retrieve and display customer information
  System.out.println ("Name: " + aCustomer.getName());
  System.out.println ("SS No: " + aCustomer.getSSNo());
  System.out.println ("Address: " + aCustomer.getAddress());
  System.out.println ("Phone: " + aCustomer.getPhoneNumber());
} // end of accept method
private void clear()
{
  tfName.setText("");
```

```
   tfSSNo.setText("");
   tfAddress.setText("");
   tfPhoneNumber.setText("");
}  // end of clear method
}  // end of NewCustomerWindow.java
```

Creating Pull-Down Menus

Next, we expand NewCustomerWindow.java to include pull-down menus. We work with three new AWT classes: <u>MenuBar</u>, <u>Menu,</u> and <u>MenuItem</u>. Although their appearance is quite different, we can do the same thing with menus we do with buttons. The user clicks them and our program responds to the click event. We use the same event handler method (**actionPerformed()**) for both <u>Buttons</u> and <u>MenuItems</u>. We determine the source object and then take the appropriate action. We keep the buttons in the new program to illustrate the similarities between button and menu events.

The window displayed by NewCustomerWindowMenus.java is

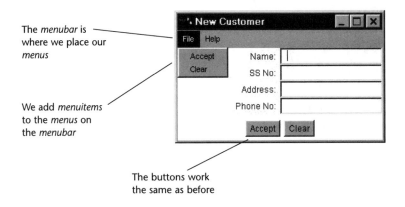

The *menubar* is where we place our *menus*

We add *menuitems* to the *menus* on the *menubar*

The buttons work the same as before

Figure 10-9. *New Customer window with menus*

The first step is to declare reference variables for the instances of MenuBar, the two Menus, and the MenuItems we are going to create

```
MenuBar mbMenuBar;        // menu bar
Menu fileMenu, helpMenu;   // menus
MenuItem miAccept, miClear;  // menu items
```

Next, we create the MenuBar instance and add it to the window:

```
mbMenuBar = new MenuBar();  // create menubar
   setMenuBar(mbMenuBar); // add menubar to window
```

Then we create the Menu instances and add them to the menu bar we just created:

```
// create file & help menus & add to menubar
   fileMenu = new Menu ("File");
   helpMenu = new Menu ("Help");
   mbMenuBar.add(fileMenu);
   mbMenuBar.add(helpMenu);
```

Now we create the MenuItem instances and add to the File menu:

```
// add items to fileMenu
   fileMenu.add(miAccept = new MenuItem("Accept"));
   fileMenu.add(miClear = new MenuItem("Clear"));
```

We then register as a listener for the menu item events:

```
// register as listener for MenuItem
eventsmiAccept.addActionListener(this);
miClear.addActionListener(this);
```

Finally, we add the event handler code to detect and respond to the event. Note, this code looks similar to the event handler code we use for button events:

```
if (event.getSource() == miAccept) // if event source is accept menu
    accept();
if (event.getSource() == miClear) // if event source is clear menu
    clear();
```

The complete program for NewCustomerWindowWithMenus.java

is shown in Listing 10-4. The code added for menus is in **boldface**.

Listing 10-4: *NewCustomerWindowWithMenus.java*

```
import java.awt.*;
import java.awt.event.*;
public class NewCustomerWindowWithMenus extends MyWindow implements
ActionListener
{
// reference variables for GUI components
Button btAccept, btClear;                              // buttons
TextField tfName, tfSSNo, tfAddress, tfPhoneNumber; // text fields
MenuBar mbMenuBar;                                     // menu bar
Menu fileMenu, helpMenu;                               // menus
MenuItem miAccept, miClear;                            // menu items
// customer attribute definitions
String name, ssNo, address, phoneNumber;
public static void main(String args[])  // main method called first
{
  NewCustomerWindowWithMenus aWindow =
    new NewCustomerWindowWithMenus();
  aWindow.setSize(300,170);        // pixels wide x pixels high
  aWindow.show();                  // display the window
} // end of main method
public NewCustomerWindowWithMenus ()   // constructor method
{
  setTitle("New Customer");      // place title
  Panel pTop = new Panel();      // two panels for the window
  Panel pBottom = new Panel();
  // add menu
  mbMenuBar = new MenuBar();     // create menubar
  setMenuBar(mbMenuBar);         // add menubar to window
  // create file & help menus & add to menubar
  fileMenu = new Menu ("File");
  helpMenu = new Menu ("Help");
  mbMenuBar.add(fileMenu);
  mbMenuBar.add(helpMenu);
```

```
// add items to fileMenu
fileMenu.add(miAccept = new MenuItem("Accept"));
fileMenu.add(miClear = new MenuItem("Clear"));
// place labels & textfields in top panel
pTop.setLayout(new GridLayout(4, 2));              // 4 rows & 2 cols
pTop.add(new Label("Name:  ", Label.RIGHT));       // Right justify text
pTop.add(tfName = new TextField());
pTop.add(new Label("SS No:  ", Label.RIGHT));
pTop.add(tfSSNo = new TextField());
pTop.add(new Label("Address:  ", Label.RIGHT));
pTop.add(tfAddress = new TextField());
pTop.add(new Label("Phone No:  ", Label.RIGHT));
pTop.add(tfPhoneNumber = new TextField());
// create & place the buttons in bottom panel
pBottom.setLayout(new FlowLayout());
pBottom.add(btAccept = new Button("Accept"));
pBottom.add(btClear = new Button("Clear"));
// place panels in the window
setLayout(new BorderLayout());
add("North", pTop);
add("South", pBottom);
btAccept.addActionListener(this);       // register for Button Events
btClear.addActionListener(this);
miAccept.addActionListener(this);   // register for MenuItem events
miClear.addActionListener(this);
} // end of constructor method
// event handler method for button and menu clicks
public void actionPerformed(ActionEvent event)
{
  if (event.getSource() == btAccept)     // if source is accept button
    accept();
  if (event.getSource() == btClear)      // if source is clear button
    clear();
  if (event.getSource() == miAccept) // if source is accept menu
    accept();
  if (event.getSource() == miClear)    // if source is clear menu
    clear();
```

```
} // end of actionPerformed
private void accept()
{
  name = tfName.getText();      // get data from textfields
  ssNo = tfSSNo.getText();
  address = tfAddress.getText();
  phoneNumber = tfPhoneNumber.getText();
  // create a customer instance
  Customer aCustomer = new Customer(name, ssNo, address, phoneNumber);
  // retrieve and display customer information
  System.out.println ("Name: " + aCustomer.getName());
  System.out.println ("SS No: " + aCustomer.getSSNo());
  System.out.println ("Address: " + aCustomer.getAddress());
  System.out.println ("Phone: " + aCustomer.getPhoneNumber());
} // end of accept method
private void clear()
{
  tfName.setText("");
  tfSSNo.setText("");
  tfAddress.setText("");
  tfPhoneNumber.setText("");
} // end of clear method
} // end of NewCustomerWindowWithMenus.java
```

Writing Applets

A Java Applet is simply a Java program that runs under control of another program such as a viewer or Web browser. The Applet is a smaller program with limited capability, a diminished application, thus Java programmers use the diminutive suffix "-let." Some argue the primary reason for Java's popularity is it can be used to write Applets. Our view, however, is Applets are only one of many reasons for Java's widespread use.

The diminished capability of an Applet is deliberately imposed to heighten security on the user's workstation. Applets are typically downloaded from another system and to restrict malevolent acts, Applets cannot access files, except on their host server. In addition, Applets do not have a title bar, so we cannot attach drop-down menus.

To run an Applet, we place an Applet html tag in a Web page. This tag identifies the Applet class name and specifies the size of the Applet window to appear on the Web page. Here, we plan to convert NewCustomerWindow.java to an Applet named NewCustomerApplet.java. The class file is named NewCustomerApplet.class and the html tag is

```
<APPLET
CODE = "NewCustomerApplet.class"
WIDTH = 400 HEIGHT = 200 >
</APPLET>
```

When the Web browser encounters this tag, it loads and executes the Applet.

An Applet and an Application are quite similar. We point out the differences here, as we convert NewCustomerWindow.java to NewCustomerApplet.java.

1. Applets extend the Applet class instead of extending the Frame class. This means we need to import the java.applet package.

   ```
   import java.applet.*;
   public class NewCustomerApplet extends Applet implements ActionListener
   ```

2. Applets do not have a **main()** method. It simply disappears. In NewCustomerWindow.java, our main method did only three things:

   • Create an instance of NewCustomerWindow

   • Establish the window size

   • Make the window visible

   The Web Browser does all this for us. The Web Browser creates the window, makes it the size indicated in the html tag, and makes it visible, thus eliminating the need for our main method.

3. Applets do not have a constructor method—instead, we place the constructor code in a method named **init()**. **init()** is automatically called when the Applet is loaded by the Browser. To make the change, we merely change the constructor method's name to **init()** and add the return type void.

   ```
   public void init () // replaces constructor method
   ```

Using a Web Browser, <u>NewCustomerApplet</u> appears as (Figure 10-10):

Figure 10-10. *New Customer Applet Window*

What is significant here is, if we wish, we can now enter customer information from any connected workstation using the Applet. From a user's perspective, the Applet functions exactly like the Application.

Summary of Key Points

1. Java includes several class libraries called *packages.* The java.awt package contains classes used to create GUIs. This chapter used the bold-face classes:

   Component (everything GUI is a component)
      Button
      Container
        Window
          Frame (our GUI applications *extend* this class)
          Panel (invisible container for other GUI components)
            Applet (Applets execute within a browser program)
          Label (used to display data)
          TextComponent
            TextField (used to display & enter data)

   MenuComponent
      MenuBar
      Menu
      MenuItem

   LayoutManager (positions GUI components in our frame)

2. A *Frame* is a Java GUI component (window) to which we can add other GUI components, such as <u>Buttons</u>, <u>Labels</u>, <u>MenuItems</u>, and <u>TextFields</u>.

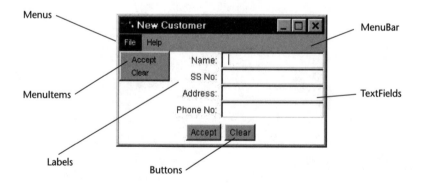

3. Both menu events and button events cause the method **actionPerformed()** to be called. Window events cause one of several window event methods to be called, depending on the specific event. For example, closing the window causes **windowClosing()** to be called.

4. Java uses Layout Managers to help arrange GUI components:

   - FlowLayout places components in successive rows. This is the default manager for the Panel & Applet classes.

   - BorderLayout places components in the borders & center (north, south, east, west, and center). This is the default manager for the Frame class.

   - CardLayout places components on top of each other (like a deck of cards).

   - GridLayout arranges components in a rectangular grid. We specify the number of rows and columns.

   - GridBagLayout is more complex than GridLayout, but it gives us more options.

5. *Panels* are invisible GUI components that we place in a Frame to hold other GUI components.

6. When Java detects a GUI event, such as clicking a button or menu item, it creates an event instance containing information about the event. If our program has registered as an event listener with the source object, Java calls an event handler method in our program. For Buttons and MenuItems, this method is named **actionPerformed()**.

7. An *interface* is similar to a class. To inherit methods from an interface, we use the keyword implements and specify the interface_name in our class header.

8. An *Applet* is a Java program that runs under control of a Web Browser. Applets may access files only on their host server, cannot have menu bars, and have an **init()** method instead of a constructor. However, Applets can run on any workstation that has access to the server where the Applet and its corresponding Web page reside. The Applet is downloaded to the workstation from the server along with the Web page.

Glossary

Applet a Java program that runs under control of a viewer or browser.

event something that happens to a GUI component, such as a user clicking a button or menu item.

event-driven programming a programming technique that responds to events.

event handler method the method called to respond to an event.

event listening a listener object that has registered with a source object is listening for events. Whenever a source object event occurs, Java calls the appropriate *event handler* method (actionPerformed() for buttons and menu items).

event registration a listener object *registers* for an event by calling a registration method in the source object. The registration method is addWindowListener() for Frames and addActionListener() for buttons and menu items.

implements Java keyword used in class header to inherit from an interface.

interface similar to a class, but with several restrictions.

layout manager Java classes used to place GUI components in a frame or panel.

listener object the object instance that responds to an event.

package a Java class library.

panel an invisible GUI component used to contain other components.

source object the object instance where the event occurs, generally a button or menu item.

this a Java keyword that refers to the current instance of the class.

Chapter 11

Object-Oriented Development Issues

Objectives

In this chapter you will study:

- OO development
- OO analysis and design issues
- Technology architecture issues

This chapter provides an overview of OO development and some of the issues you should consider when developing OO systems. Whereas the previous chapters have introduced specific programming topics, this chapter pulls together several of these topics and presents them in terms of software development. As you will see, OO development is much more than writing Java programs. The successful software developer must become familiar with, and apply, OO development techniques. OO requires more attention to analysis and design than traditional development. The payoff, however, is software that is developed more quickly and is maintained more easily. The chapter begins with an overview of OO development, followed by a brief introduction to current OO systems development methodologies. Next, we present activities commonly associated with analysis. Then we discuss various aspects of design necessary for understanding OO development and successful Java programming. We provide Java examples to enable you to compare and

249

contrast some of the basic philosophical differences between OO and traditional development approaches.

This chapter assumes you understand the following:

Java:

- OO Concepts (Chapter 2)

- Java Program Structure (Chapter 3)

- Defining Data (Chapter 4)

- Computation (Chapter 5)

- Decision Making (Chapter 6)

- Looping (Chapter 7)

- Arrays (Chapter 8)

- Data Access (Chapter 9)

- Graphical User Interfaces (Chapter 10)

Developing OO Systems

Programming is not a stand-alone process, although this has been the focus so far in this book. Writing code is only one part, albeit an important part, of software development. From a life cycle perspective, OO development is quite similar to traditional development. You still must do analysis, design, and programming to create a system, although the precise details and execution of these three phases varies. We have thus far deliberately focused on OO programming to give you a broad understanding of Java. This chapter gives you an overview of some development issues you should consider, in addition to programming.

By now, you have undoubtedly accepted the truth of a statement we made earlier in Chapter 2:

OO is a new way of thinking about the development of systems—it is not simply a programming technique.

In other words, don't view Java programming too narrowly. Understanding only the structure and syntax of Java is not sufficient. To develop OO systems successfully, you must also understand OO development, including OO analysis and design.

Like all systems development efforts, good analysis and design are essential to the success of the effort. However, where structured development permits us to bypass analysis and design and jump right to coding—essentially a code-and-fix-it development process—the OO paradigm requires us to do analysis and design. We can't begin writing code without previously identifying and defining our OO classes.

Class programs are the physical representation of classes identified in analysis and defined in design. Without proper analysis and design, knowing about the programs we must write becomes essentially impossible. The analysis, design, and programming phases are much more closely tied together in OO development than in traditional development. Using traditional structured design, the programs have little resemblance to the design documents, such as data flow diagrams and system flowcharts. In contrast, the OO design documents clearly indicate the needed class programs.

OO Methodologies

Adhering to the analysis, design, and programming phases however, does not guarantee we will produce good systems. Our projects must also follow an established formal systems development methodology (SDM). An *SDM* is a detailed guide for the development of a system, sort of a "how to" book for developing systems.

Chapter 2 introduced UML and class diagrams. UML consists of several additional diagrams, including sequence diagrams, collaboration diagrams, activity diagrams, component diagrams, package diagrams, deployment diagrams, state diagrams, and use case models. As indicated in Chapter 2, UML is actually a notation set for OO modeling. UML is not an SDM, however.

It is significant that the Object Management Group has adopted the UML notation set. UML has thus become a standard notation set for OO development and future OO SDMs are expected to use UML. Although a detailed explanation of UML diagrams is outside the scope of this book, we encourage you to familiarize yourself with UML before getting too far into OO development.

One of the first methodologies to take full advantage of the UML notation is the Unified Software Development Process (USDP), developed and published by Rational Corporation (the originators of UML). Books describing the USDP are now available.

The OO Process, Environment, and Notation (OPEN) methodology is another recent OO methodology. A consortium of 32 members developed OPEN. According to the authors of the book detailing OPEN, it "...may be used in conjunction with any OO method or notation, such as Coad, Firesmith, Odell, SOMA, or UML."

Several additional OO methodologies exist, including the Object Modeling Technique (OMT), Fusion, Coad's methodology, and Martin and Odell's methodology, among others. Additionally, several commercial OO methodologies are available. Some of these use UML and others do not.

Among the myriad methodologies, differences in basic development philosophies, phase activities, sequence of phases, and deliverables are found. Some suggest an iterative approach using prototyping and incremental class development, while others propose a more sequential technique.

Which methodology is best? Unfortunately, an easy answer does not exist to this question. In time, we hope the available methodologies will become more compatible, making this question easier to answer.

OO Analysis

In OO analysis, the objective is to determine user needs and then model these requirements. This should sound familiar because you probably do the same things now. Several ways exist to model requirements using UML. Use case models, class diagrams, sequence diagrams, collaboration diagrams, state diagrams, and activity diagrams are all used to model user requirements. Of these, the class diagram is the most important because everything revolves around the class diagram. The other diagrams all provide input to the class diagram.

Our focus during analysis is to understand the business logic (that is, problem domain) of the system. The class diagram identifies the classes we need and their relationships to each other. The use cases provide scenarios of requirements (for example, what are the steps needed to open a checking account?). Sequence diagrams illustrate interaction between the classes by modeling calls to various methods.

Overall, we want to know how the business works and what it will take to solve the users' problems. In our Community National Bank example, the class diagram depicts accounts, checking accounts, and customers. Specific user interfaces and data details are delayed until the design phase.

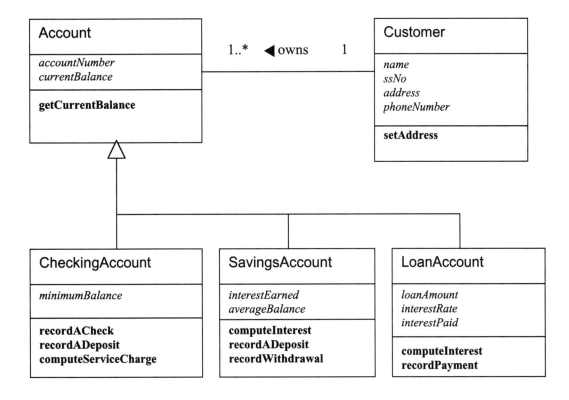

Figure 11-1. *Class diagram for Community National Bank*

OO Design

In OO design, the models created during analysis are enhanced to provide more detail. Among other things, specifications are provided for the user interface and data access aspects of the system. Additional UML models such as package diagrams, component diagrams, and deployment diagrams become useful late in the design phase of development.

With the exception of Chapters 9 (Data Access) and 10 (GUI), we have focused on the specific business logic for the Community National Bank. We developed classes to model accounts and customers, and methods to post checks, post deposits, and compute service charges. The various Account and Customer classes representing the heart of the business processing logic are called *problem domain* (PD) classes. These classes and their methods were developed while we ignored how to get data into and out of the system.

Chapter 9 added *data access* (DA) classes to store and retrieve CNB data. Then, Chapter 10 added *user interface* (UI) classes to allow the user to interact with the system. This clear separation of UI, PD, and DA classes was deliberate.

Why did we separate these classes? Isn't it simpler to combine the UI, PD, and DA tasks into a single program? You bet it is, but the short-term benefits of easier development quickly disappear when we begin maintaining the system. Good design, whether OO or structured, suggests we decompose processing into small independent modules. We want each program to be unaffected by changes to other programs in the system.

In the early days of COBOL, we wrote large programs that did numerous, sometimes unrelated, processing tasks. Specifically, we wrote programs that included a user interface, problem domain processing, and data access all in one program. The interface, processing, and data access functions were neither separated nor independent. Processing tended to be sequential with the code reflecting the sequence of execution, rather than a logical partitioning of the code. Figure 11-2 illustrates these three components graphically.

Why worry about separating these three components? On the surface, keeping the three together makes sense. For example, if we want to post checks to checking accounts, we input account number and check amount, retrieve the appropriate checking account record, subtract the

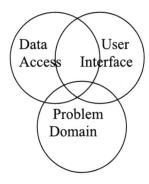

Figure 11-2. *Typical COBOL program components*

amount of the check from the account balance, and then rewrite the record. Why not put all of these tasks in one program? The answer is simple: a change in any one of the three areas (UI-PD-DA) forces us to recompile and test the entire program. For example, if we switch from a text-based user interface to a GUI, then the monolithic program must be changed and recompiled in total. Specifically, we first need to locate all the UI code, replace it with the new interface code, and then recompile and test the program. Chances are good when we wrote the original program, we tied the UI to the problem domain processing and data access code, making it difficult to locate and make all the changes needed to convert to a GUI front end.

For another example, consider the impact of changing the data file structure. We may, for example, add a field or change from an indexed file to relational database. Parts of the program must be changed and recompiled. No problem, right? Wrong! How many times have you made a change in one area of a program, only to find the change you made caused unanticipated problems in another part of the program or system? If this has happened to you, then you have experienced the problems associated with overlapping the three components. By separating these components, we are essentially isolating program functions and reducing future maintenance problems.

Three-Tier Design

Separating UI, DA, and PD is often referred to as *three-tier design* (not to be confused with "three-tier architecture," discussed later in this chapter). The three-tier design can be illustrated using UML package diagrams (Figure 11-3). Package diagrams provide a logical grouping of classes. In the following example, three packages are shown: user interface, problem domain, and data access. Packages are represented by a symbol resembling a file folder. A dashed line is used to show dependency among packages.

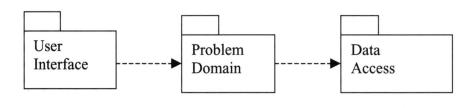

Figure 11-3. *Package diagram*

Here, we demonstrate Java three-tiered design by developing a small system for Community National Bank to post checks to customer checking accounts. This system has four class programs:

1. PostChecksGUI.java—a GUI window to permit the user to input account number and check amount.

2. Account.java—the same class program developed in Chapter 3.

3. CheckingAccountPD.java—CheckingAccount.java from Chapter 3 modified to interface with the Data Access class.

4. CheckingAccountDA.java—a new class program to provide data access using a relational database.

This example uses a Microsoft Access relational database, but the data access class effectively hides the data storage implementation from all the other classes. The UI and PD classes are totally insulated from the database.

First, we create a relational database with the five accounts shown in Figure 11-4.

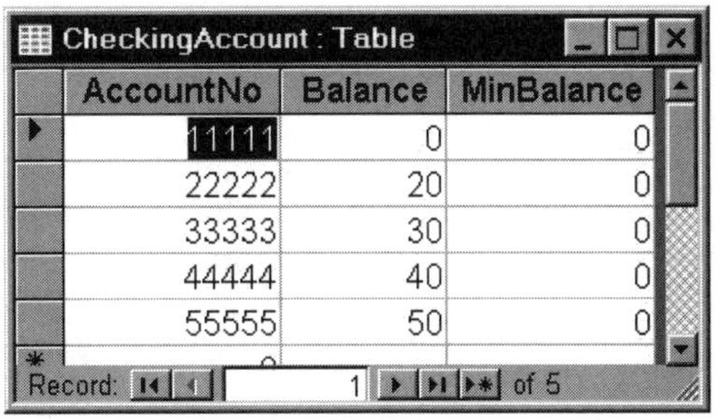

CheckingAccount : Table

AccountNo	Balance	MinBalance
11111	0	0
22222	20	0
33333	30	0
44444	40	0
55555	50	0

Record: 1 of 5

Figure 11-4. *Checking Account Database Table*

Next, we design the Data Access class program, CheckingAccountDA.java, modeling it after the DataBaseDemo.java program developed in Chapter 9.

CheckingAccountDA.java will have four class methods:

1. **initialize()**—establish the database connection
2. **terminate()**—close the database connection
3. **getAccount()**—retrieve the specified account
4. **updateAccount()**—store the account with a new balance

We then add three new class methods to our problem domain class, CheckingAccountPD.java:

1. **initialize()**—call **initialize()** in the data access class
2. **terminate()**—call **terminate()** in the data access class
3. **recordACheck()**—call **getAccount()** in the data access class and, if the account is found, call the instance method
4. **recordACheck()**. Note this new method is a **class** method. We also have the **recordACheck()** instance method.

We also make two modifications to the instance method **recordACheck()**:

1. Throw NSFException if the account does not have sufficient funds to pay the check.

2. Call **updateAccount()** in CheckingAccountDA.java to store the updated account balance in the database.

When multiple classes are interacting, one of the best ways to depict the communication between classes is the UML sequence diagram. *Sequence diagrams,* part of the UML notation package, illustrate the timing and sequence of messages between classes and objects. Sequence diagrams depict various scenarios of the system (for example, scenarios identified from use cases). Examples of scenarios from Community National Bank include opening an account, closing an account, recording checks, and recording deposits, among others.

Each object and/or class is identified at the top of the diagram using the following naming convention:

Object:Class   represents an instance of a class
  :Class represents a class (no instance)

Arrowed lines are used to show the interaction between the objects and classes. Solid lines indicate the message and arguments sent (in parentheses). Dashed lines indicate variables returned. The non-arrow end of the line marks the sender of the message; the arrowed end shows the receiver of the message. The ordering of the arrowed lines indicates the timing and sequence of interaction. The vertical line beneath each object and class represents the timeline.

Figure 11-5 shows the sequence diagram for recording checks. In this case, the sequence diagram maps the interaction between the GUI, Problem Domain, and Data Access classes. Specifically, the PostChecksGUI, CheckingAccountPD, and CheckingAccountDA classes are used; an instance of the CheckingAccountPD, named anAccount, is also used. Note, the shaded names at the top of Figure 11-5 are not part of the sequence diagram. We included them here to highlight the UI, PD, and DA objects and classes.

The sequence diagram in Figure 11-5 shows the normal course of events for recording checks. Unusual occurrences, such as overdrawn accounts or invalid accounts numbers, are not represented on this sequence diagram. Alternate sequence diagrams can be created to demonstrate the sequence of events that occur when an exception is thrown.

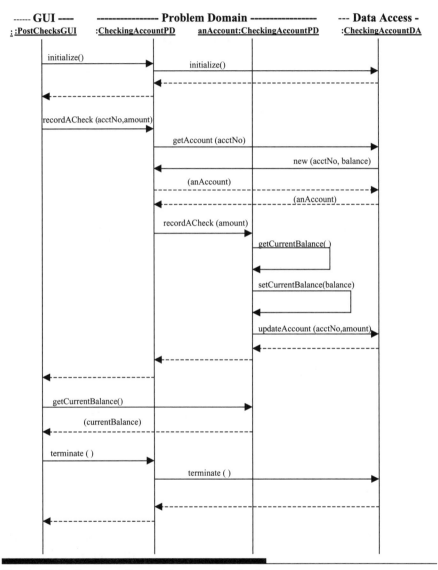

Figure 11-5. *Sequence diagram for recording checks*

The GUI window displayed by PostChecksGUI.java is shown in Figure 11-6.

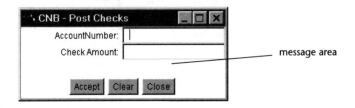

Figure 11-6. *Post Checks Window*

The **main()** method in PostChecksGUI.java creates and displays the window and then calls the class method **initialize()** in CheckingAccountPD.java.

```
public static void main(String args[])  // main method called first
{
   PostChecksGUI aWindow = new PostChecksGUI(); // create window instance
   aWindow.setSize(300,170);      // pixels wide x pixels high
   aWindow.show();                // display the window
   CheckingAccountPD.initialize(); // initialize data manager
} // end of main method
```

The **initialize()** method in the problem domain class, CheckingAccountPD.java, simply calls **initialize()** in the data access class, CheckingAccountDA.java.

```
public static void initialize()
{
   CheckingAccountDA.initialize();  // call initialize in Data Access
} // end initialize
```

The CheckingAccount**DA**.java **initialize()** method loads the database driver and then creates a connection and statement instance. We could do this each time we get an account but doing it once when we begin processing is more efficient.

```
public static void initialize() // initialize method
{
try
{   // load the jdbc - odbc bridge driver for Windows-95
    Class.forName("sun.jdbc.odbc.JdbcOdbcDriver");
    // create connection instance
    aConnection = DriverManager.getConnection(url,"Admin","JavaIsFun");
    // create statement object instance
    aStatement = aConnection.createStatement();
} // end try
catch (Exception e)
    {System.out.println("Exception caught "+ e);}
} // end initialize
```

When the user enters the account number and the check amount in the GUI window and clicks the Accept button, PostChecksGUI.java first validates the input data, and then calls the class method **recordACheck()** in CheckingAccountPD.java. This method can throw two different exceptions: <u>NoAccountFoundException</u> and <u>NSFException</u>. If either of these is thrown, the GUI class catches them and displays the appropriate error message in the message area of the GUI window. If no exceptions are caught, the resulting account balance is displayed in the message area. The PostChecksGUI code is

```
public void postCheck()
  {
  try
  {
    anAccount =
    CheckingAccountPD.recordACheck(accountNumber, checkAmount);
    lblMessage.setText("Balance is: " +
    Float.toString(anAccount.getCurrentBalance()));
  }
  catch (NoAccountFoundException e)
    {lblMessage.setText("No Account Found");}
  catch (NSFException e)
    {lblMessage.setText("Insufficient Funds");}    } // end postCheck
```

The class method **recordACheck()** in CheckingAccountPD.java first calls **getAccount()** in the Data Access class to retrieve the account entered by the user.

```
// note this is a class method - we also have an instance method with
// this name
public static CheckingAccountPD recordACheck (int accountNumber,
   float checkAmount) throws NoAccountFoundException, NSFException
{
  try
   { // ask Data Access class to get the account instance for us
   CheckingAccountPD anAccount =
      CheckingAccountDA.getAccount(accountNumber);
   anAccount.recordACheck(checkAmount);  // if successful, post check
   return anAccount;      // return the instance reference variable
   }
  catch (NoAccountFoundException e)  // No Account Found
   { throw e;}
  catch (NSFException e)       // Not Sufficient Funds
   { throw e;}
} // end class method recordACheck
```

If the account is successfully retrieved, **getAccount()** creates a <u>CheckingAccount</u> instance and returns the reference variable anAccount to the problem domain class. Note, if **getAccount()** cannot retrieve the account, a <u>NoAccountFoundException</u> is thrown by the data access class.

```
public static CheckingAccountPD getAccount(int acctNo) throws
   NoAccountFoundException
{
try
{
  String sqlQuery = "SELECT AccountNo, Balance, MinBalance FROM
   CheckingAccount WHERE AccountNo =" + acctNo;
  rs = aStatement.executeQuery(sqlQuery); // execute the SQL query
  boolean more = rs.next(); // set the cursor
  if (more)
   { // if we got the account extract the data & display
```

```
    int acctNO = rs.getInt(1);
    float balance = rs.getFloat(2);
    float minBalance = rs.getFloat(3);
    anAccount = new CheckingAccountPD(acctNO, balance); //create instance
    }
    else
    { // no account found - create & throw the exception
     NoAccountFoundException e = new NoAccountFoundException("Not Found");
     throw e;
    } // end if
  } // end try
  catch (SQLException e)
  { while (e != null) // we can have multiple exceptions here
    { System.out.println("SQLException caught "+ e);
     e = e.getNextException();
    } // end while loop
  } // end catch
    return anAccount;
  } // end getAccount
```

recordACheck() in the problem domain calls its instance method
recordACheck() to post the check to the account instance.

The instance method **recordACheck()** will throw an <u>NSFException</u>
if the account does not have sufficient funds to pay the check.

```
// instance method to post a check to this account
public void
recordACheck (float checkAmount) throws NSFException
{
  float currentBalance = getCurrentBalance(); //get the current balance
  if (currentBalance >= checkAmount)          // see if sufficient funds
  {
    currentBalance = currentBalance - checkAmount;
    setCurrentBalance(currentBalance);        // set the current balance
    // update the balance in the database

CheckingAccountDA.updateAccount(getAccountNumber(),currentBalance);
  }
```

```
else
{ // if not, throw an exception
  NSFException e = new NSFException("Not Sufficient Funds");
  throw e;
} // end if
} // end instance method recordACheck
```

If sufficient funds exist to pay the check, the class method **updateAccount()** in the data access class is called to store the new balance in the database.

```
public static void updateAccount(int acctNo, float balance)
{
  try
  {
    String sqlUpdate = "UPDATE CheckingAccount SET Balance = "
      + balance + " WHERE AccountNo = " + acctNo;
    aStatement.executeUpdate(sqlUpdate);
  } // end try
  catch (SQLException e)
  { while (e != null) // we can have multiple exceptions here
        { System.out.println("SQLException caught "+ e);
    e = e.getNextException();
    } // end while loop
  } // end catch
} // end update
```

The interaction of multiple objects and classes can get confusing. Sequence diagrams and written narratives can help eliminate the confusion by outlining the interaction. Going back to look at the sequence diagram again and to reread the Java code may be helpful now. The following narrative summarizes the interaction:

Summary Narrative for Recording Checks

1. :PostChecksGUI creates and displays the window, and then calls the class method **initialize()** in CheckingAccountPD.

2. The **initialize()** method in :CheckingAccountPD calls **initialize()** in :CheckingAccountDA to create the database connection.

3. The :CheckingAccountDA **initialize()** method loads the database driver, and then creates a connection and statement instance. We could do this each time we get an account, but it is more efficient to do it once when we begin processing.

4. The user enters the account number and the check amount in the GUI window and clicks the Accept button. :PostChecksGUI validates the input data and then calls the class method **recordACheck()** in :CheckingAccountPD. This method can throw two different exceptions: NoAccountFoundException and NSFException. If either of these is thrown, the GUI class catches them and displays the appropriate error message in the message area of the GUI window.

5. The class method **recordACheck()** in :CheckingAccountPD calls **getAccount()** in :CheckingAccountDA to retrieve the account entered by the user.

6. If the account is successfully retrieved, **getAccount()** creates a CheckingAccount instance by calling the constructor method in :CheckingAccountPD; a reference to the new Account instance, anAccount, is returned to :CheckingAccountDA. This reference variable is then returned to the :CheckingAccountPD, the initiator of this sequence of events. If **getAccount()** cannot retrieve the account, a NoAccountFoundException is thrown by :CheckingAccountDA.

7. :CheckingAccountPD calls its **instance** method **recordACheck()**, which actually posts the check to the account instance. The **recordACheck()** method then does three things: (1) calls **getCurrentBalance()** to retrieve the current balance; (2) subtracts the check amount from the current balance and calls **setCurrentBalance()** to set the balance. If there are sufficient funds to pay the check, the class method **updateAccount()** in :CheckingAccountDA is called to store the new balance in the data-

base. The instance method **recordACheck()** will throw an NSFException if the account does not have sufficient funds to pay the check.

8. When the user clicks the Close button, the class method **terminate()** in CheckingAccountPD is called. This method, in turn, calls **terminate()**in :CheckingAccountDA to close the database connection.

The complete programs are included in the enclosed CD-ROM and we encourage you to experiment with them. An excellent exercise is to modify the GUI window to post deposits as well. You need to write the **recordADeposit()** class method for CheckingAccountPD.java, but you should not make any changes to the data access class.

Architecture Issues

At some point in the design—we hope as late as possible—decisions will be made regarding the technology architecture. Specifically, issues such as platform type and number of tiers are addressed. Consideration must be given to single machine, two-tier, three-tier, or n-tiered architectures. An important OO design issue is the physical location of the classes. For single machine architecture, the answer is simple: all classes reside on the machine. For two-tiered client-server systems, several options exist. One option is to put the user interface and problem domain classes on the client and put data access on the server. For a three-tiered system that normally contains a client, an intermediate server, and a back-end or host server, several options are also available. For example, we can put the user interface on the client, problem domain on the intermediate server, and data access on the back-end. For Internet applications, which may be n-tiered, it is possible for all classes to be on the server until the user activates the browser, which then downloads the user interface, problem domain, and data access as needed.

UML provides notation to illustrate the physical distribution of objects. Deployment diagrams are useful in showing the physical location of objects, groups of objects (packages), or portions of objects (components). An example of a deployment diagram, for the Community National Bank problem, is shown in Figure 11-7. In this case, the user interface is located on the bank teller's PC, which is connected via a token ring network to an AS/400 located in the bank, which is, in turn, connected to the home office's mainframe via a T1 line. The user interface, problem domain, and data access packages are stored on these three tiers respectively.

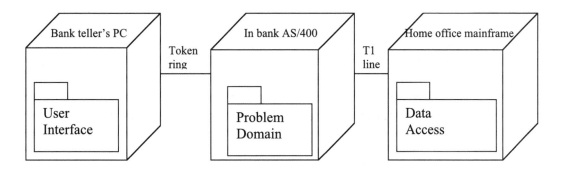

Figure 11-7. *Deployment diagram*

The physical allocation of objects to different platforms requires some mechanism for passing objects and messages between objects across the tiers. The mechanism for accomplishing this task is called an ***Object Request Broker*** (ORB). An ORB keeps track of object locations and provides the communication mechanisms to allow objects to communicate. Basically, the ORB accepts messages from objects, decides where it needs to go, and delivers it to the proper object. All this functionality is hidden from the developer. Currently, three ORB options exist:

1. Sun's Remote Method Invocation (RMI): good for communicating among Java objects on distributed sites;

2. Microsoft's Distributed COM (DCOM): good for communicating among Java and ActiveX objects in a Windows environment;

3. The Object Management Group's Common Request Broker Architecture (CORBA): a standard to allow any object of any

type to communicate across any type of platform; OMG does not sell the necessary CORBA software, but it is provided by several vendors, such as IBM and Hewlett-Packard. This is the only truly generic communicating mechanism among the three and the only one that allows, for example, Java components to communicate with Smalltalk components.

Which ORB option should be used? For simple Java-only environments, use RMI. For complex or mixed-environments, use CORBA. DCOM is restrictive because it limits the platforms (currently) to only Windows environments.

We recommend you visit the Sun, Microsoft, and OMG Web sites for more information concerning RMI, DCOM, and CORBA, respectively.

Performance Issues

OO development and Java both provide great flexibility in software development and execution. Unfortunately, some of these benefits carry a cost. Using a three-tier design of separating the user interface, problem domain, and data access requires more communication among the objects and the possibility for decreased performance. The trade-off, of course, is potential loss of performance with a three-tier design versus increased difficulty in maintaining the system without a three-tier design.

Distributed systems, such as a three-tier architecture described earlier, require additional overhead because they need an ORB. The ORB adds another layer of software to the system, which tends to hurt performance. Also, by their nature, distributed systems may have performance problems due to the physical separation of components.

Perhaps the hardest knock on Java to date has been its performance. Some of this is due to the Java environment and the portability it provides. As an interpreted language (using bytecodes and Java Virtual Machines), performance can suffer. Also, because Java is being widely used in distributed environments, many of which are Internet-based, performance has tended to suffer because of communications bottlenecks. The blame cannot be placed solely on Java. Any language in a distributed environment using ORBs may suffer somewhat, but Java is the language receiving heavy use and attention, and, thus, the criticism that comes with it.

In situations where performance is an important issue, we can use a native language compiler to produce executable Java code and bypass bytecode and eliminate the JVM. Of course, when we do this, we sacrifice portability.

Summary of Key Points

1. OO programming is only one portion of the overall OO development process. Programming cannot stand alone. To develop good OO systems, you must also use OO analysis and design.

2. **UML** is the standard notation set for OO modeling. UML is not a methodology.

3. Several OO development methodologies exist, including the **Unified Software Development Process** (by Rational Corp.) and OPEN. Commercial methodologies are also available.

4. In OO analysis, problem domain classes are identified and requirements are modeled using several UML diagrams.

5. In OO design, models created during analysis are enhanced and implementation details, such as interfaces, data access, and technology architecture considerations, are added.

6. Classes should be designed so the user interface, problem domain, and data access segments are separated (called a **three-tiered design**). These classes should communicate via messages only.

7. Consideration should be given to the physical placement of objects. The technology architecture—primarily single machine, two-tiered, three-tiered, n-tiered—impact the placement decisions.

8. **Object Request Brokers** (ORBs) are necessary to facilitate communication between objects in a multitiered architecture.

9. Potential performance problems exist with Java and OO systems in general due to the multitiered nature of many of the systems and the requisite use of ORBs and **three-tiered designs**.

Glossary

Common Request Broker Architecture (CORBA) an OMG standard to allow any object of any type to communicate across any type of platform.

data access classes the classes that allow storage, retrieval, and manipulation of data.

deployment diagrams show the physical location of objects, groups of objects, or portions of objects.

Distributed COM (DCOM) Microsoft's ORB; good for communicating among Java and ActiveX objects in a Windows environment.

Object Request Broker (ORB) keeps track of object locations and provides the communication mechanisms to allow objects to communicate.

OPEN (Object-Oriented Process, Environment, and Notation) an OO methodology developed by a consortium of 32 members; uses UML and other notation sets.

package diagrams provide a logical grouping of classes.

problem domain classes the objects and classes representing business logic.

Remote Method Invocation (RMI) a Sun Microsystems ORB; good for communicating among Java objects on distributed sites.

sequence diagrams illustrate the timing and sequence of messages between classes and objects.

systems development methodology (SDM) a detailed guide for the development of a system; a "how to" book for developing systems.

three-tier design system design where the user interface, problem domain, and data access segments are separated.

UML Unified Modeling Language; the standard object modeling notation adopted by the Object Management Group.

Unified Software Development Process (USDP) an OO methodology developed and published by Rational Corporation; this methodology uses UML.

user interface classes the objects and classes that allow the user to interact with the system.

Bibliography

Booch, G., Rumbaugh, J., and Jacobson, I., *The Unified Modeling Language User Guide*, Reading, Massachusetts: Addison-Wesley, 1999.

Chapman, D., *Understanding ActiveX and OLE: A Guide for Developers & Managers*, Redmond, Washington: Microsoft Press, 1996.

Graham, I., Henderson-Sellers, B., and Younessi, H., *The OPEN Process Specification*, Reading, Massachusetts: Addison-Wesley, 1997.

Harmon, P., and Watson, M., *Understanding UML: The Developer's Guide with a Web-Based Application in Java*, San Francisco, California: Morgan Kaufmann Publishers, Inc., 1998.

Orfali, R., and Harkey, D., *Client/Server Programming with Java and CORBA*, New York, New York: John Wiley & Sons, 1997.

Appendix

Programs on the CD-ROM

Chapter 3: Java Structure

Account.java

```
// Java For The COBOL Programmer - copyright 1999 Doke & Hardgrave
// Chapter 3 - Java Strucuture
// Program to model the Account class
// Account.java 3 JAN 99

public class Account
{
    // account attribute definitions
    private int accountNumber; // private scope limited to this class
    private float currentBalance;

    // constructor method to create an instance
    public Account (int newAccountNumber, float newCurrentBalance)
    {
        accountNumber  = newAccountNumber;
        currentBalance = newCurrentBalance;
    }
    // accessor methods
    public float getCurrentBalance ()
    { return currentBalance; }

    public int getAccountNumber ()
    { return accountNumber;}

    // mutator methods
    public void setAccountNumber(int newAccountNumber)
```

```
{accountNumber = newAccountNumber; }

public void setCurrentBalance( float newCurrentBalance)
{ currentBalance = newCurrentBalance; }
} // end account class
```

AccountProcessor.java

```
// Java For The COBOL Programmer - copyright 1999 Doke & Hardgrave
// Chapter 3 - Java Program Structure
// Program to exercise methods in CheckingAccount.java
// AccountProcessor.java 3 JAN 99

public class AccountProcessor
{
   public static void main (String args[])  // main is first method
   {
      // attribute values
      int accountNumber = 12345;
      float currentBalance = 50.00F;

      // create a checking account instance
      CheckingAccount anAccount = new CheckingAccount(accountNumber,
currentBalance);

      // retrieve and display current balance
      System.out.println ("Beginning Balance: " +
anAccount.getCurrentBalance());

      // post a $20 check then again retrieve and display current balance
      anAccount.recordACheck (20.00F);
      System.out.println ("Balance After $20 check: " +
anAccount.getCurrentBalance());
      // post a $15 deposit then again retrieve and display current balance
      anAccount.recordADeposit (15.00F);
      System.out.println ("Balance After $15 deposit: " +
anAccount.getCurrentBalance());
   }  // end main
}  // end AccountProcessor.java
```

CheckingAccount.java

```
// Java For The COBOL Programmer - copyright 1999 Doke & Hardgrave
// Chapter 3 - Java Program Structure
// Program to model the CheckingAccount class
// CheckingAccount.java  3 JAN 99

public class CheckingAccount extends Account  // superclass is account
{ // attribute definition
    private float minimumBalance; // private scope limited to this class

    // constructor method
    public CheckingAccount (int newAccountNumber,float newCurrentBalance)
    { // invoke account constructor to populate account attributes
        super (newAccountNumber, newCurrentBalance);
        minimumBalance = newCurrentBalance; // populate checkingAccount
                                            // attribute
    } // end constructor

    // accessor method
    public float getMinimumBalance ()
        { return minimumBalance; }

    // post a check to this account
    public void recordACheck (float checkAmount)
    {   float balance = getCurrentBalance(); // retrieve balance
        balance = balance - checkAmount;    // subtract check
        setCurrentBalance(balance);         // store new balance
    }  // end recordACheck

    // post a deposit to this account
    public void recordADeposit (float depositAmount)
    {   float balance = getCurrentBalance(); // retrieve balance
        balance = balance + depositAmount; // add deposit
        setCurrentBalance(balance);        // store new balance
    }  // end recordADeposit
}  // end CheckingAccount.java
```

Customer.java

```
// Java For The COBOL Programmer - copyright 1999 Doke & Hardgrave
// Chapter 3 - Java Program Structure
// Program to model the Customer class
// Customer.java 3 JAN 99

public class Customer
{ // customer attribute definitions
    private String name;  // private scope limits access to this class
    private String ssNo;
    private String address;
    private String phoneNumber;

    // constructor method to create an instance
    public Customer (String newName, String newSSNo, String newAdr, String
newPhone)
    {
        name = newName;
        ssNo = newSSNo;
        address = newAdr;
        phoneNumber = newPhone;
    } // end constructor

    // setAddress mutator method
    public void setAddress (String newAdr)
    { address = newAdr;
    } // end setAddress

    // accessor methods
    public String getName ()
        {return name;}
    public String getSSNo ()
        {return ssNo;}
    public String getAddress ()
        {return address;}
    public String getPhoneNumber ()
```

```
        {return phoneNumber;}
}  // end Customer.java
```

CustomerProcessor.java

```
// Java For The COBOL Programmer - copyright 1999 Doke & Hardgrave
// Chapter 3 - Java Program Structure
// Program to exercise the methods in Customer.java
// CustomerProcessor.java 3 JAN 99

public class CustomerProcessor
{
   public static void main (String args[])   // main is first method executed
   { // customer attribute definitions
      String name = "Jed Muzzy";
      String ssNo = "499444471";
      String address = "P.O. Box 1881, Great Falls, MT 59601";
      String phoneNumber = "None";

      // create an account instance
      Customer aCustomer = new Customer(name, ssNo, address, phoneNumber);

      // retrieve and display customer information
      System.out.println ("Name: " + aCustomer.getName());
      System.out.println ("SS No: " + aCustomer.getSSNo());
      System.out.println ("Address: " + aCustomer.getAddress());
      System.out.println ("Phone: " + aCustomer.getPhoneNumber());

      // change address then redisplay
      aCustomer.setAddress ("P.O. Box 1998, St. Louis, MO 63105");
      System.out.println ("Address: " + aCustomer.getAddress());
   } // end main
} // end CustomerProcessor.java
```

Chapter 4: Defining Data

CastDemo.java

```java
// Java For The COBOL Programmer - copyright 1999 Doke & Hardgrave
// Chapter 4 - Defining Data
// Program to demonstrate type casting
// CastDemo.java 6 JAN 99

public class CastDemo
{
   public static void main (String args[])  // main is first method executed
   {
      double answer;
      int integer1 = 3;
         int integer2 = 2;

         answer = 1.5 + integer1 / integer2;
         System.out.println ("The answer is " + answer);

         answer = 1.5 + (double) integer1 / integer2;
         System.out.println ("The second answer is " + answer);

   } // end of main method
} // end of CastDemo.java
```

StringDemo.java

```java
// Java For The COBOL Programmer - copyright 1999 Doke & Hardgrave
// Chapter 4 - Defining Data
// Program to demonstrate String methods
// StringDemo.java 6 JAN 99

public class StringDemo
{
    public static void main (String args[])  // main is first method executed
    {
        String s1 = "COBOL Programmers";
        String s2 = "can learn Java";

        System.out.println ("The length of s1 is " + s1.length());
        System.out.println ("The 7th character of s1 is " + s1.charAt(6));
        System.out.println (s2.substring (10,14) + " is FUN!");

    } // end of main method
} // end of StringDemo.java
```

Chapter 5: Computation

AccountProcessor.java

```
// Java For The COBOL Programmer - copyright 1999 Doke & Hardgrave
// Chapter 5 - Java Program Structure
// Program to exercise methods in CheckingAccount.java & demonstrate custom
// exception
// AccountProcessor.java 3 JAN 99

public class AccountProcessor
{
    public static void main (String args[])  // main is first method executed
    {
        // attribute values
      int accountNumber = 12345;
        float currentBalance = 50.00F;

        // create a checking account instance
        CheckingAccount anAccount =  new CheckingAccount(accountNumber,
currentBalance);

        // retrieve and display current balance
        System.out.println ("Beginning Balance: " +
anAccount.getCurrentBalance());
        try
        {// post a $20 check then again retrieve and display current balance
        anAccount.recordACheck (20.00F);
        System.out.println ("Balance After $20 check: " +
anAccount.getCurrentBalance());
        // post a $15 deposit then again retrieve and display current balance
        anAccount.recordADeposit (15.00F);
        System.out.println ("Balance After $15 deposit: " +
anAccount.getCurrentBalance());
        // now try posting a $100 check
        anAccount.recordACheck (100.00F);
```

```
        System.out.println ("Balance After $100 check: " +
anAccount.getCurrentBalance());
        } // end try block
    catch (NSFException e)
    {System.out.println ("Caught NSFException" + e);}
  } // end main
} // end of AccountProcessor.java
```

ArithmeticExceptionDemo.java

```java
// Java For The COBOL Programmer - copyright 1999 Doke & Hardgrave
// Chapter 5 - Computation
// Program to demonstrate ArithmeticException
// ArithmeticExceptionDemo.java  15 JAN 99

public class ArithmeticExceptionDemo
{
   public static void main(String args[])
   {
      int a = 5;
      int b = 0;
      int c = 0;
      try
      {
         c = a / b;
         System.out.println ("Successful divide by zero");
      } // end try
      catch (ArithmeticException anException)
      {
         System.out.println ("Caught ArithmeticException " + anException);
      } // enc catch
   } // end main
} // end ArithmeticExceptionDemo.java
```

CheckingAccount.java

```
// Java For The COBOL Programmer - copyright 1999 Doke & Hardgrave
// Chapter 5 - Computation
// Program to model the CheckingAccount class with Custom Exception
// CheckingAccount.java  15 JAN 99

public class CheckingAccount extends Account  // superclass is account
{ // attribute definition
   private float minimumBalance; // private scope limited to this class

   // constructor method
   public CheckingAccount (int newAccountNumber,float newCurrentBalance)
   { // invoke account constructor to populate account attributes
      super (newAccountNumber, newCurrentBalance);
      minimumBalance = newCurrentBalance; // populate checkingAccount
                                          // attribute
   } // end constructor

   // accessor method
   public float getMinimumBalance ()
      { return minimumBalance; }

   // instance method to post a check to this account
   public void recordACheck (float checkAmount) throws NSFException
   {        float balance = getCurrentBalance();
      if (balance >= checkAmount)  // see if sufficient funds
         {
         balance = balance - checkAmount;
         setCurrentBalance(balance); // store new balance
         }
      else
         {// if not, throw an exception
            NSFException e = new NSFException("Not Sufficient Funds");
               throw e;
         } // end if
   }  // end instance method recordACheck
```

```
// post a deposit to this account
public void recordADeposit (float depositAmount)
{  float balance = getCurrentBalance(); // retrieve balance
   balance = balance + depositAmount; // add deposit
   setCurrentBalance(balance);          // store new balance
} // end recordADeposit
} // end of checking account class
```

MathClassDemo.java

```
// Java For The COBOL Programmer - copyright 1999 Doke & Hardgrave
// Chapter 5 - Computation
// Program to demonstrate methods in the Math class
// MathClassDemo.java 15 JAN 99

import java.text.NumberFormat;
public class MathClassDemo
{
   public static void main(String args[])
   {
    // declare variables
    float balance = 1000F;
    float apr = .08F;
    int months = 6;
    double payment;
    payment = (balance * (apr / 12))/ (1 - 1 / Math.pow ((1 + apr/12), months));
    float roundedPayment = roundOff(payment); // round to 2 decimals
    System.out.println ("Payment = " + payment);
    System.out.println ("Rounded Payment = " + roundedPayment);
    } // end main

   // roundOff method
   static public float roundOff (double value)
   {
      value = value * 100;        // move decimal 2 places to right
      // Math.round returns long - recast to float
      float roundedValue = (float) Math.round(value);
      roundedValue = roundedValue / 100;  // move decimal back to left
         return roundedValue;
   } // end roundOff
} // end MathClassDemo
```

NSFException.java

```
// Java For The COBOL Programmer - copyright 1999 Doke & Hardgrave
// Chapter 5 - Computation
// Exception Class Program to demonstrate Custom Exception
// Not Sufficient Funds Exception
// NSFException.java

public class NSFException extends Exception
{
    public NSFException (String errorMessage) // constructor
    { super(errorMessage);}
} // end NSFException.java
```

NumberFormatDemo.java

```java
// Java For The COBOL Programmer - copyright 1999 Doke & Hardgrave
// Chapter 5 - Computation
// Program to demonstrate methods in the NumberFormat class
// NumberFormatDemo.java 15 JAN 99

import java.text.*;

public class NumberFormatDemo
{
    public static void main(String args[])
    {
        // demonstrate currency format
        NumberFormat currencyFormat = NumberFormat.getCurrencyInstance();
        String currencyNumber = currencyFormat.format(123456.78);
        System.out.println ("currencyNumber = " + currencyNumber);

        // demonstrate comma format
        NumberFormat numberFormat = NumberFormat.getInstance();
        String commaNumber =   numberFormat.format(123456.78);
        System.out.println ("commaNumber = " + commaNumber);

        // demonstrate percent format
        NumberFormat percentFormat = NumberFormat.getPercentInstance();
        String percentNumber =  percentFormat.format(0.78);
        System.out.println ("percentNumber = " + percentNumber);

        // demonstrate decimal format
        DecimalFormat decimalFormat = new DecimalFormat("##,##0.00");
        String decimalNumber =  decimalFormat.format(123456.7890);
        System.out.println ("decimalNumber = " + decimalNumber);
    } // end main
} // end NumberFormatDemo
```

WrapperDemo.java

```
// Java For The COBOL Programmer - copyright 1999 Doke & Hardgrave
// Chapter 5 - Computation
// Program to demonstrate Data Type Class Methods
// WrapperDemo.java 15 JAN 99

public class WrapperDemo
{
    public static void main(String args[])
    {
    // create & display instances of Double, Float, Integer, and Long
    Double aDouble = new Double(123.456);
    Float aFloat = new Float(123.456F);
    Integer anInteger = new Integer (123);
    Long aLong = new Long(123456);
    System.out.println("aDouble =" + aDouble);
    System.out.println("aFloat =" + aFloat);
    System.out.println("anInteger =" + anInteger);
    System.out.println("aLong =" + aLong);

    // convert numeric to String & disply
    String aStringFromDouble = new String(Double.toString(aDouble.doubleValue()));
    String aStringFromFloat = new String(Float.toString(aFloat.floatValue()));
    String aStringFromInteger = new String(Integer.toString(anInteger.intValue()));
    String aStringFromLong = new String(Long.toString(aLong.longValue()));
    System.out.println("aStringFromDouble =" + aStringFromDouble);
    System.out.println("aStringFromFloat =" + aStringFromFloat);
    System.out.println("aStringFromInteger =" + aStringFromInteger);
    System.out.println("aStringFromLong =" + aStringFromLong);

    // convert String to numeric & display
    Double aDoubleFromString = Double.valueOf(aStringFromDouble);
    Float aFloatFromString = Float.valueOf(aStringFromFloat);
    Integer anIntegerFromString = Integer.valueOf(aStringFromInteger);
    Long aLongFromString = Long.valueOf(aStringFromLong);
    System.out.println("aDoubleFromString =" + aDoubleFromString);
```

```java
        System.out.println("aFloatFromString =" + aFloatFromString);
        System.out.println("anIntegerFromString =" + anIntegerFromString);
        System.out.println("aLongFromString =" + aLongFromString);

        // do arithmetic with instances using instance methods
        double d = aDouble.doubleValue() + aDoubleFromString.doubleValue();
        System.out.println("d =" + d);
        float f = aFloat.floatValue() + aFloatFromString.floatValue();
        System.out.println("f =" + f);
        int i = anInteger.intValue() + anIntegerFromString.intValue();
        System.out.println("i =" + i);
        long l = aLong.longValue() + aLongFromString.longValue();
        System.out.println("l =" + l);
    } // end main
} // end WrapperDemo.java
```

Chapter 7: Loops

Amortizer.java
■■■■■■

```java
// Java For The COBOL Programmer - copyright 1999 Doke & Hardgrave
// Chapter 7 - Loops
// Program to compute amortization schedule
// Amortizer.java 29 JAN 99
import java.text.NumberFormat;
public class Amortizer
{
    public static void main (String args[])
    { // declare variables
        float balance = 1000F;
        float apr = .08F;
        int months = 6;
        float interestPaid = 0F;
        float principalPaid = 0F;
        float totalInterestPaid = 0F;
    // compute payment
    double doublePayment = (balance * (apr / 12))/ (1 - 1 / Math.pow ((1 +
apr/12), months));
    float payment = (float) doublePayment;    // cast to float
    payment = roundOff (payment);   // round to cents
    // print heading
    System.out.println ("Mo Payment  Interest  Principal Balance");
    // beginning of while loop
    int monthNumber = 1;
    while (monthNumber <= months)
    {
        interestPaid = roundOff (balance * apr / 12);
        totalInterestPaid = totalInterestPaid + interestPaid;
        if (monthNumber == months)
        payment = interestPaid + balance; // adjust last payment
        principalPaid =  payment - interestPaid;
        balance = roundOff(balance - principalPaid);
```

```
        System.out.print ("  " + monthNumber);   // print a line
        System.out.print (" " + payment);
        System.out.print ("  " + interestPaid);
        System.out.print ("  " + principalPaid);
        System.out.println ("   " + balance);
        monthNumber = monthNumber + 1;
    } // end of while loop
    System.out.println ("Total Interest Paid " + roundOff(totalInterestPaid));
  } // end of main method
  // roundOff method
  static public float roundOff (double value)
  {
      value = value * 100;          // move decimal 2 places to right
      // Math.round returns long - recast to float
      float roundedValue = (float) Math.round(value);
      roundedValue = roundedValue / 100; // move decimal back to left
          return roundedValue;
  } // end roundOff
} // end of Amortizer.java
```

DoLoopDemo.java

```
// Java For The COBOL Programmer - copyright 1999 Doke & Hardgrave
// Chapter 7 - Loops
// Program to demonstrate do loop
// DoLoopDemo.java 29 JAN 99

public class DoLoopDemo
{
    public static void main (String args[])
    {
    // we have an amount of money in an interest bearing account:
    // initialBalance
    // each year we make a fixed deposit to the account: annualDeposit
    // the account earns at an annual rate of interest: apr
    // how many years are required for our account to double in value: years

    // declare variables
    float initialBalance = 1000F;   // let's begin with $1,000
    float annualDeposit = 100F;     //  then deposit $100 at end of each year
    float apr = 0.05F;        // apr is 5%
    float currentBalance;     // running balance
    int numberOfYears;        // count the number of years

    // initialize currentBalance and numberOfYears
    currentBalance = initialBalance;
    numberOfYears = 0;

    System.out.println ("Output From do Loop"); // print headings
    System.out.println ("Year Balance");

    // beginning of do loop
    do
    {
        currentBalance = currentBalance * (1 + apr) + annualDeposit;
        numberOfYears = numberOfYears + 1; // increment numberOfYears
        System.out.println (numberOfYears + "     " +
```

```
Math.round(currentBalance));
    } while (currentBalance <= 2 * initialBalance);  // end of do loop

    System.out.print ("In " + numberOfYears + " years.");
    System.out.println ("The balance will be " + Math.round(currentBalance));
    } // end of main method
} // end of DoLoopDemo.java
```

ForLoopDemo.java

```
// Java For The COBOL Programmer - copyright 1999 Doke & Hardgrave
// Chapter 7 - Loops
// Program to demonstrate for loop
// ForLoopDemo.java 29 JAN 99

public class ForLoopDemo
{
    public static void main (String args[])
    {
    // we have an amount of money in an interest bearing account:
    // initialBalance
    // each year we make a fixed deposit to the account: annualDeposit
    // the account earns at an annual rate of interest: apr
    // how many years are required for our account to double in value: years

    // declare variables
    float initialBalance = 1000F;  // let's begin with $1,000 balance
    float annualDeposit = 100F;    // then deposit $100 at end of each year
    float apr = 0.05F;         // annual interest rate is 5%
    float currentBalance;      // running balance
    int numberOfYears;         // count the number of years

    // initialize currentBalance and numberOfYears
    currentBalance = initialBalance;
    numberOfYears = 0;
    System.out.println ("Output From for Loop");  // print headings
    System.out.println ("Year Balance");
    // beginning of for loop

    for (numberOfYears = 0; currentBalance <= 2 * initialBalance; numberOfYears
= numberOfYears + 1)
    {
        currentBalance = currentBalance * (1 + apr) + annualDeposit;
        System.out.println (numberOfYears + "     " + Math.round(currentBalance));
    } // end of for loop
```

```
    System.out.println ("It will take " + numberOfYears + " years.");
    System.out.println ("The balance will be " + Math.round(currentBalance));
    } // end of main method
} // end of ForLoopDemo.java class program
```

WhileLoopDemo.java

```
// Java For The COBOL Programmer - copyright 1999 Doke & Hardgrave
// Chapter 7 - Loops
// Program to demonstrate while loop
// WhileLoopDemo.java 29 JAN 99

public class WhileLoopDemo
{
    public static void main (String args[])
    {
    // we have an amount of money in an interest bearing account:
    // initialBalance
    // each year we make a fixed deposit to the account: annualDeposit
    // the account earns at an annual rate of interest: apr
    // how many years are required for our account to double in value: years

    // declare variables
    float initialBalance = 1000F;  // let's begin with $1,000 balance
    float annualDeposit = 100F;    // then deposit $100 at end of each year
    float apr = 0.05F;         // annual interest rate is 5%
    float currentBalance;      // running balance
    int numberOfYears;         // count the number of years

    // initialize currentBalance and numberOfYears
    currentBalance = initialBalance;
    numberOfYears = 0;
    System.out.println ("Output From while Loop"); // print headings
    System.out.println ("Year Balance");
    // beginning of while loop
    while (currentBalance <= (2 * initialBalance))
    {
        currentBalance = currentBalance * (1 + apr) + annualDeposit;
        numberOfYears = numberOfYears + 1;
        System.out.println (numberOfYears + "    " + Math.round(currentBalance));
    } // end of while loop
```

```
    System.out.print ("In " + numberOfYears + " years.");
    System.out.println ("The balance will be " + Math.round(currentBalance));
    } // end of main method
} // end of WhileLoopDemo.java
```

Chapter 8: Arrays

FindZipCode.java

```
// Java For The COBOL Programmer - copyright 1999 Doke & Hardgrave
// Chapter 8 - Arrays
// Program to demonstrate array search
// FindZipCode.java 30 JAN 99

public class FindZipCode
{  // findZip() accepts argument & array - returns true or false
   public static boolean findZip (int zipToFind, int []zipCode)
   {
   int index = 0;
   boolean foundIt = false;

      while (index < zipCode.length && !foundIt) // loop til found or end
      { // compare the argument to this element value
         if (zipToFind == zipCode [index])
            foundIt = true;   // set switch to true if we have a match
         else
            index = index + 1;  // else, keep looking
      }  // end of loop

      return foundIt;
      }  // end of findZip method
}  // end of FindZipCOde.java
```

OneDimArrayDemo.java

```java
// Java For The COBOL Programmer - copyright 1999 Doke & Hardgrave
// Chapter 8 - Arrays
// Program to demonstrate one dimensional array access
// OneDimArrayDemo.java 30 JAN 99

public class OneDimArrayDemo
{
    public static void main (String args[])
    {
    // declare loan array & loop counter
    int numberOfLoans [] ={39,44,45,65,72,93,14,55,67,27,46,82};
    String monthNames [] =
            {"Jan","Feb","Mar","Apr","May","Jun","Jul",
              "Aug","Sep","Oct","Nov","Dec"};
    int monthNumber;
    // print month name & number of loans for the year
    monthNumber = 0;
    System.out.println ("Loans  Month");
    while (monthNumber < 12)  // loop 12 times for 12 months
    {
        System.out.println (numberOfLoans [monthNumber] +
"           " + monthNames [monthNumber]);
        monthNumber = monthNumber + 1;
    } // end of loop
    } // end of main method
} //   end of OneDimArrayDemo.java
```

TwoDimArrayDemo.java

```
// Java For The COBOL Programmer - copyright 1999 Doke & Hardgrave
// Chapter 8 - Arrays
// Program to demonstrate two dimensional array access
// TwoDimArrayDemo.java 30 JAN 99

public class TwoDimArrayDemo
{
    public static void main (String args[])
    {// CNB wants to track number of loans made each month by loan type
        // row is type (auto, boat, home; column is month
        // declare & populate loan array & loop counter
        int numberOfLoans [] []=
        {
        {12,23,20,21,15,12,5,9,40,20,12,26}, // auto loans in row 1
        {13,10,15,25,35,41,2,16,11,1,19,31}, // boat loans in row 2
        {14,11,10,19,22,40,7,30,16,6,15,25}        // home loans in row 3
        };
        String monthNames []={"Jan","Feb","Mar","Apr","May",
            "Jun","Jul","Aug","Sep","Oct","Nov","Dec"};
        int monthNumber;
        int typeOfLoan;
        int numberOfLoansThisMonth;

        // print number of boat loans - row 2
        monthNumber = 0;
        System.out.println ("CNB Boat Loans");
        System.out.println ("Month Number");
        while (monthNumber < 12)  // loop 12 times
        {
            System.out.println (monthNames [monthNumber] + "         " +
numberOfLoans [1] [monthNumber]);
            monthNumber= monthNumber + 1;
        } // end of loop to print boat loans
        // print the sum of each column (total loans for each month)
        monthNumber = 0;
```

```
        typeOfLoan = 0;
        System.out.println ("CNB Total Loans");
        System.out.println ("Month Number");
        while (monthNumber < 12)  // loop 12 times for 12 months
        {
           numberOfLoansThisMonth = 0;
           typeOfLoan = 0;
           while (typeOfLoan < 3)  // loop 3 times to sum this column
           {
              numberOfLoansThisMonth = numberOfLoansThisMonth +
    numberOfLoans [typeOfLoan] [monthNumber];
              typeOfLoan = typeOfLoan + 1;
           }  // end of row loop
           System.out.println (monthNames [monthNumber] + "              "
    + numberOfLoansThisMonth);
           monthNumber= monthNumber + 1;
        }  // end of month loop
     }  // end of main method
  }  // end of TwoDimArrayDemo.java
```

ZipCodeProcessor.java

```
// Java For The COBOL Programmer - copyright 1999 Doke & Hardgrave
// Chapter 8 - Arrays
// Program to demonstrate array search
// ZipCodeProcessor.java 30 JAN 99

// program to exercise static method findZip in FindZipCode.java to demonstrate:
// 1. array search
// 2. static method
// 3. passing array to method
// 4. using arraay public attribute 'length'

public class ZipCodeProcessor
{
    public static void main(String args[])
    {
    // declare & populate the array
    int zipCode [] ={30309,40410,41515,65757,72701};
    int zipArgument;
    boolean foundIt;
    zipArgument = 65757;  //  we should find this value

    // call findZip method & pass zipArgument and zipCode array
    foundIt = FindZipCode.findZip (zipArgument, zipCode);
    if (foundIt)
        System.out.println ("We found " + zipArgument);
    else
        System.out.println ("We did NOT find " + zipArgument);

    // call findZip method again with a different argument
    zipArgument = 12345;  //  we should NOT find this value
    foundIt = FindZipCode.findZip (zipArgument, zipCode);
    if (foundIt)
        System.out.println ("We found " + zipArgument);
    else
        System.out.println ("We did NOT find " + zipArgument);
```

```
    } // end of main method
} // end of ZipCodeProcessor.java
```

Chapter 9: Data Access

Customer.java

▄▄▄▄▄▄▄▄▄

```java
// Java For The COBOL Programmer - copyright 1999 Doke & Hardgrave
// Chapter 9 - Data Access
// Program to demonstrate Object Persistence using Serialization
// Customer.java 7 FEB 99

public class Customer implements java.io.Serializable
{
   // customer attribute definitions
   private String name;   // private scope limits access to this class
   private String ssNo;
   private String address;
   private String phoneNumber;

   // constructor method to create an instance
   public Customer (String newName, String newSSNo, String newAdr, String
newPhone)

   {
      name = newName;
      ssNo = newSSNo;
      address = newAdr;
      phoneNumber = newPhone;
   }

   // changeAddress method
   public void changeAddress (String newAdr)
   {
      address = newAdr; ;
   }

   // accessor methods
   public String getName ()
```

```
        {return name;}

    public String getSSNo ()
        {return ssNo;}

    public String getAddress ()
        {return address;}

    public String getPhoneNumber ()
        {return phoneNumber;}
}  // end of Customer.java
```

DataBaseDemo.java

```
// Java For The COBOL Programmer - copyright 1999 Doke & Hardgrave
// Chapter 9 - Data Access
// Program to demonstrate one dimensional array access
// Program to demonstrate SQL Database Access
// DataBaseDemo.java 7 FEB 99
import java.sql.*;
public class DataBaseDemo
{
   public static void main(String args[])
   { // declare variables for the data
      String name, ssNo, address, phoneNumber;
      // declare url for the database
      String url = "jdbc:odbc:Customers";  // DB name is "Customers"
      // define the SQL query statement
   String sqlQuery = "SELECT Name, SSNo, Address, Phone FROM Customer";
      try
      { // load the jdbc - odbc bridge driver for Windows-95
         Class.forName("sun.jdbc.odbc.JdbcOdbcDriver");
   // create connection  "JavaDemo" is ID & "JavaIsFun" is password
         Connection aConnection = DriverManager.getConnection(url,
"JavaDemo", "JavaIsFun");
         // create statement object instance
         Statement aStatement = aConnection.createStatement();
         // execute the SQL query statement
         ResultSet rs = aStatement.executeQuery(sqlQuery);
         // set the cursor & get first row
         boolean more = rs.next();
         while (more) // loop while there are rows of data
         { // extract the data & display
            name = rs.getString(1);
            ssNo = rs.getString(2);
            address = rs.getString(3);
            phoneNumber = rs.getString(4);
            System.out.println("Name: " + name);
            System.out.println("SS No: " + ssNo);
```

```
                System.out.println("Address: " + address);
                System.out.println("Phone: " + phoneNumber);
                // get next row
                more = rs.next();
            } // end while loop
            rs.close();     // close everything
            aStatement.close();
            aConnection.close();
        } // end try
    catch (ClassNotFoundException e)
    {System.out.println("Exception caught "+ e);}
    catch (SQLException e)
    {   while (e != null) // we can have multiple exceptions here
        {   System.out.println("SQLException caught "+ e);
            e = e.getNextException();
        } // end while loop
    } // end catch
  } // end main
} // end DataBaseDemo.java
```

ObjectSerializationDemo.java

```
// Java For The COBOL Programmer - copyright 1999 Doke & Hardgrave
// Chapter 9 - Data Access
// Program to demonstrate Object Persistence using Serialization
// ObjectSerializationDemo.java  7 FEB 99

import java.io.*;
public class ObjectSerializationDemo
{
    public static void main (String args[])  // main is first method executed
    {  // create a File instance for Customer.dat
        File customerFile = new File ("C:/Temporary/Customer.dat");
        // create two customer instances
        String name = "Jed Muzzy";
        String ssNo = "499444471";
        String address = "P.O. Box 1881, Great Falls, MT 59601";
        String phoneNumber = "None";
        Customer customer1 =  new Customer(name, ssNo, address,
phoneNumber);
        name = "Bill Sinclair";
        ssNo = "491446543";
    address = "General Delivery, Pender Harbor, BC, Canada";
        phoneNumber = "441-8970";
        Customer customer2 =  new Customer(name, ssNo, address,
phoneNumber);
        // and store them in "CustomerFile"
        try
        {  FileOutputStream f = new FileOutputStream (customerFile);
            ObjectOutputStream o = new ObjectOutputStream (f);
            o.writeObject(customer1);
            o.writeObject(customer2);
        }
        catch (Exception event)
        {System.out.println ("I/O error during write to CustomerFile");}
        // now read them back - Note customer1 is now Bill)
        try
```

```
{ FileInputStream f = new FileInputStream (customerFile);
  ObjectInputStream i = new ObjectInputStream (f);
  customer2 = (Customer) i.readObject();
  customer1 = (Customer) i.readObject();
}
catch (Exception event)
{System.out.println ("I/O error during read from CustomerFile");}
// now display the attributes from retrieved customer instances
  System.out.println ("Name: " + customer1.getName());
  System.out.println ("SS No: " + customer1.getSSNo());
  System.out.println ("Address: " + customer1.getAddress());
  System.out.println ("Phone: " + customer1.getPhoneNumber());
  System.out.println ("Name: " + customer2.getName());
  System.out.println ("SS No: " + customer2.getSSNo());
  System.out.println ("Address: " + customer2.getAddress());
  System.out.println ("Phone: " + customer2.getPhoneNumber());
}
} // end of ObjectSerializationDemo.java
```

SequentialFileDemo.java

```
// Java For The COBOL Programmer - copyright 1999 Doke & Hardgrave
// Chapter 9 - Data Access
// Program to demonstrate Object Persistence using sequential file
// SequentialFileDemo.java 7 FEB 99

import java.io.*;
public class SequentialFileDemo
{
    public static void main(String args[])
    {
    // data for the output file
    String name = "Jed Muzzy";
    String ssNo = "499444471";
    String address = "P.O. Box 1881, Great Falls, MT 59601";
    String phoneNumber = "None";

    // create a text file containing Customer attributes
    File customerFile = new File ("C:/Temporary/Customer.txt");
    try
    {
        FileOutputStream fo = new FileOutputStream (customerFile);
        PrintStream. pw = new PrintStream(fo);
        pw.println(name);
        pw.println(ssNo);
        pw.println(address);
        pw.println(phoneNumber);
    }
        catch (Exception event)
        {System.out.println ("I/O error during write to CustomerFile");}

    // now, read it back in
    try
    {
        FileInputStream fi = new FileInputStream (customerFile);
        DataInputStream i = new DataInputStream(fi);
```

```
        name = i.readLine();
        ssNo = i.readLine();
        address = i.readLine();
        phoneNumber = i.readLine();
        System.out.println ("Name: " + name);
        System.out.println ("SS No: " + ssNo);
        System.out.println ("Address: " + address);
        System.out.println ("Phone: " + phoneNumber);
    }
    catch (Exception event)
    {System.out.println ("I/O error during read from CustomerFile");}
  } // end main
} // end  SequentialFileDemo.java
```

Chapter 10: Graphical User Interfaces

MyWindow.java

```java
// Java For The COBOL Programmer - copyright 1999 Doke & Hardgrave
// Chapter 10 - GUI
// Program to demonstrate the creation and closing of a window
//  MyWindow.java  15 FEB 99

import java.awt.*;
import java.awt.event.*;

public class MyWindow extends Frame implements WindowListener
{
    static MyWindow aWindow;  // reference variable for window instance

    public static void main(String args[]) // main method called first
    {
        aWindow = new MyWindow();  // create instance & call constructor
        aWindow.setSize(300,150);  // pixels wide x pixels high
        aWindow.setTitle("A Title for My Window"); // place title
        aWindow.show();           // display the window
    }  // end of main

     public  MyWindow ()     // constructor method
    { addWindowListener(this); // register for window events
    }  // end of constructor
    // note that aWindow is both a source object & a listener object

    // The following 7 methods are required because we implemented
    // the WindowListener interface
    // When a window event occurs, Java calls the appropriate handler
    // method below.  windowClosing is the only one we have code for.

public void windowClosing(WindowEvent event)
    { System.exit(0);       // terminate this program
```

```java
    } // end of windowClosing
    public void windowClosed(WindowEvent event)
    {}
    public void windowDeiconified(WindowEvent event)
    {}
    public void windowIconified(WindowEvent event)
    {}
    public void windowActivated(WindowEvent event)
    {}
    public void windowDeactivated(WindowEvent event)
    {}
    public void windowOpened(WindowEvent event)
    {}
} // end of MyWindow.java
```

MyWindowWithAButton.java

```
// Java For The COBOL Programmer - copyright 1999 Doke & Hardgrave
// Chapter 10 - GUI
// Program to demo creation and closing of a window with a push button
// MyWindowWithAButton.java 15 FEB 99

import java.awt.*;
import java.awt.event.*;
public class MyWindowWithAButton extends MyWindow implements
ActionListener
{
    static MyWindowWithAButton aWindow;// window reference variable
    static Button aButton;          // button reference variable

    public static void main(String args[]) // main method called first
    {
        aWindow = new MyWindowWithAButton(); // create window instance
        aWindow.setSize(400,100);      // pixels wide x pixels high
        aWindow.setTitle("A Title for My Window With My Button");
        aWindow.show();                // display the window
    } // end of main method

    public  MyWindowWithAButton ()     // constructor method
    {
        setLayout(new FlowLayout()); // arrange components in the window
        aButton = new Button ("Click Me!"); // create button instance
        add(aButton);                // add button to window
        aButton.addActionListener(this);  // register as listener
    } // end constructor

    // this is the event handler method for button click
    public void actionPerformed(ActionEvent event)
    {
        if (event.getSource() == aButton) // if event source is button
            System.out.println ("I've Been Clicked!");
    } // end of actionPerformed
```

```
} // end of MyWindowWithAButton.java
```

NewCustomerApplet.java

```
// Java For The COBOL Programmer - copyright 1999 Doke & Hardgrave
// Chapter 10 - GUI
// Program to demo using Applet with buttons, labels & textfields
// NewCustomerApplet.java  15 FEB 99

import java.awt.*;
import java.awt.event.*;
import java.applet.*;

public class NewCustomerApplet extends Applet implements ActionListener
{
    // reference variables for GUI components
    Button btAccept, btClear;              // buttons
    TextField tfName, tfSSNo, tfAddress, tfPhoneNumber; // text fields

    // customer attribute definitions
    String name, ssNo, address, phoneNumber;

    public  void init () //  constructor method replaced by init
    {
       Panel pTop = new Panel();  // make two panels for the window
       Panel pBottom = new Panel();

       // place labels & textfields in top panel
       pTop.setLayout(new GridLayout(4, 2));     // 4 rows & 2 cols
       pTop.add(new Label("Name: ", Label.RIGHT));  // Right justify
       pTop.add(tfName = new TextField());
       pTop.add(new Label("SS No: ", Label.RIGHT));
       pTop.add(tfSSNo = new TextField());
       pTop.add(new Label("Address: ", Label.RIGHT));
       pTop.add(tfAddress = new TextField());
       pTop.add(new Label("Phone No: ", Label.RIGHT));
       pTop.add(tfPhoneNumber = new TextField());

       // create & place the buttons in bottom panel
```

```
        pBottom.setLayout(new FlowLayout());
        pBottom.add(btAccept = new Button("Accept"));
        pBottom.add(btClear = new Button("Clear"));

        // place panels in the window
        setLayout(new BorderLayout());
        add("North", pTop);
        add("South", pBottom);

        btAccept.addActionListener(this); // listen for Button Events
        btClear.addActionListener(this);
    } // end of constructor method

    // event handler method for button clicks
    public void actionPerformed(ActionEvent event)
    {
        if (event.getSource() == btAccept) // if source is accept button
            accept();
        if (event.getSource() == btClear)  // if source is clear button
            clear();
    } // end of actionPerformed

    private void accept()
    {
        name = tfName.getText(); // get data from textfields
        ssNo = tfSSNo.getText();
        address = tfAddress.getText();
        phoneNumber = tfPhoneNumber.getText();

        // create a customer instance
        Customer aCustomer =  new Customer(name, ssNo, address,
phoneNumber);

            // retrieve and display customer information
            System.out.println ("Name: " + aCustomer.getName());
            System.out.println ("SS No: " + aCustomer.getSSNo());
            System.out.println ("Address: " + aCustomer.getAddress());
```

```
          System.out.println ("Phone: " + aCustomer.getPhoneNumber());
     } // end of accept method

  private void clear()
  {
     tfName.setText("");
     tfSSNo.setText("");
     tfAddress.setText("");
     tfPhoneNumber.setText("");
   } // end of clear method
 } // end of NewCustomerApplet.java
```

NewCustomerWindow.java

```
// Java For The COBOL Programmer - copyright 1999 Doke & Hardgrave
// Chapter 10 - GUI
// Program to demo using a GUI with buttons, labels & textfields
//  NewCustomerWindow.java 15 FEB 99

import java.awt.*;
import java.awt.event.*;
public class NewCustomerWindow extends MyWindow implements
ActionListener
{
    // reference variables for GUI components
    Button btAccept, btClear;                         // buttons
    TextField tfName, tfSSNo, tfAddress, tfPhoneNumber; // text fields
    Panel pTop, pBottom;                              // panels

    // customer attribute definitions
    String name, ssNo, address, phoneNumber;

    public static void main(String args[])  // main method called first
    {
        NewCustomerWindow aWindow = new NewCustomerWindow();
        aWindow.setSize(300,170);      // pixels wide x pixels high
        aWindow.show();                // display the window
    }  // end of main method

    public  NewCustomerWindow ()  //  constructor method
    {
        setTitle("New Customer"); // place title

        pTop = new Panel();  // make two panels for the window
        pBottom = new Panel();

        // place labels & textfields in top panel
        pTop.setLayout(new GridLayout(4, 2));       // 4 rows & 2 cols
        pTop.add(new Label("Name:  ", Label.RIGHT)); // Right justify
```

```
        pTop.add(tfName = new TextField());
    pTop.add(new Label("SS No:  ", Label.RIGHT));
        pTop.add(tfSSNo = new TextField());
        pTop.add(new Label("Address:  ", Label.RIGHT));
        pTop.add(tfAddress = new TextField());
        pTop.add(new Label("Phone No:  ", Label.RIGHT));
        pTop.add(tfPhoneNumber = new TextField());

        // create & place the buttons in bottom panel
        pBottom.setLayout(new FlowLayout());
        pBottom.add(btAccept = new Button("Accept"));
        pBottom.add(btClear = new Button("Clear"));

        // place panels in the window
        setLayout(new BorderLayout());
        add("North", pTop);
        add("South", pBottom);

        btAccept.addActionListener(this); // listen for Button Events
        btClear.addActionListener(this);
    } // end of constructor method

    // event handler method for button clicks
    public void actionPerformed(ActionEvent event)
    {
        if (event.getSource() == btAccept) // if source is accept button
            accept();
        if (event.getSource() == btClear)  // if source is clear button
            clear();
    } // end of actionPerformed

    private void accept()
    {
        name = tfName.getText(); // get data from textfields
        ssNo = tfSSNo.getText();
        address = tfAddress.getText();
        phoneNumber = tfPhoneNumber.getText();
```

```
        // create a customer instance
            Customer aCustomer = new Customer(name, ssNo, address,
phoneNumber);

            // retrieve and display customer information
            System.out.println ("Name: " + aCustomer.getName());
            System.out.println ("SS No: " + aCustomer.getSSNo());
            System.out.println ("Address: " + aCustomer.getAddress());
            System.out.println ("Phone: " + aCustomer.getPhoneNumber());
    } // end of accept method

    private void clear()
    {
      tfName.setText("");
      tfSSNo.setText("");
      tfAddress.setText("");
      tfPhoneNumber.setText("");
    } // end of clear method
} // end of NewCustomerWindow.java
```

NewCustomerWindowWithMenus.java

```
// Java For The COBOL Programmer - copyright 1999 Doke & Hargrave
// Chapter 10 - GUI
// Program to demonstrate Demonstrate using a GUI with Menus
// NewCustomerWindowWithMenus.java 15 FEB 99

import java.awt.*;
import java.awt.event.*;
public class NewCustomerWindowWithMenus extends MyWindow implements
ActionListener
{
    // reference variables for GUI components
    Button btAccept, btClear;              // buttons
    TextField tfName, tfSSNo, tfAddress, tfPhoneNumber; // text fields
    MenuBar mbMenuBar;                     // menu bar
    Menu fileMenu, helpMenu;               // menus
    MenuItem miAccept, miClear;            // menu items

    // customer attribute definitions
    String name, ssNo, address, phoneNumber;

    public static void main(String args[])  // main method called first
    {
        NewCustomerWindowWithMenus aWindow = new
            NewCustomerWindowWithMenus();
        aWindow.setSize(300,170);      // pixels wide x pixels high
        aWindow.show();            // display the window
    }  // end of main method

    public  NewCustomerWindowWithMenus ()  //  constructor method
    {
        setTitle("New Customer");    // place title

        Panel pTop = new Panel();       // two panels for the window
        Panel pBottom = new Panel();
        // add menu
```

```
mbMenuBar = new MenuBar();     // create menubar
setMenuBar(mbMenuBar);         // add menubar to window
// create file & help menus & add to menubar
fileMenu = new Menu ("File");
helpMenu = new Menu ("Help");
mbMenuBar.add(fileMenu);
mbMenuBar.add(helpMenu);
// add items to fileMenu
fileMenu.add(miAccept = new MenuItem("Accept"));
fileMenu.add(miClear = new MenuItem("Clear"));

// place labels & textfields in top panel
pTop.setLayout(new GridLayout(4, 2)); // 4 rows & 2 cols
pTop.add(new Label("Name: ", Label.RIGHT));   // Right justify
pTop.add(tfName = new TextField());
pTop.add(new Label("SS No: ", Label.RIGHT));
pTop.add(tfSSNo = new TextField());
pTop.add(new Label("Address: ", Label.RIGHT));
pTop.add(tfAddress = new TextField());
pTop.add(new Label("Phone No: ", Label.RIGHT));
pTop.add(tfPhoneNumber = new TextField());

// create & place the buttons in bottom panel
pBottom.setLayout(new FlowLayout());
pBottom.add(btAccept = new Button("Accept"));
pBottom.add(btClear = new Button("Clear"));

// place panels in the window
setLayout(new BorderLayout());
add("North", pTop);
add("South", pBottom);

btAccept.addActionListener(this); // listen for Button Events
btClear.addActionListener(this);

miAccept.addActionListener(this);// register as listener for MenuItem
                                 // events
```

```java
            miClear.addActionListener(this);
        } // end of constructor method

        // event handler method for button and menu clicks
        public void actionPerformed(ActionEvent event)
        {
            if (event.getSource() == btAccept) // if source is accept button
                accept();
            if (event.getSource() == btClear)  // if source is clear button
                clear();
            if (event.getSource() == miAccept) // if source is accept menu
                accept();
            if (event.getSource() == miClear)  // if source is clear menu
                clear();
        } // end of actionPerformed

        private void accept()
        {
            name = tfName.getText();    // get data from textfields
            ssNo = tfSSNo.getText();
            address = tfAddress.getText();
            phoneNumber = tfPhoneNumber.getText();
            // create a customer instance
            Customer aCustomer = new Customer(name, ssNo, address,
phoneNumber);
                // retrieve and display customer information
                System.out.println ("Name: " + aCustomer.getName());
                System.out.println ("SS No: " + aCustomer.getSSNo());
                System.out.println ("Address: " + aCustomer.getAddress());
                System.out.println ("Phone: " + aCustomer.getPhoneNumber());
        } // end of accept method
        private void clear()
        {
            tfName.setText("");
            tfSSNo.setText("");
            tfAddress.setText("");
            tfPhoneNumber.setText("");
```

```
    } // end of clear method
} // end of NewCustomerWindowWithMenus.java
```

Chapter 11: OO Development Issues

Account.java

```java
// Java For The COBOL Programmer - copyright 1999 Doke & Hardgrave
// Chapter 11 - OO Development Issues
// Program to model the Account class
// Account.java 3 JAN 99

public class Account
{
    // account attribute definitions
    private int accountNumber; // private scope limited to this class
    private float currentBalance;

    // constructor method to create an instance
    public Account (int newAccountNumber, float newCurrentBalance)
    {
        accountNumber  = newAccountNumber;
        currentBalance = newCurrentBalance;
    }
    // accessor methods
    public float getCurrentBalance ()
    { return currentBalance; }

    public int getAccountNumber ()
    { return accountNumber;}

    // mutator methods
    public void setAccountNumber(int newAccountNumber)
    {accountNumber  = newAccountNumber;  }

    public void setCurrentBalance( float newCurrentBalance)
    { currentBalance = newCurrentBalance; }

} // end account class
```

CheckingAccountDA.java

```
// Java For The COBOL Programmer - copyright 1999 Doke & Hardgrave
// Chapter 11 - OO Development Issues
// Program to demonstrate 3 tier design
// Provide access to Checking Accounts Stored in Access Database
// CheckingAccountDA.java 20 FEB 99

import java.sql.*;

public class CheckingAccountDA
{
    static String url = "jdbc:odbc:db1";  // The dB name is "db1"
    static Connection aConnection;
    static Statement aStatement;
    static ResultSet rs;
    static  CheckingAccountPD anAccount;

    public static void initialize() // initialize method
    {
       try
       {  // load the jdbc - odbc bridge driver for Windows-95
          Class.forName("sun.jdbc.odbc.JdbcOdbcDriver");
          // create connection instance
          aConnection = DriverManager.getConnection(url,"Admin","JavaIsFun");
          // create statement object instance
          aStatement = aConnection.createStatement();
       } // end try
       catch (Exception e)
          {System.out.println("Exception caught "+ e);}
    } // end initialize

    public static void terminate() // terminate method
    {
     try
     {    rs.close();     // close everything
        aStatement.close();
```

```
      aConnection.close();
   } // end try

   catch (Exception e)
      {System.out.println("Exception caught "+ e);}
   }  // end terminate

   public static CheckingAccountPD getAccount(int acctNo) throws
NoAccountFoundException
   {
   try
   {
      String sqlQuery = "SELECT AccountNo, Balance, MinBalance FROM
CheckingAccount WHERE AccountNo =" + acctNo;
      rs = aStatement.executeQuery(sqlQuery);    // execute the SQL query
statement
      boolean more = rs.next();  // set the cursor
      if (more)
      {  // if we got the account extract the data & display
         int acctNO = rs.getInt(1);
         float balance = rs.getFloat(2);
         float minBalance = rs.getFloat(3);
         anAccount = new CheckingAccountPD(acctNO, balance);
      }
      else
   { //  no account found - create & throw the exception
         NoAccountFoundException e = new NoAccountFoundException("Not
Found");
         throw e;
      }
   } // end try
   catch (SQLException e)
   { while (e != null) // we can have multiple exceptions here - print all
   { System.out.println("SQLException caught "+ e);
     e = e.getNextException();
      } // end while loop
      } // end catch
```

```
    return anAccount;
} // end getAccount

public static void updateAccount(int acctNo, float balance)

{
try
{
    String sqlUpdate = "UPDATE CheckingAccount SET Balance = "+ balance
+" WHERE AccountNo = " + acctNo;
    aStatement.executeUpdate(sqlUpdate);
} // end try
catch (SQLException e)
{  while (e != null) // we can have multiple exceptions here - print all
    { System.out.println("SQLException caught "+ e);
   e = e.getNextException();
    } // end while loop
} // end catch
} // end update
} // end CheckingAccountDA.java
```

CheckingAccountPD.java

```java
// Java For The COBOL Programmer - copyright 1999 Doke & Hardgrave
// Chapter 11 - OO Development Issues
//  Problem Domain Class for CheckingAccount
//  Interfaces with Data Access class                        //
CheckingAccountPD.java  20 FEB 99
public class CheckingAccountPD extends Account
{ // instance variable
   private float minimumBalance;  //private scope limited to this class
   public static void initialize()
{CheckingAccountDA.initialize();}     // call initialize in Data Access
   public static void terminate()
{CheckingAccountDA.terminate();}    // call terminate in Data Access
   // constructor method
   public CheckingAccountPD (int newAccountNumber,float newCurrentBalance)
   { // invoke account constructor to populate account attributes
      super (newAccountNumber, newCurrentBalance);
      minimumBalance = newCurrentBalance;  // populate checkingAccount
                                           // attribute
   } // end constructor
   // note this is a class method to record a check - we also have an instance
   // method
   public static CheckingAccountPD recordACheck (int accountNumber, float
checkAmount) throws NoAccountFoundException, NSFException
   { try
   { // ask Data Access class to get the account instance for us
   CheckingAccountPD anAccount =
CheckingAccountDA.getAccount(accountNumber);
      anAccount.recordACheck(checkAmount); // if successful, post check
      return anAccount;    // return the instance reference variable
      }
      catch (NoAccountFoundException e)  // No Account Found
      { throw e;}
      catch (NSFException e)             // Not Sufficient Funds
      { throw e;}
      } // end class method recordACheck
```

```
// instance method to post a check to this account
public void recordACheck (float checkAmount) throws NSFException
{
    float currentBalance = getCurrentBalance();
    if (currentBalance >= checkAmount)  // see if sufficient funds
        {currentBalance = currentBalance - checkAmount;
        setCurrentBalance(currentBalance);
        // update the balance in the database
CheckingAccountDA.updateAccount(getAccountNumber(),currentBalance);
        }
    else
        {
            NSFException e = new NSFException("Not Sufficient Funds");
        // if not, throw an exception
        throw e;
        } // end if
    } // end instance method recordACheck
} // end CheckingAccountPD.java
```

MyWindow.java
▬▬▬▬▬▬▬▬

```
// Java For The COBOL Programmer - copyright 1999 Doke & Hardgrave
// Chapter 11 - OO Development
// Program to demonstrate the creation and closing of a window
//  MyWindow.java  20 FEB 99

import java.awt.*;
import java.awt.event.*;

public class MyWindow extends Frame implements WindowListener
{
    static MyWindow aWindow;      // reference variable for window instance
    public static void main(String args[]) // main method called first
    {
        aWindow = new MyWindow(); // create instance & call constructor
        aWindow.setSize(300,150); // pixels wide x pixels high
        aWindow.setTitle("A Title for My Window"); // place title
        aWindow.show();           // display the window
    } // end of main

    public MyWindow ()     // constructor method
    { addWindowListener(this); // register as listener for window events
    } // end of constructor

    // note that aWindow is both a source object & a listener object
    // The following seven methods are required because we implemented
    // the WindowListener interface
    // When a window event occurs, Java calls the appropriate handler
    // method below. windowClosing is the only one we have code for.
    public void windowClosing(WindowEvent event)
    { System.exit(0);     // terminate this program
    } // end of windowClosing
    public void windowClosed(WindowEvent event)
    {}
    public void windowDeiconified(WindowEvent event)
    {}
```

```
    public void windowIconified(WindowEvent event)
    {}
    public void windowActivated(WindowEvent event)
    {}
    public void windowDeactivated(WindowEvent event)
    {}
    public void windowOpened(WindowEvent event)
    {}
} // end of MyWindow.java
```

NSFException.java

```
// Java For The COBOL Programmer - copyright 1999 Doke & Hardgrave
// Chapter 11 - OO Development Issues
// Not Sufficient Funds Exception
// NSFException.java  20 FEB 99

public class NSFException extends Exception
{
    public NSFException (String errorMessage) // constructor
    { super(errorMessage);}
} // end NSFException.java
```

NoAccountFoundException.java

___

```
// Java For The COBOL Programmer - copyright 1999 Doke & Hardgrave
// Chapter 11 - OO Development Issues
// No Account Found Exception
// NoAccountFoundException.java  20 FEB 99

public class NoAccountFoundException extends Exception
{
   public NoAccountFoundException (String errorMessage) // constructor
   { super(errorMessage);}
} // end NoAccountFoundException.java
```

PostChecksGUI.java

```
// Java For The COBOL Programmer - copyright 1999 Doke & Hardgrave
// Chapter 11 - OO Development Issues
//  Demonstrate a GUI collaborating with a PD class
//  PostChecksGUI.java 20 FEB 99


import java.awt.*;
import java.awt.event.*;
public class PostChecksGUI extends MyWindow implements ActionListener
{
   // reference variables for GUI components
   Button btAccept, btClear, btClose;            // buttons
   TextField tfAccountNumber, tfCheckAmount;  // text fields
   Label lblMessage;                 // label
   Panel pTop, pMiddle, pBottom;     // panels

   CheckingAccountPD anAccount; // other variable definitions
   int accountNumber;
   float balance, checkAmount;
   boolean goodData;

   public static void main(String args[])  // main method called first
   {
      PostChecksGUI aWindow = new PostChecksGUI();
      aWindow.setSize(300,170);      // pixels wide x pixels high
      aWindow.show();                // display the window
      CheckingAccountPD.initialize();    // initialize data manager
   } // end of main method
   public  PostChecksGUI() //  constructor method
   {
      setTitle("CNB - Post Checks");       // place title
      pTop = new Panel();           // create panels
      pMiddle = new Panel();
      pBottom = new Panel();

      // place labels & textfields in top panel
```

```
    pTop.setLayout(new GridLayout(2, 2));        //  rows & 2 cols
    pTop.add(new Label("AccountNumber:  ", Label.RIGHT)); // Right justify
the text
    pTop.add(tfAccountNumber = new TextField());
    pTop.add(new Label("Check Amount:  ", Label.RIGHT));
    pTop.add(tfCheckAmount = new TextField());

    // message label in middle panel
    pMiddle.setLayout(new FlowLayout());
    pMiddle.add (lblMessage = new Label("
 "));

    // create & place the buttons in bottom panel
    pBottom.setLayout(new FlowLayout());
    pBottom.add(btAccept = new Button("Accept"));
    pBottom.add(btClear = new Button("Clear"));
    pBottom.add(btClose = new Button("Close"));

    // place panels in the window
    setLayout(new BorderLayout());
    add("North", pTop);
    add("Center", pMiddle);
    add("South", pBottom);

    btAccept.addActionListener(this); // listen for Button Events
    btClear.addActionListener(this);
    btClose.addActionListener(this);
  } // end of constructor method

// event handler method for button clicks
public void actionPerformed(ActionEvent event)
  {
    if (event.getSource() == btAccept)  // if source is accept button
        accept();
    if (event.getSource() == btClear)   // if source is clear button
        clear();
    if (event.getSource() == btClose)   // if source is close button
```

```
        {CheckingAccountPD.terminate();  // shut down the data manager
        System.exit(0);}
    } // end of actionPerformed

 private void accept()
 {
 getInput();
 if (goodData)
    postCheck();
 } // end accept

 private void getInput()
 {
    goodData = true;
    try
    {accountNumber = Integer.parseInt(tfAccountNumber.getText().trim());}
    catch (NumberFormatException e)
    {
       lblMessage.setText("Bad Account Number Entered!");
       goodData = false;
    }
    try
    {Float f = new Float(tfCheckAmount.getText().trim());
    checkAmount = f.floatValue();}
    catch (NumberFormatException e)
    {
       lblMessage.setText("Bad Amount Entered!");
       goodData = false;
    }
 } // end getInput

 public void postCheck()
 {
    try
    {
    anAccount = CheckingAccountPD.recordACheck(accountNumber,
checkAmount);
```

```
        lblMessage.setText("Balance is: " +
Float.toString(anAccount.getCurrentBalance())));
        }
        catch (NoAccountFoundException e)
        {lblMessage.setText("No Account Found");}
        catch (NSFException e)
        {lblMessage.setText("Insufficient Funds");}
    }  // end postCheck

    private void clear()
    {
        tfAccountNumber.setText("");
        tfCheckAmount.setText("");
        lblMessage.setText("");
    } // end of clear method
}  // end of PostChecksGUI.java
```

Glossary

abstract a Java keyword used in class header to indicate the class will not have instances. Instead, we create instances of its subclass. (Chapter 3)

accessor method a method that returns an attribute value. Named with a prefix "get" plus the variable name. (Chapter 3)

aggregation a relationship among classes wherein one class is a component or part of another class. (Chapter 2)

Applet a Java program that runs under control of a viewer or browser. (Chapters 1, 10)

argument the variable or variables passed to a method. (Chapter 3)

assignment operator one of the arithmetic operators combined with the equal sign (=). (Chapter 5)

assignment statement Java uses the assignment to store a value into a variable. The expression on the right side of the equal sign is evaluated and the result is placed in the variable on the left of the equal sign. (Chapter 3)

association a connection (not considered inheritance or aggregation) between two or more classes. (Chapter 2)

attributes the things an object knows about itself; an object's data. (Chapter 2)

Bean (aka JavaBean) an independent, reusable software component. Java Beans can be combined to create an application. (Chapter 1)

binary association an association involving two classes. (Chapter 2)

Boolean variable a variable whose value is either true or false. (Chapter 6)

byte stream a flow of data in Unicode format. (Chapter 9)

case structure a multiple-direction decision structure that can often replace nested if statements. Implemented in COBOL with the EVALUATE verb and in Java with the switch statement. (Chapter 6)

casting the process to change the data type of a variable in an assignment statement to override a potential truncation error. (Chapter 4)

catch an exception using the catch block to intercept an exception that has been thrown. (Chapters 1, 3, 5, 10)

character stream a flow of data in the system's native format, automatically converted back to Unicode when it comes into our program. (Chapter 9)

class header the first line in a class definition containing accessibility, class name, and other keywords. (Chapter 3)

class method a static method; a method that provides services for the class and not for a specific instance of the class. (Chapter 8)

class program a Java program written to model a class. The program contains the attribute definitions and method code for the class. (Chapters 2, 3)

class scope applies to variables in a class that are accessible by all methods within the class. (Chapter 4)

class a group of objects that share common attributes and common methods. (Chapter 2)

Common Request Broker Architecture (CORBA) an OMG standard to allow any object of any type to communicate across any type of platform. (Chapter 11)

compiled code machine-readable code, converted from computer language syntax via a compiler. (Chapter 1)

complex data type an object instance—not one of the eight Java primitive data types (see primitive data type). (Chapter 4)

compound condition two conditions joined with the Java logical operators || (or) or && (and). (Chapter 6)

condition a logical expression. (Chapter 6)

condition name the name of a COBOL condition defined as a level 88. (Chapter 6)

conditional operator a Java coding shortcut to writing simple if statement. Its format is: variable = logical expression ? value-1 : value-2;. (Chapter 6)

constant a variable defined using the keyword final. Its value cannot be changed. (Chapter 4)

constructor method a method to create object instances. It has the same name as the class. (Chapter 3)

custom exception Java has several standard exceptions. You can write a custom exception class for conditions unique to your program. (Chapter 5)

custom method a method designed and written to do some custom processing. (Chapter 3)

data access classes the classes that allow storage, retrieval, and manipulation of data. (Chapter 11)

data type classes same as wrapper classes. (Chapter 5)

data type the type of data that must be explicitly stated when declaring a variable. Java has eight primitive types. (Chapters 3, 4)

decrement operator Java has two decrement operators predecrement (--i) and postdecrement (i--). (Chapter 5)

deployment diagrams show the physical location of objects, groups of objects, or portions of objects. (Chapter 11)

Distributed COM (DCOM) Microsoft's ORB; good for communicating among Java and ActiveX objects in a Windows environment. (Chapter 11)

dynamic binding classes and methods are not validated until runtime. (Chapter 2)

encapsulation (aka information hiding) the hiding of an object's internals from everything outside the object. (Chapter 2)

event handler method the method called to respond to an event. (Chapter 10)

event listening a listener object that has registered with a source object is listening for events. Whenever a source object event occurs, Java calls the appropriate event handler method (**actionPerformed()** for buttons and menu items). (Chapter 10)

event registration a listener object registers for an event by calling a registration method in the source object. The registration method is **addWindowListener()** for Frames and **addActionListener()** for buttons and menu items. (Chapter 10)

event something that happens to a GUI component such as a user clicking a button or menu item. (Chapter 10)

event-driven programming a programming technique that responds to events. (Chapter 10)

exception an instance created to deal with a condition. The instance contains information about the condition. (Chapter 5)

expression a combination of operators, variables, and values that evaluates to a result. (Chapter 5)

final a Java keyword used to define constants. (Chapter 4)

hybrid object-oriented language a language that uses an existing language as its base and adds OO features and syntax. (Chapter 1)

identifier a term used for the name associated with Java programs, classes, methods, and variables. (Chapter 3)

implements a Java keyword used in class header to inherit from an interface. (Chapter 10)

increment operator Java has two increment operators pre-increment (++i) and post-increment (i++). (Chapter 5)

index a variable containing a value that points to a specific element in a Java array. Java index values begin with 0 for the first element. In a two-dimensional array, the first index refers to the row and the second to the column, relative to zero. (Chapter 8)

inheritance a relationship among classes wherein one class shares the attributes and/or methods defined in other classes. (Chapter 2)

instance method a method that provides services for a specific instance of the class. (Chapter 8)

instance name (aka instance pointer) a unique identifier for a specific object instance. (Chapter 2)

instance reference variable a variable that refers to or points to an instance. (Chapter 5)

instance a specific object. (Chapter 2)

instruction scope a variable declared within a statement has statement scope. (Chapter 4)

interface similar to a class, but with several restrictions. (Chapter 10)

Java Archive files (JAR files) a Java file format used for compressing many files into one to improve transmission speed across network connections. (Chapter 1)

Java Development Kit (JDK) Sun's software development environment for writing Applets and applications in Java. (Chapter 1)

Java Integrated Development Environment (IDE) a complete Java development environment including compilers, debuggers, interpreters, and so forth. (Chapter 1)

Java Virtual Machine (JVM) a Java interpreter; responsible for interpreting bytecodes. (Chapter 1)

JavaScript a Web scripting language developed by Netscape; has similar constructs to Java, but is a separate language. Typically used for user interface features within HTML documents, but can also be used on the server side. (Chapter 1)

layout manager Java classes used to place GUI components in a frame or panel. (Chapter 10)

listener object the object instance that responds to an event. (Chapter 10)

logical expression an expression that evaluates to a Boolean value—true or false; a condition. (Chapter 6)

logical operator Java operators used in writing logical expressions (<, >, <=, >=, ==, &&, ||, !, !=). (Chapter 6)

message an operation that one object performs upon another; usually consists of the object's name, a method name, and required parameters. (Chapter 2)

method header the first line of a method definition indicating accessibility, return data type, method name, and parameter list. (Chapter 3)

method scope a variable declared within a method has method scope. It is accessible only within the method. (Chapter 4)

method signature the method name and its parameter list. (Chapter 3)

methods the things an object can do; its behavior. (Chapter 2)

multiple inheritance a subclass (child) with more than one superclass (parent). (Chapter 2)

multiplicity an indication of the number of instances of a class involved in a relationship. (Chapter 2)

mutator method a method that changes the contents of an attribute. Named with a prefix "set" plus the variable name. (Chapter 3)

n-ary association an association involving n classes (usually more than three). (Chapter 2)

object instance an area of memory containing values for a specific member of a class. (Chapter 3)

object interface what others outside the object see of the object; usually the object name, method name, and required parameters. (Chapter 2)

object persistence the technique of storing object instances or their attribute values, so they may be reconstructed at a later time. (Chapter 9)

Object Request Broker (ORB) keeps track of object locations and provides the communication mechanisms to allow objects to communicate. (Chapter 11)

object serialization a Java technique introduced with JDK 1.1 used to store complete instances in a file. These instances can then be retrieved intact as if they were just created. (Chapter 9)

object an entity containing both data (what it knows about itself) and behavior (what it can do). (Chapter 2)

object-based language a programming language that supports some OO concepts, but does not support inheritance. (Chapter 2)

object-oriented language a programming language that supports all OO concepts including inheritance. (Chapter 2)

one-dimensional array an array that has only one dimension, a row of elements. A Java array is really an instance and is referenced with an instance reference variable. (Chapter 8)

OPEN (Object-Oriented Process, Environment, and Notation)—an OO methodology developed by a consortium of 32 members; utilizes UML and other notation sets. (Chapter 11)

package diagrams provide a logical grouping of classes. (Chapter 11)

package a Java class library. (Chapter 10)

panel an invisible GUI component used to contain other components. (Chapter 10)

parameter the variables received by a method. (Chapter 3)

passing by reference passing a reference variable as an argument to a method is called passing by reference because we pass a reference to the data instead of a copy of the data. Note, when a method receives a reference variable, it has access to the instance referenced by the variable. (Chapter 8)

persistent instance an instance that exists longer than the execution of the program, an instance, or its data stored in a file. (Chapter 9)

polymorphism the same message can elicit a different response, depending on the receiver of the message. (Chapter 2)

portability the capability to run an application on different platforms without making changes to the code. (Chapter 1)

post-test loop a loop whose terminating condition is tested at the end of the loop. (Chapter 7)

pre-test loop a loop whose terminating condition is tested at the beginning of the loop. (Chapter 7)

primitive data type one of the eight basic types of data in Java (int, short, long, byte, float, double, char, boolean). (Chapter 4)

private access only this program has access to this method or variable. (Chapter 3)

problem domain classes the objects and classes representing business logic. (Chapter 11)

public access any program has access to this method or variable. (Chapter 3)

pure object-oriented language a language in which everything is represented as an object and all major characteristics of object-orientation such as inheritance, classes, and polymorphism are supported. (Chapter 1)

reference variable a variable that points to an object instance. (Chapter 3)

Remote Method Invocation (RMI) a Sun Microsystems ORB; good for communicating among Java objects on distributed sites. (Chapter 11)

restricted access only this program and its subclasses have access to this method or variable. (Chapter 3)

return a Java statement that returns a specified variable to the calling program. (Chapter 3)

scope the accessibility of a variable. Java variables have class, method, or instruction scope. (Chapter 4)

sequence diagrams illustrate the timing and sequence of messages between classes and objects. (Chapter 11)

Servlet similar to an Applet, but is located on the server; provides added functionality to Java-enabled servers. (Chapter 1)

single inheritance a subclass (child) with only one superclass (parent). (Chapter 2)

socket an instance of the Socket class is used to establish communication between a client and a server. (Chapter 9)

source object the object instance where the event occurs, generally a button or menu item. (Chapter 10)

SQL Structured Query Language, a standardized (ANSI) database language. Java uses classes in the java.sql package to execute SQL statements. (Chapter 9)

static binding all classes and methods are validated at compile time. (Chapter 2)

static method a class method, a method that provides services for the class and not for a specific instance of the class. (Chapter 8)

static a Java keyword meaning only one copy is to exist. Static variables are sometimes called class variables. (Chapter 4)

stream a flow of data either into or out of a program. (Chapter 9)

String a supplied Java class whose instances contain character string data. These instances are complex data type. (Chapter 4)

subclass (aka child) inherits attributes and/or methods from another class. (Chapter 2)

subscript a COBOL term corresponding to a Java index. It points to an element in an array. (Chapter 8)

superclass (aka parent) is inherited from by other classes. (Chapter 2)

systems development methodology (SDM) a detailed guide for the development of a system; a "how to" book for developing systems. (Chapter 11)

ternary association an association involving three classes. (Chapter 2)

this a Java keyword that refers to the current instance of the class. (Chapter 10)

three-tier design system design where the user interface, problem domain, and data access segments are separated. (Chapter 11)

throw an exception the process of sending an exception instance is called throwing and uses the keyword throw. (Chapter 5)

transient instance an instance that is erased when the program terminates. (Chapter 9)

two-dimensional array an array that has only two dimensions, elements arranged into rows and columns. A Java array is really an instance and is referenced with an instance reference variable. (Chapter 8)

type casting changing data type. (Chapter 5)

UML Unified Modeling Language; the standard object modeling notation adopted by the Object Management Group. (Chapter 11)

unary association an association involving only one class. (Chapter 2)

Unicode a standard character set used by Java. Each Unicode character requires 2 bytes. (Chapter 4)

Unified Software Development Process (USDP) an OO methodology developed and published by Rational Corporation; this methodology utilizes UML. (Chapter 11)

user interface classes the objects and classes that enable the user to interact with the system. (Chapter 11)

variable a place in memory used to store data. The data can be either a value or a pointer to an object instance. (Chapter 3)

wrapper classes Java classes for each of the primitive data types. (Chapter 5)

Bibliography

Booch, G., Rumbaugh, J., and Jacobson, I., *The Unified Modeling Language User Guide*, Reading, Massachusetts: Addison-Wesley, 1999.

Booch, G., *Object-Oriented Analysis and Design with Applications*, The Benjamin/Cummings Publishing Company, Inc., Redwood City, CA, 1994.

Booch, G., "Object Oriented Development," *IEEE Transactions on Software Engineering*, SE-12 (2), February 1986, 211-221.

Brown, D., *Object-Oriented Analysis: Objects in Plain English*, John Wiley & Sons, New York, NY, 1997.

Chapman, D., *Understanding ActiveX and OLE: A Guide for Developers & Managers*, Redmond, Washington: Microsoft Press, 1996.

Dietel, H. M., and Dietel, P. J., *Java: How to Program*, Upper Saddle River, NJ: Prentice Hall, 1997.

Doke, E. R., and Hardgrave, B. C., *An Introduction to Object COBOL*, John Wiley & Sons, New York, NY, 1998.

Douglas, D. E., and Hardgrave, B. C., "The Changing Language Mix in Information Systems Curricula," *1998 Proceedings of the National Decision Sciences Institute*, November 1998.

Fowler, M. and Scott, K., *UML Distilled, Applying the Standard Object Modeling Language*, Addison Wesley Longman, Inc., New York, NY, 1997.

Garside, R., and Mariani, J., *Java: First Contact*, Cambridge, MA: Course Technology, 1998.

"Glossary of Java and Related Terms," available at *http://java.sun.com/docs/glossary.print.html*

Gosling, J., Joy, B., and Steele, G., *The Java Language Specification*, available at *http://java.sun.com/docs/books/jls/html/index.html*

Gosling, J., and McGilton, H., "The Java Language Environment: A White Paper," available at *http://java.sun.com/docs/white/langenv/*

Graham, I., Henderson-Sellers, B., and Younessi, H., *The OPEN Process Specification*, Reading, Massachusetts: Addison-Wesley, 1997.

Harmon, P., and Watson, M., *Understanding UML: The Developer's Guide with a Web-Based Application in Java*, San Francisco, California: Morgan Kaufmann Publishers, Inc., 1998.

Harrington, J. L., *Java Programming: An IS Perspective*, New York, NY: John Wiley & Sons, Inc., 1998.

Henderson-Sellers, B., and Edwards, J., *Book Two of Object-Oriented Knowledge: The Working Object*, Prentice-Hall, Englewood Cliffs, NJ, 1994.

Kay, A. C., "The Early History of Smalltalk," *SIGPLAN Notices*, 28 (3), March 1993, 69-95.

Nilsen, K., "Adding Real-Time Capabilities to Java," *Communications of the ACM*, 41 (6), June 1998, 49-56.

Orfali, R., and Harkey, D., *Client/Server Programming with Java and CORBA*, New York, New York: John Wiley & Sons, 1997.

Radding, A., "Tool Immaturity Tempers Java Buzz," *Software Magazine*, 17 (8), July 1997, 51-54.

"Retraining COBOL Programmers for Client-Server," available at *http://www.alchemy-computing.co.uk/coboltrn.htm*

Singhal, S., and Nguyen, B., "The Java Factor," *Communications of the ACM*, 41 (6), June 1998, 34-37.

"The Java Language: An Overview," available at *http://java.sun.com/docs/overviews/java/java-overview-1.html*

Tyma, P., "Why Are We Using Java Again?" *Communications of the ACM*, 41 (6), June 1998, 38-42.

Index

C

C, 3, 5, 7
    use in higher education, 11
C++, 3, 5, 6, 7, 16, 23, 43
    use in higher education, 11
calling a method, 14, 61–66
calling a subprogram, 14
call statement, 73
capabilities, 16
CardLayout, 226
case sensitivity, of Java, 57
case statements, 137
case structure, 136–140, 144, 344
CASE Tools, 24
casting, 87–89, 92, 93, 345
catch an exception, 121, 345
CD–ROM, Java programs on, 275–342
char, 79, 81, 91
character, 79, 91, 137, 142
character set, 93
character stream, 192, 214, 215, 345
character strings, 81, 83, 84
checks, recording of, 265–266
child. *See* subclass
class, 6, 37, 39, 43, 72
    definition of, 25–26, 45, 345
class attribute, 72
class diagram, 26–34, 90, 252
class header, 50, 72, 74, 346
class library, 14, 192–193
class method, 184, 189, 346
class names, 58
class program, 26, 45, 50–55, 72
    definition of, 74, 346
class relationships, 34–38, 43
class scope, 82, 91, 93, 345
class symbol, examples of, 27, 28, 29
class variable, 72, 82, 93
client–server model, 2
Coad/Yourdon, 23, 252
COBOL, 5, 7, 8, 42, 55, 254
    attributes of programmers for, 12
    compared to Java, 2, 10–13, 14
    program components of, 255
    strength of, 10–13

subprogram compared to Java
    method, 62, 73
terms in, 50
use in higher education, 11
COBOL-XX, 10, 55, 172
code, shortcuts of, 111, 112
code-and-fix, 251
collaboration diagram, 251, 252
column restrictions, 55, 72
comma format, 96, 118
comments, 53, 55–57, 72
Common Request Broker Architecture
    (CORBA), 267–268, 271, 345
Community National Bank Case, 21–75,
    89–90, 100–104, 115, 124–164,
    168–182, 200, 217, 253, 254–267
compiled code, 17, 345
compiler, 8
complex data type, 83, 93, 345
component diagram, 251, 254
components, 246, 248
compound condition, 130, 144, 345
computation, 95–121, 284–293
    programs for, 284–293
compute, 14, 110
condition, 14, 125, 144, 345
conditional operator, 130–131, 143,
    144, 345
condition name, 131–132, 142, 144, 345
CONSISTS-OF. *See* aggregation
constant, 58, 83, 93, 345
constant names, 58
constructor method, 59, 73, 74, 346
continue statement, 130, 160–161, 165
CORBA. *See* Common Request Broker
    Architecture (CORBA)
createStatement method, 204
creating an object instance, 58–61
currency format, 118
custom exception, 346
custom method, 68–70, 73, 74, 346

D

Dahl, Ole-Johan, 23
data access, 191–215

End-User Agreement

Purchase of this book, *Java for the COBOL Programmer,* entitles you to a non-exclusive, non-transferable license to use the accompanying CD-ROM on a single terminal for the purposes and in the manner described in the book and in the license agreement supplied by Symantec on the CD-ROM. Access to the CD-ROM by more than one user simultaneously is forbidden. The software contained on the CD-ROM is in copyright and is for personal use only. The publisher accepts no responsibility for any loss or damage consequent upon use of the software.